WELLESLEY STUDIES IN CRITICAL THEORY,
LITERARY HISTORY, AND CULTURE
VOL. 5

REGIONALISM
RECONSIDERED

GARLAND REFERENCE LIBRARY
OF THE HUMANITIES
VOL. 1698

WELLESLEY STUDIES IN CRITICAL THEORY, LITERARY HISTORY, AND CULTURE

WILLIAM E. CAIN
General Editor

REGIONALISM RECONSIDERED

New Approaches to the Field

edited by

David Jordan

GARLAND PUBLISHING, Inc.
New York & London / 1994

Library of Congress Cataloging-in-Publication Data

Regionalism reconsidered : new approaches to the field
/ edited by David Jordan.
    p.   cm. — (Garland reference library of the
humanities ; vol. 1698. Wellesley studies in critical
theory, literary history, and culture ; vol. 5)
  Includes bibliographical references (p.).
  ISBN 0–8153–1289–X
  1. Literature, Modern—History and criticism.
2. Regionalism in literature. 3. Setting (Literature)
4. Local color in literature.   I. Jordan, David.
II. Series: Garland reference library of the humanities ; vol. 1698.   III. Series: Garland reference library
of the humanities. Wellesley studies in critical theory,
literary history, and culture ; vol. 5.
PN710.R375   1994
809'.922—dc20   94–20701
                                        CIP

Printed on acid-free, 250-year-life paper
Manufactured in the United States of America

Contents

General Editor's Introduction

The volumes in this series, Wellesley Studies in Critical Theory, Literary History, and Culture, are designed to reflect, develop, and extend important trends and tendencies in contemporary criticism. The careful scrutiny of literary texts in their own right remains today a crucial part of the work that critics and teachers perform: this traditional task has not been devalued or neglected. But other types of interdisciplinary and contextual work are now being done, in large measure as a result of the emphasis on "theory" that began in the late 1960s and early 1970s and that has accelerated since that time. Critics and teachers now examine texts of all sorts—literary and non-literary alike—and, more generally, have taken the entire complex, multi-faceted field of culture as the object for their analytical attention. The discipline of literary studies has radically changed, and the scale and scope of this series is intended to illustrate this challenging fact.

Theory has signified many things, but one of the most crucial has been the insistent questioning of familiar categories and distinctions. As theory has grown in its scope and intensified in importance, it has reoriented the idea of the literary canon: there is no longer a single canon, but many canons. It has also opened up and complicated the meanings of history, and the materials and forms that constitute it. Literary history continues to be vigorously written, but now as a kind of history that intersects with other histories that involve politics, economics, race relations, the role of women in society, and many more. And the breadth of this historical inquiry has impelled many in literary studies to view themselves more as cultural critics and general intellectuals than as literary scholars.

Theory, history, culture: these are the formidable terms around which the volumes in this series have been organized. A number of these volumes will be the product of a single author or editor. But perhaps even more of them will be collaborative ventures, emerging from the joint enterprise of editors, essayists, and respondents or commentators. In each volume, and as a whole, the series will aim to highlight both distinctive contributions to knowledge and a process of exchange, discussion, and debate. It will make available new kinds of work, as well as fresh approaches to criticism's traditional tasks, and indicate new ways through which such work can be done.

William E. Cain
Wellesley College

Introduction

After languishing on the periphery of critical discourse for several decades, regionalism has recently begun to contribute a significant voice to some of the most urgent debates of our day. As we witness nations being torn apart by warring factions, each claiming a particular parcel of land as its native soil; as industry and environmentalists square off over development versus protection of ecosystems; as once-common assumptions about universal humanist values come increasingly under question, it has become clear that regionalism is more than just nostalgic "local color," but that it comprises a dynamic interplay of political, cultural, and psychological forces. As notions of cultural homogeneity become increasingly outdated, and as humanity's tenuous place in the natural world seems in peril, regionalists have begun to speak out, contributing to a sporadic dialogue that spans the past century. The purpose of this volume is to bring together contributions from a wide array of critical interests, all of which add to a rich history of regionalist studies, and which reflect regionalism's contribution to current debates about such topical issues as multiculturalism, environmentalism, and literary pedagogy.

In the late nineteenth century, the United States experienced a collective cultural crisis: as the country began to emerge as an industrial world power, it was still bound by colonial ties to Old World culture, and critics and artists sought an indigenous art form that would reflect a unique American identity. Regionalism seemed to be the answer: detailed depictions of unique American environments and the communities that inhabited them were thought to be the means of forging a distinctly American art.[1] William Dean Howells voiced the popular sentiment when he declared that in order for American culture to break free from its British ancestry, "the arts must become democratic," and praised authors who chronicled the daily lives of common citizens (66). He described the careful observation of local details as a "vertical" examination of national character, which he opposed to the "horizontal" sweep of heroic fiction typical of such British writers as Sir Walter Scott (67). Comparing America's "rarefied and nimble air full of shining possibilities and radiant promises" to "the fog-and-soot-clogged lungs of those less-favored islanders," he was certain that verisimilar depictions of local environs would produce a unified image of the national character (61, 62). Hamlin Garland, a young writer whom Howells had taken under his wing, echoed Howells in describing as "crumbling idols" the classic works that littered the history of English literature.

Although the logic of Howells's solution to America's cultural crisis seemed irrefutable, some regionalist authors confronted contradictions in trying to apply Howells's realist methods to their own depictions of regionalism. The first of these problems was the question of exactly what is to be represented in regionalist fiction. In trying to describe what drew him to San Francisco as the subject of his fiction, Frank Norris explained that his motivation sprang not from a desire to catalogue local artifacts, but from the desire to capture what he described as an "indefinable air" that gave San Francisco a distinct character (1112). Hamlin Garland encountered a similar problem when he discovered that regionalism does not originate *out there* in an external world of local artifacts, but within the artist, in a deep personal affinity with a particular place, which he or she calls home. Garland explains that "it is the most natural thing in the world for the young writer to love his birthplace, to write of it, to sing of it," and goes on to describe the lasting effects of this attachment to one's birthplace when he says that the mature author "carries with him consciously or unconsciously a compelling sense of its power, its beauty, its significance" ("The Vital Element," 43).

Garland confronted another, even more profound contradiction between the kind of local-color realism that Howells advocated and his own regionalist art. For Howells, regionalism had been a means to an end. The ultimate goal of all art, Howells believed, was to reveal a universal truth that would overcome differences. "Men are more like than unlike one another," Howells declared, and the aim of all fiction is to "make them know one another better, that they may all be humbled and strengthened with a sense of their fraternity" (87). Garland, however, found this humanist idealism at odds with his regionalist art, for he seems to have intuitively recognized regionalism as a literature of difference. In his criticism, Garland returns repeatedly, almost obsessively, to the importance of representing difference: in one article he describes local color as "the differentiating element" ("The Vital Element," 43); elsewhere he says that "it is the differences which interest us; the similarities do not please" ("Local Color in Art," 57); and in yet another article he goes so far as to proclaim that "in the space of that word 'difference' lies all the infinite range of future art" ("The Local Novel," 78).

For Garland, this startling foreshadowing of Derridian deconstruction was merely a vague intuition; he ignored his own fledgling insight and proceeded to write the kind of pedestrian local-color realism that Howells advocated, and that many readers today still associate with regionalism. Garland did, however, point the way to important insights that would be developed by future generations of regionalists.

In the 1920s and '30s, the industrial might that only a decade ago had promised limitless prosperity had now become an engine of death and destruction. The technology that had fueled the Great War was now a divisive force, alienating individuals and communities from the land they inhabited, and dissolving communal ties that assure each individual a secure place in the world. Once again, regionalism was central to popular debates, offering an antidote to the prevailing mood of alienation and despair.

Regionalist movements sprang up spontaneously throughout North and South America. Regionalism was far more popular in South America, where *regionalismo* movements proliferated, and sparked fierce debates with more Eurocentric purveyors of modernist ideas and techniques. Regionalism had less cultural force in the United States, and it would never again attain the popular appeal that it had in the late nineteenth century, but regionalist movements did arise throughout the country, and voiced opposition to the prevailing tendency toward cosmopolitanism, or what John Crowe Ransom described as the prevailing trend toward "progressivism, industrialism, free trade, interregionalism, internationalism, eclecticism, liberal education, the federation of the world, or simple rootlessness" (293–94). For the most part, these regionalist movements were confined to local communities and were served by small magazines with readerships in the hundreds.[2] One of these groups, however, gained brief national notoriety, and added a significant voice to popular debates over cultural despair in general, and national identity in particular.

In the early 1920s, a group of young writers that included John Crowe Ransom, Allen Tate, Donald Davidson, and Robert Penn Warren gathered at Vanderbilt University in Nashville, and together published a magazine called *The Fugitive*. The magazine itself was short-lived, but its contributors went on to defend regionalism in publications with such inflammatory titles as *I'll Take My Stand, The Attack on Leviathan,* and *Who Owns America? A New Declaration of Independence.* Despite their preoccupation with regressive agrarian politics, some of these writers addressed the issue of representing difference that the previous generation of regionalists had only been vaguely aware of, and in so doing unearthed profound implications that would be further pursued by regionalist authors.

Donald Davidson presaged deconstruction by half a century when he revealed the hidden ideology underlying Howells's realism. If America were to have an art of its own, Davidson argued, it would not be the "democratic" voice of the people that Howells had described as rising up in a unified chorus, but it would reside in diversity. Davidson traced the popular perception of a national literature back to the previous century, when the same "old men" Garland had described as clinging to the "crumbling idols" of the English canon had used nationalism as, in Davidson's words, "an attempt to rationalize a cultural tradition which it became almost a point of honor to label as a distinctive possession" (272). The British had used this reasoning, Davidson continues, to justify the evolution of an increasingly pompous national literature:

> If the modern Englishman had evolved from a one-cell organism up to the state of Victorian complexity represented in Mr. Gladstone, then English literature had to be exhibited as mounting nobly up the evolutionary ladder from amoebic verse to the lofty periods of Alfred, Lord Tennyson. (272)

Following this logic, American regionalism would be a minor step toward a great literature: just as a great nation had evolved from a smattering of colonial outposts, a great national literature would evolve from lesser regional literatures. Not only was such thinking outdated, Davidson argued, but it was entirely unsuited to the American political and cultural context:

> Regionalism is a name for a condition under which the national American literature exists as a literature: that is, its constant tendency to decentralize rather than to centralize; or to correct overcentralization by conscious decentralization. (269)

John Crowe Ransom rescued regionalism from naive local-color realism by formulating a theory that defends regionalism on aesthetic grounds. Ransom's theory of an aesthetics of regionalism begins with economic necessity; when a community is first settled, he reasons, its means of production are determined by locally available materials. As a community progresses beyond mere subsistence and begins to develop an aesthetic sensibility, these same local materials will be woven into distinct local art forms. For Ransom, regional art is the *only* art; he defines the opposite of regionalism as eclecticism, and while for him regionalism is synonymous with culture, eclecticism is synonymous with everything that opposes culture: "In contrast with the regional view . . . eclectic minds are doubtless good for something, but they are very dangerous for the health of the arts" (299). Ransom generally associates eclecticism with urbanization, but he suggests that not all cities are necessarily built "upon indifferent and eclectic foundations" (299–300); without specifically referring to urban regionalism, Ransom implies that a city that develops naturally around local commerce and that does not deny its history can maintain its regional aesthetic.

Ransom stops short of explaining how this regional aesthetic might be expressed other than in literal representations of local artifacts, but Robert Penn Warren hints at an alternative to realist poetics when he praises some contemporary regionalists whose works "represent deviations from the ordinary fictional norm of reported actuality" (*Southern Harvest*, xvi). Warren offers an alternative to the distant perspective of empirical observation when he observes that these writers "have attempted to assume the responsibility of creating characters from the inside out; they have not been content with the routine process of penetrating the surface of reported actuality" (*Southern Harvest*, xvi). Warren criticizes traditional regionalist fiction by describing two typical fallacies: "descriptive" and "historical" regionalism. Davidson describes "descriptive" regionalism as merely a superficial treatment of local space that is divorced from historical context, and says that this kind of descriptive fiction "does not provide a framework in which human action has more than immediate and adventitious significance" ("Not Local Color," 154). According to Warren, "historical" regionalism, in the novel-of-manners tradition, ignores the vital interaction between human communities, and "manners tend to be substituted for value, and costume and *décor* for an essential relationship between man and his background" ("Not Local Color," 154). To Warren, local-color descriptive realism and historical novels of manners both deny the important fact that for the regionalist, "time and place are one thing" ("Not Local Color," 154). Donald Davidson echoes this necessary interdependence of time and place in his insistence that rather than "dwell among the artifacts" belonging to a region, the regionalist author must "from his region, confront the total and moving world" (277).

The advent of the new criticism diverted the agrarians' attention from regional concerns before they had pursued the implications of their important insights, and the country's headlong rush into yet another national war effort soon eclipsed what proved to be a short-lived public debate between regionalists and nationalists. This brief regionalist movement made considerable contributions to the rudimentary understanding of regionalism offered by the previous generation, though: in offering an alternative to the prevailing trend toward "rootlessness," these critics and authors freed regionalism from the constraints of naive realism; they repudiated common assumptions about a homogeneous national identity; and they suggested that a harmonious interaction between a human community and the environment it inhabits need not be an anachronism, even in developed industrial societies. The dialogue that the fugitive-agrarians had taken up where Howells and his contemporaries had left off would not be picked up again for another half century, when regionalism would once again offer significant contributions to urgent cultural debates.

Today, the essential sense of community that assures each individual a place in the world is once again threatened by technology: not only by the machinery that drove Victorian industry and that fueled the two world wars, but also by electronic communication, which would seem to make regional loyalty an anachronism. Horrifying accounts of holes in the atmosphere, aerial photographs of the deforestation of entire continents, ethnic riots in the United States, neo-Nazism in Germany, "ethnic cleansing" in the former Yugoslavia: these all give weight to end-of-the-century prophesies of doom. And once again, regionalism is surfacing as a counter-voice to cries of alienation and despair.

Various fields of study have addressed these themes individually: feminism examines the familial sense of belonging that has been suppressed by the kind of patriarchal discourse that is perhaps less blatant today than it was when Howells spoke of the "fraternity" that binds all cultures, but that still persists; nature writing has recently provided fruitful examinations of humanity's relation to the environment it inhabits; and cultural studies have examined ways in which social communities are marginalized by discourse that suppresses the representation of difference. As the essays in this collection will demonstrate, regionalism encompasses all of these issues: it is born of a sense of identity and belonging that is shared by a region's inhabitants; this sense of community springs from an intimate relation to the natural environment; and since a region is by definition a small part of a larger whole, a regional community is necessarily a marginal community. The contributors to this collection bring insights stemming from feminism, environmentalism, cultural studies, and literary theory to bear on a comprehensive understanding of regionalism's role in contemporary critical discourse.

The collection begins with Francesco Loriggio, who draws on recent contributions from literary theory to fully explore the implications of what for Garland had been a naive intuition that regionalism is a literature of difference. Loriggio starts with the premise that the world that regionalist authors strive to represent is not a homogeneous space governed by universal laws, but is a distinct reality governed by local forces. Bringing possible-worlds theory and narratology to his examination of regionalism's quest to portray difference, Loriggio observes that "once we admit that worlds are multiple and coexist . . . we also admit that the question of what regionalist fiction is becomes not a secondary question, but very nearly the question of what fiction is."

Michael Kowalewski applies recent critical and theoretical insights to explaining the personal sense of place that underlies regionalism. Kowalewski looks more closely at the intimate relation between human community and natural environment that gives rise to a distinct local reality, and at the localized world view, or "bioregional perspective," that results. Drawing on contributions from the emerging field of bioregionalism, Kowalewski establishes regionalism's central place in current discussions of environment and ecology.

Marjorie Pryse pursues the implications of regionalism as a literature of difference by showing how regionalism's de-centered world view can be inscribed in regionalist texts. Referring to examples from late nineteenth- and early twentieth-century women regionalist authors, Pryse explains how readers conditioned by more traditional views of culture often find themselves "in uncertain territory" on entering the regionalist text, and how these texts can teach us to read "differently," or how to recognize cultural differences that are excluded from more traditional representations of national culture. Pryse draws on her own classroom experience to offer practical insights into the current debate over what we should be teaching in our literature courses, and how we should be teaching it.

The de-centered perspective that Pryse describes distinguishes regionalism from other depictions of local communities (such as nature writing or travel writing), and exactly who has access to this regionalist perspective has always been a contentious issue.[3] Two of the contributors to this collection illustrate how the regionalist "insider's" experience is represented in fiction by contrasting paired treatments of a region: one by a region's native inhabitant, and the other by an outside observer.

Mark Schlenz contrasts two treatments of the same region—one by Mary Austin, an inhabitant of the American Southwest, and the other by Willa Cather, a curious visitor. By adapting Kristeva's concept of *chora* to regionalist poetics, Schlenz shows how Austin's novel reflects a semiotic fusion of culture and environment. In both novels a character experiences an epiphanic vision in the New Mexico desert, but whereas the protagonist of Cather's novel hastens to erect a cathedral— starkly incongruous with the desert landscape—to commemorate his vision, Austin's protagonist finds confirmation at home, in the family. Rather than erect a spire, the boy returns to the landscape, where he finds that the mountains and desert are inseparable from the patterns of his home.

Jill Franks's comparison of two treatments of the same isolated region in Sardinia offers a similar contrast between the insider with privileged access to regional culture and the curious outsider. D. H. Lawrence's *Sea and Sardinia* and Grazia Deledda's *La madre* describe the same place, but whereas the stark cliffs that frame the village are for Deledda redolent with cultural connotations, for Lawrence, these same cliffs symbolize only the stark emptiness of the Sardinian peasant's world. Similarly, the clothing and demeanor that for Deledda represent centuries of cultural heritage are for Lawrence merely exotic embellishments on common stereotypes.

Regional identity is seldom contained within arbitrary political borders. Warren Johnson proves this point by examining depictions of regional identity in Alsace-Lorraine, which has retained its culture despite being the object of political disputes involving several different political states. Johnson shows how although each of these warring states would contribute to regional identity, Alsace-Lorraine nevertheless retains a culture entirely its own. A pair of nineteenth-century authors known popularly as Erckmann-Chatrian portray conflicting political and ideological forces on a human scale, through characters that blend in with their environment to share an ideological framework shaped by both indigenous beliefs and by influences borrowed from warring factions that would claim Alsace-Lorraine as their own.

Peter Caccavari reminds us that the United States is not exempt from the kind of regional warfare that has for centuries buffeted Alsace-Lorraine and that today is tearing apart nations in Europe and elsewhere. Caccavari examines conflicts between regional and national borders evident in two novels by Albion Tourgee, a "carpetbagger," or Northerner who moved to the South following the Civil War. The two novels illustrate two possible ways of reconciling regionalism and nationalism: Tourgee's earlier work offers the more traditional view of nationalism as an overarching ideology that subsumes regionalism, yet his later *Bricks Without Straw* suggests a positive role for regionalism, portraying it as a dynamic cognitive process rather than a static, organic object.

Regional conflicts have traditionally been limited to struggles between powerful centers of culture and commerce and marginal rural communities. The conflict is compounded when regionalism is put in the broader context of postcolonialism: New World regions are doubly marginalized by virtue of falling in the shadow of Europe's centuries-old cultural authority. New World regionalism is further complicated when one considers that an urban setting might be the site of a distinct culture that has arisen in close contact with its natural surroundings. Rosa Sarabia explores the complex and paradoxical implications of urban New World regionalism in her discussion of a group of Buenos Aires writers in the 1920s.

Ricardo Kaliman looks at another group of 1920s South American writers, one that does not fit any conventional definitions. The south-central Andes region that several 1920s avant-garde writers describe is not enclosed within a single national boundary, so their writing falls outside of traditional anthologies of national literature; their directly referential aims exclude these writers from traditional studies of avant-garde literature; and their own form of indigenism does not suit themes common in South American criticism (indigenism as saviour of the oppressed, for example, or as the champion of agrarian reform). Kaliman proposes a systems theory that would see regionalism not as a "school" or "movement," but instead as an artistic and social configuration that defies the traditional classifications of critical discourse.

Petar Ramadanović provides a poignant example of contemporary regionalism in his discussion of Milorad Pavić's *Dictionary of the Khazars*, a novel written in Serbo-Croat (and subsequently translated into several languages), a language that has become a casualty of regional strife in the former Yugoslavia. Ramadanović shows how postmodern poetics of self-reference and indeterminacy portray a distinct regional culture that survives despite losing its language and its land.

My search for colleagues whose research could shed light on new approaches to regionalism brought together ten scholars from diverse backgrounds, all of whom were examining the literary representation of marginal cultures whose identities are defined primarily by an intimate interaction with the natural environment. Many of these scholars had been pursuing their interest in regionalism in isolation, or as a tangential aspect of other, more firmly established fields of research. We have all been gratified to find that our interest is shared not only by the other contributors, but also by the many scholars identified in the list of works cited accompanying each of these essays. The rudimentary history that I have sketched here indicates that these essays contribute to a dialogue that goes back at least a century, and that promises to play a significant role in decades to come.

David Jordan

NOTES

1. Conditions were very different in South America, but the result was the same: as it became clear that poverty and underdevelopment were not transitory stages on the road to development, but were endemic, South American authors sought means of breaking the cycle of exploitation and violence that had marked their history since the conquest. Realistic depictions of rural communities became popular means of both portraying the effects of colonial exploitation and forging an autochthonous literature. See Cândido.

2. See Reigelman for an excellent discussion of the role of the small magazine in general, and of one magazine in particular.

3. Garland declared defiantly that the regionalist novel (or what he referred to as "the local novel") "could not have been written in any other place or by any one else than a native" ("Local Color in Art," 64). More recently, Walter Wells offers more moderate criteria when he says that "What counts is that a writer, whatever his regional tenure, know the region intimately, and that this intimacy find its way into the aesthetic makeup of his writing." Wells contradicts Garland's claim that nativity is the only legitimate criteria of regionalism by pointing out that Robert Frost was born in California, and Robinson Jeffers was born in Pennsylvania (7–8).

WORKS CITED

Cândido, Antônio. "Backwardness and Underdevelopment: Its Repercussions in the Writer's Consciousness." *Latin America in Its Literature*. Eds. César Fernández and Julio Ortega. Trans. Mary G. Berg. New York: Holmes and Meier, 1980. 263–282.

Davidson, Donald. "Regionalism and Nationalism in American Literature." 1938; rpt. *Still Rebels, Still Yankees and Other Essays*. N.p. Louisiana State University Press, 1972. 267–278.

Garland, Hamlin. "Local Color as the Vital Element of American Fiction." Proceedings of the American Academy of Arts and

Letters and the National Institute of Arts and Letters. No. 4 (1910–1911). 41–45.

————. "Local Color in Art." Crumbling Idols; Twelve Essays on Art and Literature. 1894; rpt. Gainesville, FL: Scholars' Facsimile and Reprints, 1957. 57–66.

————. "The Local Novel." Crumbling Idols. 69–79.

Howells, William Dean. "Criticism and Fiction." Criticism And Fiction and Other Essays. Eds. Clara Marburg Kirk and Rudolf Kirk. New York: New York University Press, 1959. 9–87.

Norris, Frank. "An Opening for Novelists: Great Opportunities for Fiction Writers in San Francisco." 1897; rpt. Novels and Essays: Frank Norris. Ed. Donald Pizer. New York: Library of America, 1986. 1112–1114.

Ransom, John Crowe. "The Aesthetics of Regionalism." American Review 2 (1934). 290–310.

Reigelman, Milton M. The Midland; a Venture in Literary Regionalism. Iowa City: University of Iowa, 1975.

Warren, Robert Penn. "Not Local Color." The Virginia Quarterly Review 1 (1932). 153–60.

————. Intro. A Southern Harvest. Boston: Houghton-Mifflin, 1937.

Wells, Walter. Tycoons and Locusts: A Regional Look at Hollywood Fiction of the 1930s. Carbondale and Edwardsville: Southern Illinois University Press, 1973.

REGIONALISM
RECONSIDERED

Regionalism and Theory

Francesco Loriggio

There are a number of reasons why, after decades of neglect,
literary regionalism should suddenly retain our attention. Most
of them have to do with events with which we are, by now, all
too familiar. We live in a period that has redrawn its atlases over
and over again, that is constantly reconfiguring its surroundings;
and if the process we are witnessing seems to be leading toward
always greater global unity, it is also, and as blatantly, leading
toward greater and greater fragmentation. The fall of the Berlin
wall occurred while the Soviet empire was breaking down; the
increasingly longer reach of multinational companies, the
planetarization of the economy and of modes of communication
has resulted not in more cohesion and/or uniformity but in the
creation of trading blocs (the EEC, the Pacific Rim states, the
North American Free Trade Area, etc.) and in the revival of the
debate on identity and the politics of ethnicity. The call for a new
world order in politics only rekindles our awareness of the
various other macrodivisions we have been living with, and
which pit North against South, underdeveloped against
developed countries, or the West against practically every other
cardinal direction. Within these larger areas, other middle-size or
smaller-size entities appear and disappear, crisscrossing the lines
politics and trade create.

   In short, the reassessment of literary regionalism, in its
most cogent aspects, goes hand in hand with the reconsideration
of space as an analytical category, itself a compelling exercise in
revision, and a major project of our *fin-de-siècle*. It is with an

account of the relevance of geography, after and in spite of our long, obsessive preoccupation with time, that recent literary critics and social scientists have prefaced their analyses of what is undoubtedly the salient occurrence of the century, i.e., decolonization, the rise of independent, Second- and Third-World states and cultures (Said, "Representing"). And, not surprisingly, their accounts dwell often on the concomitant, puzzling, and perhaps necessary presence of both continuity and discontinuity, on the give and take between amalgamation and dissolution, centripetal and centrifugal forces (Said, *Culture*). No sooner do new nations emerge than new linkages form. Linkages are established, and other discontinuities come to the surface. Borderlines intersect other borderlines. Divisions operating on the basis of one criterion overlap divisions governed by other criteria. Places are deterritorialized and quickly reclaimed to some other sort of territory. Just as it is becoming clear that there was more cultural resistance to the colonial, metropolitan powers during colonialization than hitherto believed, it is also becoming clear that independence does not abolish contact with the colonizing countries: the interested parties remain conjoined by the past, by what *has* happened between them. Paradoxically, this means that new, additional separations come to bear. The old French and British empires give way to the "francophonie" or to "the English-speaking world," but French and English appear today in many subvarieties, depending on the location of the speakers.

The historical and political inscription of geographical space, its ambivalences: this is a premise which any contemporary recanvassing of regionalism must address and inevitably return to. Space is—there's no denying it—the dimension of power and resistance: besides postcolonialist criticism, the works of philosophers, historians, and sociologists (Foucault and Goffman come to mind) on prisons, asylums, and clinics have taught us that the cityscape, no less than the landscape, is a hodgepodge of sites, each with a different institutional status and a different relation to the machinery of domination. Yet to anchor the concept of regionalism too strictly to the vicissitudes of the geography that is mentioned on the evening news or that we pass by with blinkered eyes in our daily routine would be to impoverish both its intellectual scope and the intellectual scope of geography. Critics such as Edward Said, who have been instrumental in steering the agenda of literary studies toward a better appreciation of the role of space, have rightly insisted on the worldliness of literature and the categories adopted by those discourses and disciplines that interpret literary texts (Said, "Introduction"). In so doing, they have rescued literature and geography (and, ergo, regionalism) from the web of literary and cultural movements we have labeled postmodernism. They have disjoined them from philosophies which, having proclaimed the advent of the local, have seemed unable to do anything with it, other than to re-ontologize it, to reintegrate it in those signifying processes that celebrate the very universalist priority of language and the linguistic over history.[1] But the secular realm is itself a macroregion: it is *this* world as opposed to the *other* world or to the other worlds that history has also had to contend with, and to eschew these other worlds from history is also to unduly limit the width and the breadth of history, along with much of its pathos.

Let me be more precise. Here in the West, references to Heaven or Hell or Purgatory or Eden or Hades are still quite common in everyday conversation and in the speech-genres of certain special occasions (prayer, religious ceremonies). Non-Christian mythologies provide their own spate of similar allusions from which to derive imagery and vocabulary. Nor is it only texts concerned with beginnings and endings, with first and last events, cosmogonies and religious texts, that have contributed to the diffusion and authority of such second-order or third-order geographies. Literature too has helped to bring into being and to promote imagined localities: Arcadia, the land of shepherds, the refuge for so many characters of plays, poems, stories about the disillusionment of city life appeared on the scene with Virgil's *Eclogues*; Parnassus, the mountain home to the Muses, was the most citable of a panoply of topographies pertaining to writing that the writers of ancient Greece bequeathed to posterity; and, of course, Utopia has been the repository of all that which societies in history cannot or dare not contemplate, cannot or dare not look squarely in the face, ever since Thomas More's work of the same title. Even if nothing were to be said about the family resemblances between the supernatural and the fictional domains, and the secret history that joins and disjoins them, the spaces they propose would have to be taken into account.

Along with the horizontal dimension that maps consign to us, there is a vertical dimension to consider. Churches, sanctuaries, sacred grounds, places devised to facilitate contact with the other world, topographies which give access to the topographies above or below, dot the everyday human habitat. And one need only think of how often the image of the earthly paradise recurs in the writings of the first explorers of the American continent, or later—properly intertwined with its corollary, the city on a hill—in the homilies of the first Pilgrim preachers, to appreciate how the geography of the supernatural has impinged on the descriptions of America, how it has insinuated itself in U.S. history. By the same token, a lot of the history of South Africa, novelist J.M. Coetzee has noted (3), would be better understood if it were telescoped back to those initial conditions which did not permit the deployment of the myth of the return to Eden and to innocence (the early settlers of the Cape knew they were in Africa, and therefore in an old and not a new world).

Viewing geography as a two- or three-tiered field, as a combination or dialectic of what there is and what people believe or imagine there is, lends credence to the solicitations coming from possible-world semantics, and especially to the suggestion that world-making, world-creating is at the core of all intellectual activity. Philologists, theologians, and historians have been able to trace the painstaking efforts that went into the invention of Purgatory in the Middle Ages (Le Goff): they, and the research already available on Arcadia, teach us that history is often not much more than the effect of semantic persuasion, the result of a process that naturalizes a world that is merely possible, turning into a world that is actual-like. Certainly, Said's concern about the theologizing penchant of deconstruction would gain some force by being restated in these terms. For a long time the two subdivisions of otherworldliness—the supernatural and the fictional—acted in tandem. By virtue of its prestige—because it dealt with beginnings and endings—religious mythology was initially the more influential of the two domains. It was the source or, in Frye's phrase, the "great code" of the fictional, as embodied by literature. Thus Arcadia can be seen as a lower-scale version of the Garden of Eden. In centuries closer to the present, the order has been reversed. The fictional is now predominant: interpreters of religious texts now more often than not approach them with the critical tools they use for poetry or prose or theater and which they borrow from literary criticism. The danger Said rightly warns against is one whereby an historical shift in taste, in philosophical attitude becomes, for all intents and purposes, the excuse for a usurpation, so that literature, the purveyor of fictional worlds, transmogrifies into religion, the purveyor of revealed worlds, and critics into aspiring ministers, into dispensers not of words, but of the Word. Deconstruction, in this respect, is the culmination of an enterprise that has its roots in the art-for-art's sake movement: it merely bestows on to the critic the qualities first associated with the text and the author (Orphic character, professionalization, outsider status vis-à-vis ordinary society to be achieved through dandyness, la bohème, proper asceticism etc.). It is, at any rate, on initial, preliminary distinctions of this sort that rest even the secular hybridisms to which some of the most sophisticated fiction of recent decades has accustomed us. The mixture of history and make-believe, the trans- or interworld narration we encounter in the works of Borges, Doctorow, Timothy Findlay or the best of science fiction (in Philip José Farmer's *To Your Scattered Bodies Go*, Sir Richard Burton, the writer-explorer, meets with Hermann Goering, Neanderthal men, the real-life model of Carroll's Alice, and a variety of improbable beings from the future) would be unthinkable if we first could not posit the existence of separate worlds, hence of a plurality of worlds.

And equally difficult to imagine would be all those works that dwell on the fictionality of fiction, on the "unreality" of stories, whose plots and events and personnel, different as they are from the stone-like concreteness of the everyday world, need to be properly accessed in order for them to become available: Calvino's *If on a Winter Night a Traveler* invites, right in the first chapter, the reader who has opened its pages to relax, turn down the light, sit in a comfortable sofa and a comfortable posture, and disregard the surrounding noise before continuing, before going on to the pages in which the characters begin to appear. Topographical markers or spatial metaphors creep in almost unawarely in literature about literature, or texts about texts. In Jean Cocteau's films, mirrors are the entrance gates to mythical or otherwordly dimensions. The protagonist of Woody Allen's *The Purple Rose of Cairo* is a film character who, tired of the vapid, superficial narratives to which he is assigned, plunges through the screen and into the life of some of the individuals watching him in the audience. One of Pirandello's short fictions tells of an author who refuses the pleas of a character to write his story; the character, a fragile, weary, older gentleman, devised the "technique of the upside-down binoculars": when he finds himself offended by life, he acts as if he is looking at it from the wrong side of binoculars, so that things will shade off into the distance and become less real; to his entreaties, the author responds by suggesting that he, the character, apply the same principle to himself and to the author's unwillingness to acknowledge his narrative potential. A suggestion which could very well have come from semanticists themselves: whereas some philosophers have warned about depicting fictions as if they were out there somewhere (Kripke, 147), we do run into philosophical works that wonder how "far" invented worlds are from the real world (Walton).

All this, it bears repeating, is important for a reappraisal of regionalism in literature. For, to pursue to its conclusion the syllogism adumbrated in what I have said thus far, once we admit that worlds are plural and coexist, however much they may encroach on one another, we also admit that the question of what regionalist fiction is becomes not a secondary question, but very nearly the question of what fiction is. The specific and apparently minor topic is directly and forcefully entangled with, and perhaps emblematically recapitulates, some of the more relevant larger theoretical issues.

To note the obvious, the fictional, the supernatural, and the actual worlds, which are regions of the possible, may be, in turn, themselves regionalized. That is, the fragments and pieces that ultimately portray these realms may elicit further segmentation. A contemporary semanticist begins his survey of fictional worlds by distinguishing between homogeneous (uniregional) and heterogeneous (pluriregional) worlds, stable and unstable worlds. With the insertion of a few other qualifications (regions are either pure or contaminated, realistic or fantastic, etc.) he is able to calculate that the simple permutation of all qualities would result in forty-four classes of fiction (Martinez-Bonati, 193). If we were to limit the list to pluriregional worlds alone, we would still be left with substantial numbers. But most of all, it is evident that to locate each of the regions of a world within that world would entail various operations, operations of the kind required to locate each of the worlds within the realms of possibility. As many devices are needed to establish the singularity of Faulkner's Yoknapatawpha County as are needed to properly represent the life of another planet in fiction, or the "realness" of realistic, actual-like worlds, or the "fictionality" of a fictional world, or the "supernaturalness" of supernatural worlds.

In the parlance of semanticists, worlds must be "furnished," they and the characters inhabiting them must be endowed with properties, no more and no less than regions,[2] or vice versa. This activates a host of typically *literary* problems, involving all the components and all the phases of the text, from production to reception. Besides the decisions about how to render the world to be narrated, the writer must grapple with his/her (or his/her textual stand-in's) relation to the world and the relation of the readers.

One example may suffice, among the many. In 1881, Italian novelist Giovanni Verga published a short story entitled "Cavalleria rusticana." It is a tale that he later adapted into a play and which inspired composer Pietro Mascagni to produce the opera of the same title. The plot of both the narrative and the theatrical piece follows the development of a love triangle: a young man just returned from military service finds that the woman of his past is now married to another man and, deaf to the entreaties of his current betrothed, attempts to rekindle the old flame. This is the stuff the novel of manners and drawing-room drama were made of in Europe during the last decades of the nineteenth century. Except that Verga's backdrop is rural Sicily, and events that in middle-class metropolitan surroundings would have led only to a psychological denouement, to all sorts of psychological, "civilized," save-the-appearances compromises, now bring out elementary passions and end in blood: incited by the vengeful proddings of the scorned woman and the coquettish acquiescence of her married rival, the two men finally settle their differences in a duel which costs one of them his life. Moreover, the action of the tale or the play takes place outside, in the village square, hence in the public sphere, rather than inside, in the privacy of the home. And it has a definitively ritualistic tinge to it: the two men fight during the Easter festivities, and after having communicated their intention to do so in very strongly coded exchanges (the "rustic chivalry" the title alludes to: in the episode in which the time and the location of their duel are arranged, the younger man bites the ear of the man he has offended in order to show that he accepts his challenge, a gesture the implications of which all the bystanders are aware).

The dilemma the tale's regionality posed for Verga was almost directly proportional to the advantages. Novelty was ensured, but there were demands. To emphasize too peremptorily the characters' difference, the rawness of their passions, would be to risk losing the audience outside of Sicily, to irk readers or spectators accustomed to situations in which passions were manifested in small dosages, at best, in the guise of sublimated sentiment, and to whom the tensions, the violence of the tale might seem exaggerated, unmotivated, and hence unrealistic. To appease the audience, and nuance the cultural difference, would be to betray the story, to give an edulcorated, polite, folkloric version of the emotions of the characters. And when they communicated verbally how were the characters to speak? Italian was still essentially a literary language, unknown in the peasant setting of the tale. And Sicilian was a regional speech, a dialect incomprehensible outside of Sicily. The balancing act was not an easy one. Verga, who did not entirely trust theater directors, spent enormous energies supervising the early stagings of his play. As for language, he had to invent an idiom which allowed the regionality to at least resonate. The characters' cues were in an Italian understood by all Italian readers but which contained the odd Italianized Sicilian expression and faithfully reproduced Sicilian syntax and speech rhythms.

Verga's efforts aimed at transcending the double insider/outsider positioning regionalist writing unavoidably generates. In his endeavours, he was helped by the fact that he was both a Sicilian and had lived on the metropolitan Continent for several years. More than perhaps any major figure of his time, he realized that, for the author no less than for the reader, fiction activates identificational mechanisms which could not be overlooked. To the very careful linguistic blending his novels and short stories undertake, whereby the characters speak in their voice and are spoken by some other voice, corresponds the equally careful, meticulous practice of the author: through a method which may be called approximation and distanciation, Verga, who during his writing years lived in Florence or Milan, would first travel to Sicily to the locations he planned to describe in the text he was researching, then, when it was time to begin writing, he would return to the Continent, to the hustle and bustle of the city environment. The empathy or sympathy with which he approached the peasant culture on the verge of being swept away by impending industrialization was tempered by an objectivity which alone could yield the overall picture, could situate the peasants in history. As he used to say, the writer "should be able to see his characters in the flesh, like God made them" but "[he] will never be as openly and as validly truthful as when he proceeds by mental reconstruction and substitutes the mind to the eyes" (Verga, quoted in Bertacchini, 232; the translation is mine).

Possible-world semantics provide, I believe, the most on-the-spot theoretical back-up for a reassessment of the nature of regionalist fiction. No doubt this stems from the geographical analogies that the notion of world encourages and which in literary criticism can be put to service, *pace* the objections of some semanticists, without trivialization. And perhaps in an age such as ours, in which disciplines are constantly finding long lost or unexpected supporters in other areas of research, one could do worse than to underscore the interests that semanticists share with geographers and literary critics. Geographers, too, have recently been comparing notes and conducting exchanges with writers and critics.[3] But within literary studies, proper crucial intimations about regionalism, its literariness, and interdisciplinary commerce come also from narratology. Not so much the mainstream, classical, structuralist-oriented version that had its heyday in France during the 1960s, as the more off-the-center, peripheral reflection of the Tartu school, and of Jurij Lotman in particular.

Most attractive about this work, which has been strangely unacknowledged by influential contemporary critics, is its reconceptualizing of narration directly by way of topology rather than chronology, in terms of space rather than time. Lotman initiates his remarkable foray into the theory of narration by distinguishing between unplotted and plotted texts. For it to have plot, a narrative must comprise at least two spaces. The event, the basic unit of plot, occurs when there is a "shifting of a persona across the borders of a semantic field," when a character goes beyond a set of rules, a world picture, a delimited (and hence culturally bound) topography (Lotman, 233).

Not surprisingly, it is the protagonist who is charged with the task of inaugurating the plot in a text: "Rastignac making his way to the top; Romeo and Juliet crossing the border that divides their warring houses; the hero breaking away from the home of his fathers to take his vow at a monastery and become a saint; or a hero breaking away from his social milieu and going to the people to make a revolution" (Lotman, 238). The disjunction between plotted and unplotted texts presupposes a disjunction between the characters. Just as plotless texts "establish a certain world and its mode of construction" (236) and secure borders, and plotted texts narrate the trespassing and the transgression of borders and constitute the "'revolutionary element' in relation to the world picture" (238), so characters are either immobile ("not permitted to cross the borders" [238]) and mobile ("[have] the right to cross the border" [238]). In contrast with the latter, who are allotted active functions and are the heroes, the agents of the story, the immobile personae, when they appear in plotted texts have an essentially classificatory, passive, subordinate role: they simply confirm the rules of the world they people, the criteria which determine its borders.

Lotman's formulations open up a whole set of issues, many of which are complementary to those raised by semantics. For one thing, switching the emphasis from the notion of world to the notion of world picture alters the idea of literature. A literary text, in this more semiotic approach to meaning, is a model of the reality to which it refers. To echo a parallel Lotman himself often uses, it stands to the world as maps do to territory. Further, the insistence on the theoretical centrality of the "world picture" reasserts the *narrative* (instead of the semantic) primacy of space and region. As Lotman tells it, plotted narration requires the copresence of at least two spaces, two worldviews that are oppositional *and* properly sequenced (a character must move from one to the other). It follows, then, that narration with plot is always "a layer superimposed on a basic plotless structure" (238). Before transgression can occur, the system of rules to be transgressed upon, the borders of the "semantic field," must be defined. Texts that strive precisely to sketch out perimeters and parameters have logical priority over texts that contemplate more than one system of rules. No less importantly, the narrative priority Lotman grants to space and region rests on the complicities he uncovers not simply between plot and space, but between plot, space, and the characters. One's affinities with, one's dependence on a particular environment or a particular community impact on one's status or one's actions, as does one's independence or one's departure.

Literarily, the upshot here is, for all intents and purposes, a vindication of description. If the semantic field is a "world picture" and is configured spatially, if the establishing of location is indirectly (rules) or directly (when the story is given distinctly topographical or geographical coordinates) the preliminary narrative gesture, one does not merely fill in the background (or the setting, the landscape, etc.). Description is not an embellishment, an ornament, an adjunct to narration; it is, on the contrary, the condition of its possibility. Without it there can be none of the other features which go with stories *qua* stories.

This amounts to saying that regionalist writing exposes the originary plotlessness of narration. All fiction must include references to place (to be is to be somewhere). Generally,

narratives do not do much with the specificity of a site, which—
left inert, unthematized—stands for all space, serving merely to
testify of the existence of a backdrop. Regionalist writing
accentuates that specificity by encrusting it over the characters
and on their actions. When we label a novel "Southern fiction,"
or, in Canada, "Prairie fiction," we are implying that no matter
how much the text may be replete with events, no matter how
much the characters may be spurred on by private or personal
motivation, their behavior will be seen as a function of their
relation with the place in which they live, hence, ultimately, as
the manifestation of a state. Action which remains confined
within the bounds of a particular place is not, for narratology,
action, but an inclination, an embodiment, something to be
described. It is the principle of the *genius loci*, whether one
conceives it as rigid positivist determinism (according to which
individual strivings "reflect" the laws of a milieu) or in line with
the more loose and more complex interactive symbiosis between
individual and ecosystem that earth scientists and geographers
have recently been talking about. The looming, umbrageous,
dilapidated Italian castles of Anne Radcliffe's Gothic novels,
Hardy's majestic Egdon Heath (in *The Return of the Native*),
Flaubert's monotonous provincial landscapes (especially in
Madame Bovary) are presences that cannot be ignored: they affect
the development of the narrative no less than the characters.

Or, to recapitulate from a slightly different angle, texts
without plot are narration of identity, narration whose primary
task is to label the characters and shed light on the mechanics by
which the labeling is carried out. In actively reinstalling setting
into the story, in narrating, as Kenneth Burke would state it, the
scene-act and the scene-agent ratios (in lieu of any of the other
ratios a fiction may summon: agent-act, agent-purpose, agent-
agency etc.; *Grammar*, xvii-xxv), regionalist writing becomes the
prototype par excellence of that narrative mode. Against the
fiction of plot, which focuses on movement, suspends or
minimizes identity in favor of freedom, it roots the items or the
individuals whose fates fall within its compass.

But the issue of identity closes the circle, brings us back to
where we started. As befits a venture that models its object of
study—and therefore must keep it well in sight—world–picture

narratology ends somewhere in the vicinity of history and the historical. It reconnects the discussion of the literariness of regionalist fiction to the spirit of the times.

For all the actuality of space, this is not an easy affair, something that goes by itself. Against the obstreperous, intrusive messiness of history, the logic of forms and structures appears too neat to a fault. How does a world exactly relate to the behavior of characters? Is it the world that provides the identity of the characters or the characters that provide the identity of the world? Transferred to regionalism such queries can have embarrassing intellectual and political codas. When Eudora Welty declares that place exerts "the most delicate control" (122) over characters, defining them by confining them, her words can acquire several meanings. They can be interpreted as the indication of sensitivity toward nature, landscape, and/or the ecosystem in general, as the indication of a materialistic conception of life and the world or as a kind of Heideggerian abeyance of the modern forgetfulness of being. All are attitudes or principles with more sanguine and deterministic variants: among them are the positivistic ideology of milieu and the philosophies of the soil that the past century has propounded. If we instead equate the region with the manners and the behavior of the community occupying it, as Flannery O'Connor has done (in *Mystery*), the physicality of place tends to be diminished. We would have to agree with those geographists who assert that a region consists of the sum of the modifications human beings impose on a given environment (and hence that region can be described simply in terms of development and underdevelopment [Entrikin]) or, in the long run, with the neo-anthropomorphists, with those scientist-philosophers who believe that the earth is a living, spirit-pervaded, cell-like entity.

Especially, identity forces us to ponder more carefully the implication of mixture. In works which narrate the overlapping of actual and fictional worlds, individual vicissitudes unfold within ontological limits that cannot be sidestepped. The character who in Woody Allen's *The Purple Rose of Cairo* jumps from the limber celluloid space of the screen to the space of Depression America can be only the properties his role permits him to be. As a character in a romance-story formula film, he cannot lose a fight, nor know how to deal with prostitutes. In his foray into the "real" world he displays his unpreparedness. Mixture here is more akin to juxtaposition, to adjacency. A one-to-one correspondence obtains between the world and the characters. By contrast, in secular actual-world novels, characters can not only cross borders, but can engage another culture without relinquishing their own. Cultural bifocality, bidimensional topologies, can be contemplated. Modern maps are double, triple geographies. In North America, such cities as New York, New Orleans, Syracuse, Ithaca, London, Messina, Waterloo, Kitchener or such provinces and states as Nova Scotia, New Brunswick, New Hampshire, to cite at random, betray the European memory that was grafted on and still hovers over the sheer physicality of the land. Together with the Little Italies, the Chinatowns that dot the North American urban landscape, they bespeak the strategy of duplication that underlies the construction of America and Canada. Because they are there, the indigenous names of cities and provinces—the various Saskatchewans, Mississaugas, Temiskamings, Oshawas, Ottawas, etc.—become endowed with their own particular saliency (they stand for pre-European history). Cultural hybridism is more and more the normal condition of communities, individuals, and literatures. It is congenital to the climate in which the activity and discourse of criticism must be carried out.

In this respect, the linear, sectionalizing, and essentializing penchant of regionalist fiction and the theories most useful for its study are vulnerable to some of the charges voiced by current postmodernist critiques of rootedness and of the arboreal imagery pervading discourses of or about identity (Deleuze and Guattari; Malkki, 24–44). In dealing with the scene-act or act-scene ratios, semantics and narratology fail to address the possibility that societies may be itinerant or may comprise deterritorialized customs, manners that pertain also to other spaces. And without cultural cohesion the transparency and the singularity of the region cannot be guaranteed. The philosophies which have advocated nomadism, migrancy, movement, or that have upheld the subordination of space to the many protheses, the many extensions of the human sensorium that technology has made available, are the conceptual litmus test of regionalism.

At the heart of the problem posed when regionalist fiction and semantic and narratological theories are reinjected into history is the notion of boundary. It is usually taken in the univocal, unequivocal, straightforward sense of enclosure. But by the mere act of cutting off, of separating, boundaries also evoke, bring into play, other spaces. Theoretically and politically, the question is whether the plotted texts/unplotted texts opposition is a dichotomy, whether it is both a dichotomy and a dyad, whether it can be both exclusionary and inclusionary.

What is interesting about regionalist literature is that such ambivalence, the dialectic to and fro which seems peculiar to our age, has been the staple ingredient of its history, from the outset. Secular regionalism, regionalism as it is usually intended in common critical discourse, emerged in fiction in significant coincidence with a number of other fundamental developments: the rise of the modern nation-state and nationalism, the idea of national literature, realism, and the consolidation of European (French and British first and foremost) imperialist expansionism. Nineteenth-century adepts of actual-world fictions swayed between opposing tensions. In abiding by the mandate of realism, that no slice of life should be outside the ken of the novelist, in deeming the slums and the lower classes, the untypical spaces of metropolitan topography, amenable to literary depiction, in charting the countryside or alluding to the existence of the *outremer*, the overseas dominions, Dickens, George Eliot, Hardy, Balzac, Flaubert, George Sand, Zola, and Verga were at once surveying the internal and external territory of the state, paying homage to the ruses and the technology that ensured its reach, *and*, unwittingly, pointing to the chinks in the machinery, the fault line in nation and empire. When Balzac affirms that the novelist should *"faire concurrence à l'Etat-Civil"* (1: 52), we can perhaps appreciate more than he ever could, the irony of his program. Novelists entered in competition with the state by leaving no stone unturned, by planning totality, by writing sagas, epic frescoes, or, more radically, by authoring narrative cycles, many-volumed (often near a hundred) stories which, as Balzac's *Comédie humaine* or Zola's *Les Rougon-*

Macquart, aspired to be the big, definitive fictional anthropologies of the times. But by entering into competition with the state through the mapping and inscription of hitherto unnamed spaces, unnamed "semantic fields," they also disclosed the artificial, cultural nature of the homogeneity the state promoted: centralized territories were composed of margins, of a myriad hinterlands, each of which provoked its own allegiances, its own enthusiasms. In literature the nation ceased being the basic unit of geography the very instant recognition of it occurred.

This stage of the continuous dialectic between globalization and localism within the nineteenth-century realistic novel is again perhaps best illustrated by Verga. In *I Malavoglia*, a work translated into English as *The House by the Medlar Tree*, the state region antinomy appears in raw form. The narrative traces with relentless completeness the effect of Italy's freshly-achieved unification on a small community of Sicilian fishermen. New taxes, new laws, a new bureaucracy, countless other social obligations: Verga provides a complete inventory of the apparatuses by which modern, modernized governments exercise control over a territory. In addition, history itself, in the guise of the telegraph, steamboats, newspapers, trains, intrudes on and disrupts the insular, insulated, and still very traditional life of the village. For the Malavoglias, the family whose vicissitudes the novel spotlights, the impact has disastrous consequences. Their fortunes take a quick downward slide when the eldest son, who has returned from military service on the Continent duly dazzled by metropolitan life, can no longer accept the patriarchal structures and the harsh struggle-to-make-ends-meet daily toil his brothers, sisters, parents, and grandparents have had to tolerate. The family splits, with some of the members leaving the village; the family dwelling is lost to creditors. Only the youngest son, the one most attached to the lore passed on by the older generation, is able, after long tribulations, to reconstitute what is left of the group and retake possession of the house. Although Verga cannot but acknowledge the impact of history and progress, his story does hold out some hope. The lesson individuals such as the Malavoglias must learn, he observes in a short story that anticipates the plot structure of his novel, is the lesson fishermen learn from mussels, which survive if they cling to the rock they inhabit, and will be eaten by bigger fish if they venture out ("Fantasticheria," 155). However defensive and conservationist (not merely conservative) the ideology, it slows down and perhaps somehow deflects history's, or the state's, awesome power.

The caution accompanying the discovery of the local and the identity of reduced radius soon gives way to more affirmative attitudes. In the twentieth century, the growing suspicion that the processes by which nations achieve and maintain their hold on their margins transcend national borders sparked off a remediation of the attachment to place. Sociologists have been warning us for the last two or three decades that the bureaucratization of everyday life produces "homeless minds," minds disengaged from any commitment to community, along with the equalities and equanimities typical of democratic societies (Berger). Long before them, in an essay entitled "Provincialism," which has to be the most impassioned and most lucid statement about the function of region in modern culture, American philosopher Josiah Royce had already singled out the "frequent changes in dwelling-place" (69), the "dead level of harassed mediocrity" (74) and the "mob-spirit" (81) as the three "evils" facing twentieth-century and, all the more so, American civilization. Mobility, technology, the massification of behavior, the instruments of the state, he argued, threaten not just the region: being unresponsive to geographical barriers, they threaten the state itself. Without provinces (i.e., the space of a national domain "sufficiently unified to have a true consciousness of its own unity, to feel a pride in its own ideals and customs, and to possess a sense of its distinction from other parts of the country") and without provincialism (i.e., "the tendency of [a] province to possess its own customs and ideals," "the totality of these customs and ideals" and "the love and pride which leads the inhabitants of a province to cherish as their own these traditions, beliefs, and aspirations" (69), there can be no identity, without identity there is no loyalty, and without loyalty, the nation ultimately loses its cohesiveness. To lose touch with the local, with small groups, is, for Royce, to forsake the qualities which also strengthen an individual's allegiance to the remote, to the larger social entities. Nations and regions are spaces of a different order, but socially they need not be at odds. In the heavily mediated, heavily depersonalized world of modernity, the ability to identify with others is among the most urgent prerequisites. The state, whose own identity is beleaguered, whose powers are being eroded by mass culture, would do well not to encourage the province "to forget itself," since neighborliness is the cornerstone of nationhood (99).

The reversal of the paradox of the nineteenth century, by which one now envisages the nation through the region, by which attachment to place is a fully positive trait, is probably North America's most significant original contribution to the dossier on regionalism. Royce's pronouncements today call to memory various other polemics. *Provincialism* plays *Gemeinschaft* against *Gesellschaft*, and is tinged by melting-pot politics, by the very travailed early twentieth-century American concern with the assimilation of newcomers, or "wanderers" and "sojourners," as Royce likes to designate them. Still, after reading his essay, it is easier to understand why such an eminent representative of late twentieth-century American fiction as Flannery O'Connor would answer those who complained about Southern alienation by claiming that the problem of the American South was, quite the contrary, that it was not "alienated enough," that its manners and the customs were not as self-evident as they might or should be (28). Or why her contemporary, Eudora Welty, concludes her analysis of the role of place in fiction—of its impact on characters, on the writer's point of view—by insisting that the place in which the writer has his or her roots should become the "first and primary proving ground" (129) of his or her fiction and that the writing which "speaks most clearly, explicitly, directly and passionately from its place of origin will remain the longest" (132).

It is not, of course, without significance that in the European and American novel regionalism should be an intranational affair, despite the references to the empire. Or that the enemy should be a diffused, faceless, ubiquitous one: progress, technology, and mass culture. One does not—and one cannot, without stepping out of one's skin—regionalize Europe or the West, except, perhaps, in foundational and hence imperceptible fashion (as the cradle of civilization or the source of the white man's burden). Only in our age, now that it, after long and painful introspection, is on the verge of unification, has Europe been able to see itself as a province in a decentralized world.

As I have already mentioned, the history of regionalism culminates with postcolonialism, whose task it has been to expose in full the geographical incidence of regionalist duality. In writing about Nigeria, Chinua Achebe detaches it from empire, regionalizes it; his cultural nationalism continues a tradition of resistance that, as literary scholarship has shown, goes back to colonial times (Said, *Culture*). In writing in English, he, like the Third-World authors who write in French or Spanish, rejoins his country's sovereignty to the residues of empire, to the past which clouds his country's and the West's history. Precisely because with postcolonialist literature the region is situated within an international or intercontinental and even interracial horizon, the geopolitical dimension of the ambivalence comes to the fore more emphatically. In the Third World, technology and mass culture are instruments wielded by certain states.

The most striking aspect of the history I have outlined is that regionalism has always been presented and has always presented itself as a reaction to and an offshoot of the central developments of the two last centuries, modernization and empire. But if region and state, nation and empire, deterritorialization and reterritorialization feed on one another, then theories of narration sympathetic to geography need to be equipped with features that capture the processual, interactive functioning of border-making and border-unmaking. Outright transgression of frontiers is only one option; spaces can be resettled or remembered.

The introduction of process changes the slant of the debate on regionalism. The value we attribute to any theoretical view may depend on circumstance, on where we locate it, on whether we believe that attachment to space or the overlapping of spaces occurs in the deterritorializing or the reterritorializing phase in the always ongoing history of border adjustment. Are stories about nation and nationhood to be read as being about repossessions of space, hence as critiques of regionalism? Or is regionalism a critique of the deterritorializing devastations of national unification? Are theories that propose errancy and nomadism as ideals a reaction to excessive faith in roots, and therefore an indirect reterritorializing, a reshuffling of borders in which the frontier coincides with the planet? Or are they illustrations of the deterritorializing effects of modernity, of a period in which individuals are by definition "homeless," already "nomadized" by bureaucracy and mass communications?

Such a revision would, of course, have significant repercussions on literature as well. Regionalist fiction is in many ways the modern novelistic revisitation of two of the classical Aristotelian unities of space, action, and time (whereas plotted, non-regionalist fiction which narrates the crossing from one semantic field to another tells the story of the repudiation of the unities). But in the twentieth century, we have seen that time insinuates itself within space. The new worlds that European explorers "discovered" and European settlers colonized contain shorter and longer durations, are a collage of different pasts. Duplication does not annul consecution. Memory conflates two spaces by inventing similarities between them, but also establishes chronological sequence. In some occasions borders are geographical *and* temporal signposts. In *The Lion's Mouth*, a novel by Canadian writer Caterina Edwards, the Venetian characters who have migrated to Alberta view their struggle to survive in the prairie flatlands and the struggle of the pioneers before them as analogous to the struggle of the individuals who managed to build Venice out of an equally precarious terrain, the marshes of the northeastern coast of Italy. What keeps divergences alive is time: Alberta may be like Venice, but for the Venetian immigrants, it comes after. Inverting one of Bakhtin's neologisms, which both amends and preserves the century's bias in favour of time,[4] we could say that regionalism today needs to be approached *topochronically*, needs to privilege space but without disavowing time.

It is by properly theorizing these slippages that the discourse on regionalism can reassume its role in criticism. Regionalism, in other words, is not a throwback to yesteryear.

But if it is nostalgic, defensive, restorative, it can claim for its anachronism the appropriate hermeneutic status. It is within modernity, one of its results, and without, one of its antinomies. As the latter, it has always held toward actuality and it manifests an interrogatory, dialogical stance. In one of his more soberingly prophetic passages of "Provincialism," Royce states: "As our country grows in social organization there will be, in absolute measure, more and not less provincialism" (66). His remark reminds us that regionalist literature and thought rehearses *avant la lettre*, and finds wanting most of the shibboleths of the postmodernist reflection on place, from cosmopolitanism to nomadism to metropolitanism, that regions are the strategic, ideological reply to placelessness.

Indeed, the notion of region is, I would submit, among those which best puts in relief some of the blind spots of postmodernist thought. Quite aside from other elements (there does seem to be a contradiction between the deconstruction of master narratives and globalizing ideologies and nomadism), nomadism may itself be an instance of a strong, if paradoxical, scene-act ratio: it does, after all, thrive in certain specific environments where the terrain facilitates mobility (plains, the steppes) or renders it compulsory (shifting sand deserts). And in any case, it is one thing to suggest that one should become nomadic philosophically or culturally and quite another to be nomadic, to constantly suffer the constraints whereby one cannot but lead a nomadic life. The criterion of choice would already bring about some sort of division. In a similar vein, the deterritorialization incurred by Third World inhabitants goes beyond the experience of Westerners, regardless of how great the influx of refugees and immigrants is or how painful the achievement of national unification was; British or French or Spanish nationals will never have to speak Hindi or one of the Arabic or Andean languages. While it is true that borders are artificial constructs, they are constantly reduced, rerouted, enlarged, rebuilt, rather than abolished. Given the functioning of regionalism, given that the crisis of regionalism is due to changes in the demographic balance of communities, it would seem more appropriate to deduce that what must be rethought, in order to revive the idea of region, is not only the relation between human beings and environment, but also togetherness and social life.

As far as literary theory is concerned, history does not confute the logical priority narratology accords to unplotted texts, since in fiction as in everyday doings there is mixture only if there is the material to mix. History does dispute the criteria that erect clear-cut barriers between plottedness and unplottedness.

In actual literary practice both plot and plotlessness have positive and negative versions that elicit the other term. Identity, as would attest the many anti-heroes twentieth-century fiction has spawned, can hang on a character like an albatross. Together with a pathos of freedom, there is a pathos of rootedness. Clym Yeobright, the protagonist of *The Return of the Native,* is disappointed by his sojourn in the city and seeks to refurbish his links to Egdon Heath; Eustacia Vye, who has always been living there, longs to get away. Emma Bovary, unlike her husband, who is in his proper element, feels trapped in the small town where she spends her life and dreams only of the glamour of the big city, of Paris. The history of the novel Gyorgy Lukacs has delineated is dominated by plotted texts and teems with alienated characters, forever marked by the "transcendental homelessness" which is, for Lukacs, the epitome of modernity (41). A good slice of the plot of twentieth-century existentialist fiction can be summarized by the dictum which declares human beings to be condemned to freedom.

As a consequence, the weightings of the mobility/ immobility dyad that both Lotmanian narratology and postmodernist philosophy sponsor appear unjustified. More often than not norms are negotiated: rarely are they only received, inherited. Even obedience to rules can turn into a willful, deliberate response, if it is the expression of solidarity, of participation in a group. As Royce explains in "Provincialism," immobility may be a desirable alternative, may be yearned for, *especially* in the modern and postmodern world. When transgression, anomie, facelessness are the order of the day, when borders have to be constantly reestablished over and against movement, over and against modernity or postmodernity, characters sensitive to locality are no longer passive figures, but agents, active individuals. And what about those stories in which characters cross borders under duress, the fiction of slavery, abduction, forced emigration? A final swerve, pulling in the direction of ethics, traverses the various antinomies. Unplotted texts are primary not only because they are the prelude to narration, but also because they can be its epilogue.

NOTES

1. I am thinking here of Jean-François Lyotard and his *The Postmodern Condition*, but also of Michel Foucault, who on this score has been even more explicit. Neither the critique of master narratives, of globalizing ideologies, nor Foucault's denouncements of the "tyranny of globalizing discourses" and his plea on behalf of "particular, local, regional knowledge" (82–83) have resulted, in my view, in any appreciable theorizing of the local, which has been instead absorbed by other interests. I am not forgetting that within postmodernism there are other approaches to space, including the very influential ones promoted by Gilles Deleuze and Felix Guattari in their *A Thousand Plateaus*. But their concerns bypass the local and actually could be seen as a repudiation of it. The target of Deleuze and Guattari is, again, globalizing structures, but especially the tendency of any structure of essentialize, to solidify into forms of power, into permanency. This makes the local and the regional as suspect as the universal.

2. Good overall surveys of possible-world semantics and the features of greatest interest for literary criticism can be found in Allen and Pavel.

3. Of great usefulness are the anthologies by William E. Mallory and Paul Simpson-Housley and Douglas C.D. Pocock.

4. I am referring here to the notion of the chronotope. See Bakhtin.

WORKS CITED

Achebe, Chinua. *No Longer At Ease*. London: Heinemann, 1960.

Allen, Sture, ed. *Possible Worlds in Humanities, Arts and Sciences*. Berlin and New York: De Gruyter, 1989.

Bakhtin, Mikhail. "Forms of Time and of the Chronotope in the Novel." *The Dialogic Imagination*. Trans. C. Emerson and M. Holquist. Austin: University of Texas Press, 1981. 84–258.

Balzac, Honoré de. *La comédie humaine*. 12 vols. Paris: Seuil, 1965.

Berger, Peter. *The Homeless Mind: Consciousness and Modernization*. New York: Random House, 1973.

Bertacchini, Renato, ed. *Documenti e prefazioni del romanzo italiano dell'800*. Roma: Studium, 1969.

Burke, Kenneth. *A Grammar of Motives* and *A Rhetoric of Motives*. 1946. Cleveland: World Publishing Company, 1962.

Calvino, Italo. *If on a Winter Night A Traveler*. Trans. William Weaver. New York: Harcourt, 1981.

Coetzee, J.M. *White Writing*. New Haven: Yale University Press, 1988.

Deleuze, Gilles, and Felix Guattari. "Treatise on Nomadology: The War Machine." *A Thousand Plateaus*. Trans. B. Massumi. Minneapolis: University of Minnesota Press, 1987. 351–423.

Edwards, Caterina. *The Lion's Mouth*. Edmonton, Alberta: NeWest Press, 1982.

Entrikin, Nicholas J. *The Betweenness of Place: Towards a Geography of Modernity*. London: Macmillan, 1991.

Farmer, José Philip. *To Your Scattered Bodies Go*. Berkeley, CA: Berkeley Medallion Books, 1971.

Flaubert, Gustave. *Madame Bovary*. Trans. Paul De Man. New York: Norton, 1965.

Foucault, Michel. *Power/Knowledge*. Trans. Colin Gordon et al. New York: Pantheon, 1980.

Hardy, Thomas. *The Return of the Native*. New York: Harper, 1966.

Kripke, Saul. "Identity and Necessity." *Identity and Individuation*. Ed. M.K. Munitz. New York: New York University Press, 1971.

Le Goff, Jacques. *La Naissance du Purgatoire*. Paris: Gallimard, 1981.

Lotman, Jurij. *The Structure of the Artistic Text*. Trans. R. Vroon. Ann Arbor: University of Michigan Press, 1977.

Lukacs, Gyorgy. *The Theory of the Novel*. Trans. Anna Bostok. London: Merlin, 1971.

Lyotard, Jean-François. *The Postmodern Condition*. Minneapolis: University of Minnesota Press, 1984.

Malkki, Lisa. "National Geographic: The Rooting of Peoples and the Territorialization of National Identity Among Scholars and Refugees." *Cultural Anthropology* 7.1 (1992). 24–44.

Mallory, William E., and Paul Simpson-Housley, eds. *Geography and Literature*. Syracuse, NY: Syracuse University Press, 1986.

Martinez-Bonati, Felix. "Towards a Formal Ontology of Fictional Worlds." *Philosophy and Literature* 7.1 (1983): 182–195.

O'Connor, Flannery. *Mystery and Manners*. New York: Farrar, Straus, & Giroux, 1969.

Pavel, Thomas. *Fictional Worlds*. Cambridge: Harvard University Press, 1986.

Pavese, Cesare. *The Moon and the Bonfire*. Trans. Louise Sinclair. London: Owen, 1974.

Pirandello, Luigi. "La tragedia di u personaggio." *Novelle per un anno*. Vol. I. Milano: Mondadori, 1956. 713–719.

Podock, Douglas C.D. *Humanistic Geography and Literature*. Totowa, NJ: Barnes & Noble, 1981.

Royce, Josiah. *Race Questions, Provincialism, and Other American Problems*. Freeport, NY: Books for Libraries, 1967.

Said, Edward. "Introduction: Secular Criticism." *The World, the Text, and the Critic*. Cambridge: Harvard University Press, 1983.

———. "Representing the Colonized: Anthropology's Interlocutors." *Critical Inquiry* 15 (Winter 1989): 203–225.

———. 1993 *Culture and Imperialism*. New York: Knopf, 1993.

Verga, Giovanni. "Cavalleria rusticana." *Tutte le Novelle* Vol. 1. Sixth Ed. Milano: Mondadori, 1969. 139–144.

———. "Fantasticheria." *Tutte le Novelle*, 149–155.

———. *The House by the Medlar Tree*. Trans. R. Rosenthal. Berkeley: University of California Press, 1983.

Walton, Kendall. "How Remote Are Fictional Worlds from the Real World?" *Journal of Aesthetics and Art Criticism* 17 (1978): 11–23.

Welty, Eudora. *The Eye of the Story*. New York: Random House, 1978.

Bioregional Perspectives in American Literature

Michael Kowalewski

> On [the American poet] rise solid growths that offset the
> growths of pine and cedar and hemlock and liveoak and
> locust and chestnut and cypress and hickory and limetree
> and cottonwood and tuliptree and cactus and wildvine
> and tamarind and persimmon . . . and tangles as tangled
> as any canebrake or swamp . . . and forests coated with
> transparent ice and icicles hanging from the boughs and
> crackling in the wind . . . and sides and peaks of
> mountains . . . and pasturage sweet and free as savannah
> or upland or prairie . . . with flights and songs and
> screams that answer those of the wildpigeon and highhold
> and orchard-oriole and coot and surf-duck and
> redshouldered-hawk and fish-hawk and white-ibis and
> indian-hen and cat-owl and water-pheasant and qua-bird
> and pied-sheldrake and blackbird and mockingbird and
> buzzard and condor and night-heron and eagle. To him
> the hereditary countenance descends both mother's and
> father's.
>
> Walt Whitman
> *Preface to* Leaves of Grass (1855)

Regionalism in the United States has conventionally been defined in geographical, historical, and cultural terms, with individual areas of the country featuring distinctive economies, urban centers, dialects, folklore, styles of cooking, and voting patterns. Large regions, like "the Midwest" and "the South" are often spoken of as if they display readily identifiable traits and boundaries. But as Howard Odum and Harry Moore suggested as early as 1938, American regions are more accurately described as a complicated set of predefined, overlapping domains:

> There are regions of government and regions of commerce. There are regions of literary achievement and regions of agricultural adjustment. There are regions of land and of water, of forests and of minerals, of flora and of crops. There are regions of educational institutions and football arrangements; regions of wholesale trade and of Rotary and Kiwanis. There are regions within regions, subregions and districts. (5–6)

American literary regionalism has played an important part in defining this diversity of regional identity. Historically, literary regionalism has been a self-conscious attempt to evoke the flavor and distinctiveness of life in rural areas of the country removed from urban centers of power and money. Literary regionalism, as the novelist Marilynne Robinson puts it, "is the product of a cultural bias that supposes books won't be written in towns you haven't heard of before" (65). Though "the idea of a regional literature is an odd one," Robinson says:

> it contains a blessing: it makes people feel that they live in a peculiar place. Of course, people, by definition, do live in a peculiar place. But if they become aware of this peculiarity as something exceptional they are stimulated to an enriching interest in the particulars of their own lives. A characteristic of all regional writing is a deep sensitivity to detail that would be a virtue in any writing. The idea that a place is significant by virtue of being the place that it is makes literature about that place possible. (65–66)

An enriching interest in the particulars of specific places also marks an aspect of contemporary environmentalism called bioregionalism. Bioregionalism emphasizes the fact that human behavior and ethical deliberation take place within the context of local communities, both human and biotic. Individuals and communities, in such a view, come into consciousness *through*, not apart from, the natural environments they inhabit. Bioregional definitions of healthy communities are ecological, seeing identity as relational and interactive and occurring within specific bioregions, territories defined by natural boundaries rather than abstract governmental designations. While bioregionalism is a relatively recent environmental movement, one connected with notions of "deep ecology," the roots of a bioregional vision of human identity can be traced in American literature of the last 150 years. Writers like Gary Snyder, Barry Lopez, Wallace Stegner, and Wendell Berry, along with many American Indian and Latino authors, have offered richly textured understandings of human interactions with the land and other life-forms. Bioregional writers emphasize an awareness of "place" as a living, interactive force in human identity. They attempt to counter the rootless and displaced character of contemporary American society by illuminating the complex ecology of local environments and how those environments affect the life of those who live within them.

"As Americans," Barry Lopez has recently argued:

> we profess a sincere and fierce love for the American landscape, for our rolling prairies, free-flowing rivers, and "purple mountains' majesty"; but it is hard to imagine, actually, where this particular landscape is. . . . In the attenuated form in which it is presented on television today, in magazine articles and in calendar photographs, the essential wildness of the American landscape is reduced to attractive scenery. We look out on a familiar, memorized landscape that portends adventure and promises enrichment. . . . [It is] a homogenized national geography, one that seems to operate independently of the land, a collection of objects rather than a continuous bolt of fabric. ("Geographies" 116, 123)

The real American landscape, Lopez says, is a realm of "almost incomprehensible depth and complexity," a mosaic of local biotic and geographical environments: "the ponderosa pine forests and black lava fields of the Cascade Mountains in western Oregon . . . the ephemeral creeks and sun-blistered playas of the Mojave Desert. . . . [T]he anomalous sand hills of Nebraska, the heat and frog voices of Okefenokee Swamp, the fetch of Chesapeake Bay, the hardwood copses and black bears of the Ozark Mountains" (117, 118). No one of these places can, perhaps, be fully fathomed, either biologically or aesthetically. But they can be lovingly evoked and lived in by those who have gained a "local knowledge" of a specific environment: an intimacy with a place that "rings with the concrete details of experience" (119). Local knowledge, Lopez says, is a form of particularized geographical perception that might first seek to understand a community by its wild nuts, fishing lures, fences, and history of storms before advancing that understanding in museums and libraries (131).

"Bioregionalism" in the United States is a grass-roots environmental movement which exemplifies Lopez's respect for down-sized ecological systems and local relationships with the land. As Kirkpatrick Sale puts it in explaining the ethics of environmental action in *Dwellers in the Land*:

> The issue is not one of morality . . . but of *scale*. There is no very successful way to teach, or force, the moral view, or to insure correct ethical responses to anything at all. The only way people will apply "right behavior" and behave in a responsible way is if they have been persuaded to see the problem concretely and to understand their own connections to it directly—and this can be done only at a limited scale. It can be done where the forces of government and society are still recognizable and comprehensible, where relations with other people are still intimate, and where the effects of individual actions are visible; where abstractions and intangibles give way to the here and now, the seen and felt, the real and known. Then people will do the environmentally "correct" thing not because it is thought to be the *moral*, but rather the *practical*, thing to do. (53)

The optimal scale at which ecological consciousness and healthy human communities can be developed, Sale argues, is the bioregional. The earth, he says, is organized "not into artificial states but natural regions" of varying size (55). These natural areas, or bioregions, are defined by "particular attributes of flora, fauna, water, climate, soils, and landforms, and by the human settlements and cultures those attributes have given rise to" (55), though Sale quickly adds that the borders of bioregions are inevitably indistinct and interpenetrating. Bioregions "are not only of different sizes but often can be seen to be like Chinese boxes, one within another [morphoregions within georegions within ecoregions], forming a complex arrangement from the largest to the smallest, depending upon which natural characteristics are dominant" (56).

Regionalism, in such a definition, requires explicit links between the natural world and human communities and the issue of how cities and congested urban areas fit into such reimaginations of geography remains problematic. Nevertheless, bioregional definitions of place do not stress the biotic dimensions of environments exclusively. They underscore the formative interrelationship of both human and nonhuman forms of life. Bioregionalism, Judith Plant says, involves "learning to become native to place, fitting ourselves to a particular place, not fitting a place to our predetermined tastes. . . . As Peter Berg and Raymond Dassmann [have said], . . . 'It means understanding activities and evolving social behavior that will enrich the life of that place, restore its life-supporting systems, and establish an ecologically and socially sustainable pattern of existence within it'" (216). "The ideas of bioregionalism are being practiced all over the world," Plant reminds us, but they are "just rarely referred to as such" (217).

Martin Lewis has criticized what he sees as a neoprimitivist romanticization of rural areas in much bioregional thinking and he reminds us that "small-scale communities are seldom as humane and ecologically sound" as some eco-theorists imply they are (91). Still, the bioregional perspective, with its emphasis on the role of "place" and a community politics informed by a knowledge of shared ecology, offers an appealing means for promoting political education, multicultural understanding, and ecological consciousness.

One of the important models for this conceptualization of geo-cultural difference in the United States is the place-based character of traditional American Indian culture, in which boat design, musical scales, and immunology might all intimately reflect the spiritual interactions of a tribe with a specific natural environment. In discussing her own tribe, the Laguna Pueblo of New Mexico, novelist Leslie Marmon Silko says that the spirit dimensions of landscapes and animals form an integral part of Pueblo beliefs. "So long as the human consciousness remains *within* the hills, canyons, cliffs, and the plants, clouds, and sky," she says, "the term *landscape*, as it has entered the English language, is misleading . . . [for] this assumes the viewer is somehow *outside* or *separate from* the territory he or she surveys. Viewers are as much a part of the landscape as the boulders they stand on" (84).

Though not as explicitly spiritual in its stance toward the land as traditional tribal practices, bioregionalism does, at the very least, help articulate a new vision of nature and a reexamination of what proper human stewardship of nature might entail. As Peter Sauer says, the "quintessentially American idea of pristine wilderness" is now being challenged by ethnobotanists and biologists who are showing that "lands once thought of as untouched by human culture reveal patterns, often millennia old, of complex cultural-natural interactions" (2). Living with this new, altered sense of nature, however, is not an easy or untroubled matter. For writers especially, Sauer says, it is not enough to assert that humanity and nature have been inextricably bound in a reciprocal relationship for centuries:

> It is not enough to "prove" that the forests of the Amazon, or those of the northern Appalachians, are the products of interaction between people and land. These are essentially facts about nature and do not say enough about *us*. . . . Facts about nature have implications for our passions, politics, religion, and art. Science never was conceived as an instrument for investigating these aspects of being human. Science cannot say what we must do in order to settle up with a spirit we have wronged or to reforge the poetry that orders our lives. These are tasks that require all the faculties of our humanity. (14)

Bioregional writing forms an important aspect of a new cross-disciplinary investigation of "place"—in psychology, urban planning, geography, cultural history, and environmental studies. In exploring the ways environment and place shape identity and define consciousness, contemporary bioregional writers are also firmly in the American grain. Bioregionalism has been less a formalized movement in recent American writing—though Gary Snyder, in *The Practice of the Wild* (1990), has begun to formulate it as such—than an impulse, an orientation, or a practice (in the Zen Buddhist sense of the term). Bioregionalism, Snyder says, "is the entry of place into the dialectic of history." But not "place" defined in exclusively human terms. "We might say," he continues, "that there are 'classes' which have so far been overlooked—the animals, rivers, rocks, and grasses—now entering history" (41).

However vagrant an impulse bioregionalism might initially seem to exemplify (and the term itself is apt to make some critics' eyes roll), its centrality becomes clearer when we remember that the struggle of American writers to imaginatively come to terms with a new continent began with the very first accounts of the New World: a struggle that did not reap immediate rewards. Until the middle of the nineteenth century, the central dilemma of American literature was how to divine and adequately honor the spirit of places whites ostensibly owned more and more of, but did not yet imaginatively possess. Unable or unwilling to appreciate American Indians' deep consciousness of and identification with their lands, early writers felt they lived in an ahistorical landscape devoid of the emotional identifications which might have infused and inspired an indigenous literature. They "quickly felt the existential void of the unknown land like a draft upon their souls," Frederick Turner says, and:

> [f]or them, imaginative entry into the country was perhaps even more difficult than it was for the trailblazers, Indian fighters, fort builders, missionaries. The land in which they now found themselves, though it had from the first been invested with the dreams of the Old World, appeared to be utterly lacking in mythic associations or any visible aids to reflection. . . . Trees there were in the unnumbered millions of the climax forests of the east and west coasts and snarling mountain ranges, too, that barred access to the broad interior. But about none of these hung the least whisper of any understandable human past, and their silent presence was mighty and oppressive. (14)

There was tremendous optimism in the 1820s and thereafter about the potential influence of geography in shaping new art forms and a distinctive American character. "America is a poem in our eyes; its ample geography dazzles the imagination," Ralph Waldo Emerson announced in 1844. "The northern trade, the southern planting, the western clearing, Oregon, and Texas, are yet unsung. . . . [And they] will not wait long for meters" (465). Writers seduced by imitative fashions and filled "with wine and French coffee," Emerson warned, would find "no radiance of wisdom in the lonely waste of the pinewoods" (461). Unfortunately, huckster critics often made too loud and insistent a connection between literary and geographical destiny. Complaining in 1849 about a kind of topographical determinism that supposedly predisposed the merit of an author's work, James Russell Lowell mockingly suggested that instead of filling their title pages with "the names of previous works, or of learned societies to which they chance to belong," authors should supply readers "with an exact topographical survey of their native districts" (118).

Lowell usefully reminds us that there is no necessary relationship between landscape and writing. Yet barely five years after Lowell's essay appeared, Henry David Thoreau included a map, "a reduced plan" of Walden Pond—complete with cross-section profiles and measurements of "area," "circumference," "greatest length," and "greatest depth" (550)— as a part of his new, unclassifiable book, *Walden; or Life in the Woods* (1854). Literary bioregionalism might be said to originate in Thoreau's detailed accounts of his woodland experiment in self-sufficient living. Thoreau charts and records the literal sights, sounds, and textures of Concord's pastures and ponds. But he also endows those natural details with a luminous metaphorical life as he uses them to explore and understand human consciousness and "the nuances of his own identity" (41). That last phrase is Scott Slovic's, who uses it to describe Thoreau's multivolume *Journal*, a work he and others see as more rewardingly full of Thoreau's "vivid primary experience" of nature and self-awareness than *Walden* (41).

Yet wherever we find it in Thoreau's work, his experiences of the nonhuman realm of nature become experiments in self-perception and the psychology of awareness. This fusion of internal and external realities marks not only the Thoreauvian tradition of American nature writing (as Slovic incisively demonstrates), but bioregional writing more generally. The process of observing nature becomes not an account of objectivity but one of interaction, one in which, as Slovic says, the "attunement of the mind to external reality results in a sudden emotional charge, a confirmation of awareness" (44). Whether night-fishing for perch, inspecting the thawing sand patterns of a railroad embankment, or finding that he grew, in sunny moments of summer solitude, "like corn in the night" (411), Thoreau assumes the interrelatedness of what Wallace Stevens would later call inner and outer weather.

Observed phenomena in nature tends to offer up analogies for observation itself. This is why the mutual interaction of epistemology, consciousness, and place remains a given in Thoreau's writing, as he delineates what Kenneth Burke once termed a "metabiology" (Donoghue, 64). "The speculations, intuitions, and formal ideas we refer to as 'mind,'" Lopez says, "are deeply influenced by where on this earth one goes, what one touches, the patterns one observes in nature—the intricate history of one's life in the land. . . . [T]the shape of the individual mind is affected by land as it is by genes" ("Landscape," 65). Thoreau shares a similar belief in a spiritual ecology that blurs distinctions of "inner" and "outer," and of nature and mind. His wacky imperative, "I was determined to know beans" (451), testifies to his sense that the most ordinary processes of growth and nurture are more elusive than we might expect. "Making the yellow soil express its summer thought in bean leaves and blossoms rather than in wormwood and piper and millet grass, making the earth say beans instead of grass—this was my daily work" (447). Knowing beans (whatever that might entail) proves no less remarkable an activity than the earth's act of "expressing" its thoughts; not least because the pun in the word *expressing* (the earth both articulates its thought and exudes or pushes it out) itself illustrates how the fertility of landscape sometimes seems to be already composting in the language used to describe it. I think Thoreau would agree with Snyder's challenge of the American "delusion that we are each a kind of 'solitary knower'—that we exist as rootless intelligences without layers of localized contexts. Just a 'self' and the 'world'" (60). Beans, philosophy, snowstorms, perch, literature, flute music, and loon calls are what, Snyder might say, Thoreau *thinks* with.

Thoreau also seems to be the prototype of a bioregional writer in that he writes primarily in nonfictional prose. Though a more complete survey of literary bioregionalism would include a wide range of poetry and fiction, much of this writing tends to be nonfiction, often of a hybridized, cross-generic character, mixing nature writing with cultural history, travelogue, personal memoir, spiritual autobiography, and the prose poem. This partially explains why the debate about the quality and credibility of the regional literature that flourished in the post-Civil War period in the United States does not always bear as importantly upon the concerns of bioregionalism as one might wish. The critical discussion of this body of work still tends, as it did at the time, to focus on fiction alone and the question of whether or not it "realistically" represented the lives of people theretofore marginalized because of gender, ethnicity, or regional prejudice.

Furthermore, the very terms in which contemporary calls for regional artistry were put forth introduced telling contradictions. Take, for instance, Hamlin Garland's essay "Local Color in Art" (1894), which argued that local color was not "a forced study" of picturesque scenery but a quality of texture and background in fiction, a quality that *"will* go in, because the writer naturally carries it with him half unconsciously, or conscious only of its significance, its interest to him" (54). Garland imagined this local color in organic terms, not as "a forced rose-culture" but as "a statement of life as indigenous as the plant-growth" (51, 54). Yet the new spontaneity and simplicity that Garland said were helping "raise" local literature to "the level of art" came about only after the large-scale despoliation of the very indigenous landscape Garland used as a metaphorical base in championing local color. "Expression rose to a higher plane," he says, "as the pressure of the forest and the wild beast grew less" (51).

Bioregional writers tend to be more aware—often elegiacally—of the lost potential of American places and the native cultures they supported, places now eroded, filled with stumps and toxic ponds, or bulldozed into submission. "Looking back over all those eras when we . . . supposed Earth had nothing to do with her own story," Reg Saner says, "we can see, now, that had historians not left the green world absolutely *invisible* to consideration, or at very best had they not treated it as a painted backdrop for armed kings, that green world might have been admitted into history sooner, and so become visible. Now 'conquered,' it's a nature whose very defeat imperils its conquerors" (56).

Mary Austin is closer to a bioregional perspective when she reminds us that the white designation of arid land as "desert" defines that region by what, from a human standpoint, it is *not* (that is, inhabited, cultivated, "civilized"). Austin prefers the Indian term "the land of little rain." That phrase comprises a more neutral, climatologically accurate description of the land, just as "the Paiute fashion of counting time . . . by the progress of the season" (by when the trout begin to leap, when the piñon harvest ends, when the deep snows begin) gets "nearer the sense of the season" (*Land*, 106–07).

It was Austin who argued, in *The American Rhythm* (1923), that "verse forms are shaped by topography and the rhythm of food supply" (19). She said that she "could listen to aboriginal verses on the phonograph in unidentified Amerindian languages, and securely refer them by their dominant rhythms to the plains, the deserts, and woodlands that had produced them" (19). It was also Austin, as Esther Stineman notes, who "felt no responsibility to resort to scholarly evidence to prove the existence of an 'American rhythm'" (172). ("This general snootiness of the classic tradition [to] primitivism calls for a response in kind on my part," Austin once complained to an unsympathetic reader [Stineman, 173].) Yet even if the evidence Austin adduces to support her claims in *The American Rhythm* seems ultimately unconvincing, her notion that a writer's (or singer's) sensibility bears the footprints, as it were, of the local environment in which it has been nurtured articulates a theme that unifies subsequent bioregional writing.

Attempts to define a bioregional mode of imagination are complicated by the fact that writers we might class as "bioregional" all exist within larger regional alignments (the Southwest, New England, the South, and so on) which tend to be traditionally defined in terms of a common cultural or historical consciousness that may have only incidental connections to particular landscapes and ecosystems. Bioregionalists generally seek to stress not the common qualities of American places but the distinctive ones, the aspects of local identity taken to be most indelible and unreproducible elsewhere. This introduces an intriguing paradox, for the bioregional imagination of a watershed in Maine might, for instance, actually resemble a similar description of Oregon or Missouri more than it does an account of another New England setting imagined in strictly sociocultural terms. This is not because Maine is necessarily *like* Missouri but because they have both been represented—or elicited—in similar ways. Bioregional evocations of the land implicitly challenge the usefulness not only of national identities but of larger regional identifications that break loose of what Lopez calls local geography. Bioregionalists in general are wary of what Wendell Berry calls "a regionalism of the mind" (81), one which can result in "a map without a territory" (82), a literature of place without a place to evoke.

Different writers, of course, see the influences of natural environments on human history and behavior (and vice versa) differently. For some those influences are nuanced, impalpable, and elusive; for others they are direct, unavoidable, and overwhelming. Nevertheless, the basic premises of bioregional writing—that literature should be a place-based art form and (Snyder again) that "wild nature is inextricably in the weave of self and culture" (68)—unites what might otherwise seem a radically divergent body of work.

Barry Lopez's exploration of Arctic tundras and ice floes, *Arctic Dreams* (1986); Sallie Tisdale's search for "home" in the Pacific Northwest, *Stepping Westward* (1991); Linda Hasselstrom's writings from the ranches and coffee shops in the interior of the American West, *Land Circle* (1991); Wendell Berry's profusion of essays from his Kentucky hill farm; Terry Tempest Williams's account of birdlife and self-healing at the Great Salt Lake, *Refuge: An Unnatural History of Family and Place* (1991); John McPhee's geological tetralogy (*Basin and Range* [1981], *In Suspect Terrain* [1983], *Rising From the Plains* [1986], and *Assembling California* [1993]); David Rains Wallace's forays into a unique area of Florida woodlands, *Bulow Hammock: Mind in a Forest* (1988); Kathleen Norris's portrait of life on the high plains in *Dakota: A Spiritual Geography* (1993); William Least Heat-Moon's *Prairy-Erth* (1991), a 600–page exploration of a single county of tall-grass prairie in the Kansas Flint Hills; C. L. Rawlins's account of his wilderness work along the Continental Divide, *Sky's Witness: A Year in the Wind River Range* (1993); the writings about the boreal forests of northern Minnesota collected in John Henricksson's anthology, *North Writers: A Strong Woods Collection* (1991): the sense of place that emerges from these and dozens of other recent works that might be termed bioregional is one in which landscape, in effect, becomes cultural ecology. Informed by an ecologist's sense of the interdependence and interconnectedness of all living systems and the process of constant adaptation in individual environments, bioregional writers picture specific localities as complex, multilayered palimpsests of geology, meteorology, history, myth, etymology, family genealogy, agricultural practice, storytelling, and regional folkways.

Bioregional visualizations of place frequently utilize pre-settlement boundaries and markings rather than recently imposed political demarcations. The territory defined by these new boundaries is also imagined in new ways. William Least Heat-Moon's subtitle for *Prairy-Erth*, "A Deep Map," aptly characterizes the three-dimensional quality that generates a sense of imaginative volume and depth in much bioregional writing. Bioregional "mappings" of local environments have increasingly involved an interest in metaphors of depth, layering, resonance, root systems, habitats, and interconnectedness—factors that not only connect different aspects of a place but that seem to put them into motion, making them move within their own history (both human and nonhuman). The effect, as Patricia Hampl puts it in *Spillville*, is to pitch us harder into the landscape: "There is no forest, but there is the sensation that now we're going deeper. The *deeper* of characters in fairy tales who set off from home and, sooner or later must enter a deep wood" (40).

This sense of extension and depth is likely to be simultaneously spatial and temporal and to occur in sudden epiphanies. Take, for instance Verlyn Klinkenborg's musings in

Making Hay (1986) as he wanders through a farm field near the Rock River in southwestern Minnesota:

> As I walked through the alfalfa, watching it dry to the baling point, inspecting the damp green on the underside of the windrows, I found it possible to believe that the genetic substance of seeds is the genuine stuff of human culture. That is an old idea, one every plant breeder knows, but it takes some grasping. It means that a direct line of culturing (or as Milton would have said, "manuring"—working with hands) descends from alfalfa's proximate source, eaten millennia since by a primeval grazer, to Janelle and Louie's field. I am used to the kind of culture whose antiquity can be found looking ancient in manuscripts and codices and books, in the shifts of language. If I could see an antique alfalfa plant alive, it would not be figured in majuscule script or Baskerville type. It would look like an ancient constellation of molecules coming up (today!) on an oceanic plain in Minnesota, cut, drying, waiting to have its leaves bound. (76–77)

Klinkenborg's momentary revelation that alfalfa is both now and history offers a small but compelling example of the search for a usable past in bioregional writing. He is aware that not only something called Western Culture but his own books rely on "majuscule script or Baskerville type," and thus exemplify a notion of antiquity particularly unsuited for understanding certain natural phenomena and experience. But Klinkenborg at the same time suggests just the opposite, for he deftly demonstrates—in words, in type—that the very abstraction embodied in print culture is still capable of evoking a vision of genetic or molecular "history" best sensed in the damp feel of cut hay rather than in print on the page.

The best way out, Robert Frost once said, is through—an insight that characterizes the best bioregional writing. The motivation for that writing seems multiple and complex and not without attendant dangers. Too deep a suspicion of urban or suburbanized landscapes (where the majority of Americans now reside), too willed or insistent a determination to become "one with the land" (or be convinced that one knows what that means), too crude or deterministic a sense of how environments shape individuals and communities: any of these pitfalls can compromise the insight or wisdom of a given piece of bioregional writing, often revealing, in the process, more about the psychic needs of the writer than the landscape he or she evokes.

Further, replacing larger, more homogenous entities (whether states or regions) with the more flexibly defined microregions bioregional writers propose will inevitably seem a form of Balkanization to some, a final form of fashionable fragmentation in imagining the self. Strangely enough, the opposite seems to be the case, at least insofar as a contemporary literature of place implicitly testifies. Imagining "deep maps" of smaller, more specific places actually offers what W.J. Keith calls "a welcome limitation of possibility" (10), one that allows for a richer understanding of individual wholeness—one, in Hampl's words, that feels like sanity. The most compelling bioregional works attempt to establish imaginative title to specific American places, to reimagine a numinous landscape beneath a desacralized, irradiated, and overdeveloped one. A grounded emotional identification with the land informed by local knowledge is not easy to come by, but that simply makes it worth the effort. What William Least Heat-Moon has said of travel writing applies as aptly to bioregional imaginations of the land: "A traveler's careful examination of any detail should reveal how little we see of a thing, how poorly we have understood it, how ineffectually we have let it touch our lives. It is this close examination that creates the traveler's ultimate excitement: the realization that if he but has the perception, he is a *perpetual* stranger in a strange land" ("Journeys," 21).

That a new, informed sense of "strangeness" forms one kind of antidote for estrangement from the land is a paradox bioregional writers invite us to ponder. Sharply observed details of landscape, weather, and animal life can lead us back into history, not away from it. They can lead us, as the pun would have it, to where history takes place. By offering a multi-dimensional vision of identity and landscape, bioregional writing provides a cue for a new place-based American literary criticism, one designed to rectify critical absenteeism in regard to physical environments. No longer can "place" in writing be adequately thought of as simply a conceptual index of social attitudes or the projection of a writer's psychic needs. No longer can it be thought of as merely a backdrop for the actions of isolated selves in the foreground. "Place" must be reimagined as a texture, a metabolism, a temperament, an etiquette. In undertaking that task, bioregional writing might help counteract both an American amnesia about history and a related, often deep-seated unresponsiveness to the places in which Americans live. "In a culture with so little regard for its lands and still less for the histories enacted in those lands," Turner says, "[literary] works in their places remind us to remember and to care." Such acts of memory and perception remain crucially important, for "the end of that remembering is to know again that we do not live in some moral and biological vacuum—and never have" (x, xi).

WORKS CITED

Austin, Mary. The American Rhythm: Studies and Reëxpressions of Amerindian Songs. Boston: Houghton Mifflin, 1930.

———. The Land of Little Rain. Albuquerque: University of New Mexico Press, 1903.

Berry, Wendell. "Writer and Region." What Are People For? San Francisco: North Point, 1990. 71–87.

Donoghue, Denis. Reading America: Essays on American Literature. New York: Knopf, 1987.

Emerson, Ralph Waldo. "The Poet." Ralph Waldo Emerson: Essays and Lectures. Ed. Joel Porte. New York: Library of America, 1983. 445–68.

Garland, Hamlin. "Local Color in Art." Crumbling Idols: Twelve Essays on Art Dealing Chiefly with Literature, Painting, and the Drama. Ed. Jane Johnson. Cambridge, MA: Belknap-Harvard University Press, 1960. 49–55.

Hampl, Patricia. Spillville. Minneapolis: Milkweed Editions, 1987.

Heat-Moon, William Least. "Journeys Into Kansas." Temperamental Journeys: Essays on the Modern Literature of Travel. Ed. Michael Kowalewski. Athens: University of Georgia Press, 1992. 19–24.

Keith, W.J. Regions of the Imagination: The Development of British Rural Fiction. Toronto: University of Toronto Press, 1988.

Klinkenborg, Verlyn. Making Hay. New York: Vintage Books, 1986.

Lewis, Martin W. Green Delusions: An Environmentalist Critique of Radical Environmentalism. Durham, NC: Duke University Press, 1992.

Lopez, Barry. "The American Geographies." Finding Home: Writing on Nature and Culture from Orion Magazine. Ed. Peter Sauer. Boston: Beacon Press, 1992. 116–32.

———. "Landscape and Narrative." Crossing Open Ground. New York: Vintage Books, 1989. 61–71.

Lowell, James Russell. "Nationality in Literature." Literary Criticism of James Russell Lowell. Ed. Herbert F. Smith. Lincoln: University of Nebraska Press, 1969. 116–31.

Odum, Howard W., and Harry Estill Moore. American Regionalism: A Cultural-Historical Approach to National Integration. New York: Henry Holt, 1938.

Plant, Judith. "Searching for Common Ground: Ecofeminism and Bioregionalism." Learning to Listen to the Land. Ed. Bill Willers. Washington, DC: Island, 1992. 212–19.

Robinson, Marilynne. "Talking About American Fiction" (interview). Salmagundi 93 (Winter 1992): 61–77.

Sale, Kirkpatrick. Dwellers in the Land: The Bioregional Vision. San Francisco: Sierra Club, 1985.

Saner, Reg. "What Does 'Nature' Name?" Ohio Review 49 (1993): 45–64.

Sauer, Peter. "Introduction." Finding Home: Writing on Nature and Culture from Orion Magazine. Ed. Peter Sauer. Boston: Beacon Press, 1992. 1–17.

Silko, Leslie Marmon. "Landscape, History, and the Pueblo Imagination." On Nature: Nature, Landscape, and Natural History. Ed. Daniel Halpern. San Francisco: North Point, 1986. 83–94.

Slovic, Scott. Seeking Awareness in American Nature Writing: Henry Thoreau, Annie Dillard, Edward Abbey, Wendell Berry, Barry Lopez. Salt Lake City: University of Utah Press, 1992.

Snyder, Gary. The Practice of the Wild. San Francisco: North Point, 1990.

Stineman, Esther Lanigan. *Mary Austin: Song of a Maverick*. New Haven: Yale University Press, 1989.

Thoreau, Henry David. *Walden; or Life in the Woods*. *Henry David Thoreau: A Week on the Concord and Merrimack Rivers, Walden; or Life in the Woods, The Maine Woods, Cape Cod*. Ed. Robert F. Sayre. New York: Library of America, 1985. 321–587.

Turner, Frederick. *Spirit of Place: The Making of an American Literary Landscape*. San Francisco: Sierra Club, 1989.

Whitman, Walt. "Preface to Leaves of Grass" (1855). *Walt Whitman: Complete Poetry and Collected Prose*. Ed. Justin Kaplan. New York: Library of America, 1982. 5–26.

Reading Regionalism
The "Difference" It Makes

Marjorie Pryse

As Michael Steiner and Clarence Mondale have observed, since the 1960s and the beginnings of various civil rights, women's rights, environmental activism, and gay rights movements, both intellectuals and the general public in the United States have expressed "a revived popular interest in region, as the spatial dimension of cultural pluralism" (x). My own interest in regionalism has emerged from an attempt to reclaim a body of neglected American women writers who published roughly between 1850 and 1910, and who wrote with a consciousness of region as a cultural concept. Judith Fetterley and I have recently published *American Women Regionalists*, in which we anthologize nineteenth-century literary regionalism and explore the literary contexts and the formal features of the sketches that comprise the tradition. The feminist movement of the 1970s clearly energized our early work in compiling this anthology; more recently, in the process of theorizing regionalism in larger terms and in teaching regionalist texts in the classroom, we have discovered ongoing connections between the fictions regionalist writers produced more than a century ago and the cultural questions and critiques of our own era.

From the perspective of literary history, regionalism as we have defined it describes a particular body of texts produced primarily by women writers who wrote against the grain of the "local color" fiction of their day—even though their own work has been (mistakenly, we believe) often categorized by literary historians as "local color." Like Steiner and Mondale, who distinguish between regionalism, which they define as "region as concept," and region, which they define as "region as object of study," we have also noted the distinction between literary regionalism, which features an empathic approach to regional characters that enfranchises their stories and cultural perceptions, and "local color," which represents regional life and regional characters as objects to be viewed from the perspective of the nonregional, often urban Eastern reader, and frequently offered for that reader's entertainment.[1] Regional literature and regionalist literature are not the same: regionalism denotes a particular *view* of American culture, a view from the perspective of marginalized persons, as well as a consciousness of difference. Unlike "classic" American fiction, regionalist texts include few middle-class white male protagonists; rather, poor, elderly, unmarried, and sometimes "dark" women take center stage, as in Mary Wilkins Freeman's "Sister Liddy." Although most women in regionalist fiction are marginalized by virtue of rural and class origins, race figures in this body of literature in the way that regional persons are sometimes viewed by visiting outsiders as "other" than themselves, especially by virtue of the dialects they speak, and in the fictions by the 1890s which represent Native American, Creole, Chinese American, and African American characters. Regionalism often shifts the center of our perception as readers of American literature to questions of disenfranchisement, of voice, and above all, of approach to regional and other differences.

In the empathic approach regionalist narrators take to representations of region and the lives of women, of older persons, of impoverished groups, and of people who have formed relational alliances that deviate from what the twentieth century has defined as "traditional," their texts often reveal an implicit pedagogy that teaches some readers how to approach regional characters differently than they are represented in "classic" American fiction, particularly in "local color." Celia Thaxter's *Among the Isles of Shoals* (1873), an "invisible" text in American literary history, gives us the language to theorize the approach that characterizes regionalist texts and distinguishes them from other nineteenth-century American fictions about region. *Among the Isles of Shoals* disrupts our expectations concerning what a book-length narrative will include, it subordinates the acts of speaking and writing to the acts of listening and reading, and it sets up self-consciousness about "approach"—to the islands themselves, to its own peculiar relationship to history, to its nonhuman inhabitants—as a central aspect of its story. Thaxter presents the bird, plant, rock, and marine life on White Island, the few acres of rock that housed the lighthouse her father kept to make his living, as different from human life and writes a narrative in which "readers" of the Shoals and readers of the *Shoals* must develop "ears made delicate by listening" in order to "hear" the different sounds, or notes, of the waves at different points on the shore, and indeed, to approach any aspect of the islands and their narrative with understanding (*AWR*, 162).[2] Delicacy, listening, respect, the ability to move in slowly or not at all in observing, a willingness to see with another's eyes rather than to *look at* the "other," all characterize Thaxter's text (and the texts of regionalism in general). Lines near the opening of the work characterize what happens when a reader allows an "other" place or person to differentiate itself. Thaxter writes, "sailing out from Portsmouth Harbor with a fair wind from the northwest, the Isles of Shoals lie straight before you, nine miles away—ill-defined and cloudy shapes, faintly discernible in the distance," but that "as you approach they separate, and show each its own peculiar characteristics" (*AWR*, 157). As readers approach the texts of regionalism as well, "they separate, and show each its own peculiar characteristics," for regionalism takes up the question of the "peculiar" characteristic rather than what is "universal" or even what is "American." Thaxter's interest in her own readers' "approach" to the islands epitomizes the care with which the narrators of regionalist texts prepare their readers to approach regional subjects. Regionalist texts promote reading "differently," as a skill that must precede any attempts at cross-cultural understanding or communication. They were readers as much as writers; in reading their work, we read "with" them.

In the process of taking a different approach, they tell a different story. In many works of American literature, regional characters serve the function of humor for condescending

urbanites, or for wealthy, white, and often male readers
(consider, for example, the portraits of rural male characters as
well as women in the fiction of the "humorists of the Old
Southwest," especially George Washington Harris and Johnson
Jones Hooper); however, in regionalist texts, regional characters
engage in acts of resistance that challenge their definition, and
dismissal, by writers more in the mainstream, or aspiring to be.
As I have discussed elsewhere ("'Distilling Essences'"),
regionalist texts construct a critique of the subordinate positions
created for, then occupied by, rural, elderly, poor, female, un- (or
unconventionally) married, often untutored persons; and they
particularly imply a critique of the "separate sphere" to which
white middle-class women were relegated in the nineteenth
century. Early writers in the regionalist tradition transform
"woman's sphere," a regionalized, contained "space" for
nineteenth-century American women, into "women's culture," a
"rhetorical construction" (Kerber, 21) and "the ground upon
which women stand in their resistance to patriarchal domination
and their assertion of their own centrality in shaping society"
(Lerner, 53). Regionalist texts share a rhetorical awareness of the
ways the dominant culture creates and maintains hierarchies
based on gendered and "separate spheres"—and on the other
excluding discourses of class and race—in the name of region.
Writing in the regionalist mode created for the authors of these
texts a rhetorical space "within" those excluding discourses.

Differences abound in regionalist texts, and they range
across a wide spectrum, loosely denoted by "gender." For
example, women characters and their stories receive a great deal
of attention in the texts of regionalism, and some of the most
memorable characters are young girls (Jewett's Sylvy in "A
White Heron," Grace King's "Pupasse," Zitkala-Sä's narrator in
"Impressions of an Indian Childhood") or old women (Charlotte
and Harriet Shattuck in Freeman's "A Mistaken Charity,"
Jewett's Mrs. Blackett in *The Country of the Pointed Firs*, Cather's
"Old Mrs. Harris"). And women engage in many activities in the
texts of regionalism, but courtship and marriage are rarely
highlighted as goals. Indeed, most of the women in these texts
are single, widowed, or unhappily married—or the relationship
the narratives explore focuses on female friendship, sisterhood,

mother-daughter or neighbor pairs, or women in community groups rather than the protagonist's relationship to a husband or father. This is not to say that fathers and husbands do not appear in the texts of regionalism; some of the most memorable fictions explore the difficulties of patriarchal fathers and husbands (Cooke's "Freedom Wheeler's Controversy with Providence" and "How Celia Changed Her Mind"), or simply subordinate a female protagonist's relationship with a man to other issues, of self-definition and self-esteem (Freeman's "A New England Nun," Dunbar-Nelson's "The Goodness of Saint Rocque," Sui Sin Far's "Mrs. Spring Fragrance" and "The Inferior Woman"). Regionalism offers stories of female development across the life cycle, and suggests that female development might also serve as a model for males. Stowe's portrait of James Benton in her earliest published sketch, "Uncle Lot," Jewett's Elijah Tilley from *The Country of the Pointed Firs*, Chopin's Ozème in "Ozème's Holiday," and Dunbar-Nelson's M'sieu Fortier all provide models of men who share some of the values the nineteenth century associated with "women's culture."

Regionalist writers across decades and regional and color lines create visionary women, herbalist-healers, not as marginal freaks, but as central to the narratives and to the different perspective regionalism offers. Indeed, the New England women Stowe describes as "women of faculty" provide early prototypes of the cultural healer. In *The Pearl of Orr's Island*, Stowe calls Aunts Roxy and Ruey "cunning women," referring to its Biblical use (Jeremiah 9.17), as well as women of "faculty," and makes Roxy and Ruey central to the development of the fiction's child-protagonist Mara Lincoln. Jewett creates Mrs. Todd, in *The Country of the Pointed Firs*, as a healer with communal and spiritual powers. Charles Chesnutt's "conjure woman" (from his 1899 collection *The Conjure Woman*), Dunbar-Nelson's "Wizened One" in "The Goodness of Saint Rocque," and Austin's Basket Maker all serve to extend the concept of healer across racial lines in regionalism. "Woman of faculty" and "conjure woman" may be terms that emerge from different regions with different cultural origins, but in the texts of regionalism, these women serve the same function: to critique so as to heal.[3]

The texts of regionalism offer an approach to "reading" difference. An examination of specific sketches or short fictions in more detail illustrates that although the regionalists did not themselves theorize their work (with the exception of Mary Austin, in "Regionalism"), they yet were self-conscious about their different approach. In one early work, Alice Cary's "Uncle Christopher's," a narrator snowbound against her will in the home of Christopher Wright conveys compassion and attempts to advocate for an abused boy. She is aware throughout the story that she takes a different perspective than most of the other characters, particularly of Uncle Christopher, "one of those infatuated men who fancy themselves to be 'called' to be teachers of religion, though he had neither talents, education, nor anything else to warrant such a notion, except a faculty for joining pompous and half scriptural phrases . . ." (*AWR*, 66). Taking this different perspective allows her to empathize with the two boys in Uncle Christopher's care: "Both interested me at once, and partly, perhaps, that they seemed to interest nobody else" (*AWR*, 66). When Uncle Christopher monopolizes the light, heat, and right to speak, "no one questioned his right to do so" (*AWR*, 73) except the narrator, who undermines Christopher's authority in showing kindness to young Mark. Although she cannot prevent Mark's death by exposure after Christopher has sent him outside and abandoned him to the snow, she can offer her own story as a different "approach" to the boy's abuse, locating its source in patriarchal domination, class exploitation, and a religious fanaticism used to bolster Christopher's cruelty that remains unchallenged by his wife and daughters, all cowed and regulated to his rule.

In Mary Murfree's "The Star in the Valley," hunter-outsider Reginald Chevis "looks at" Celia Shaw but does not see her. Chevis brings into Tennessee's Cumberland Mountains an attitude toward nature and the entitlements due white men of a certain class position that Murfree critiques. Chevis can afford to pass long days "hunting deer, with horn and hounds, through the gorgeous autumnal forest; or perchance in the more exciting sport in some rocky gorge with a bear at bay and the frenzied pack around him; or in the idyllic pleasures of bird-shooting with a well-trained dog; and coming back in the crimson sunset to a well-appointed tent and a smoking supper of venison or wild turkey—the trophies of his skill" (*AWR*, 257). From his campsite, Chevis looks down on a gleam of light that shines from mountaineer Celia Shaw's house and fancies that "the charm of that bright bit of color in the night-shrouded valley added a sort of romantic zest to these primitive enjoyments, and ministered to that keen susceptibility of impressions which Reginald Chevis considered eminently characteristic of a highly wrought mind and nature" (*AWR*, 257). Because he considers himself superior to his companions, one a fellow sportsman and the other "the gawky mountaineer whose services he had secured as guide" (*AWR*, 256), he keeps his romantic fancies to himself. However, Murfree's story demonstrates that "infinite as was the difference" Chevis believes separates himself from others in this story, including the "country girl," Celia Shaw, in fact, Chevis only "flattered himself" (*AWR*, 262). To Murfree's narrator, Chevis "had not even a subacute idea that he looked upon these people and their inner life only as picturesque bits of the mental and moral landscape; that it was an aesthetic and theoretical pleasure their contemplation afforded him; that he was as far as ever from the basis of common humanity" (*AWR*, 262). While Chevis flatters himself that he "sees" the mountaineers, Murfree takes a different view of his self-flattery. Chevis's "idle comings and goings" cause Celia a "strange, vague, unreasoning trouble," for while she also looks up at his campfire, she "knew nothing of the life he had left, and of its rigorous artificialities and gradations of wealth and estimation" (*AWR*, 263). Without knowledge of the social and class hierarchies that "separate" Celia from Chevis, she is powerless to defend herself against "heart-break" when he leaves to return "to his former life" (*AWR*, 270); the "wide contrast" between their lives, and their perspectives, kills Celia, Murfree suggests; Chevis fails as a model of an "approach" to difference. For all of his romanticism, he "hunts" Celia as certainly as he hunts the animals he kills, and understands her as little as he understands them.

In "The Star in the Valley," Murfree offers Chevis as an example of an approach to regional characters that does not allow them to emerge from stereotype. One of the pedagogical "devices" of regionalism includes offering such examples, and suggests a self-consciousness within regionalist texts of constructing an alternative to the approach of a character like Chevis, or like the ornithologist in Sarah Orne Jewett's "A White Heron," the tourist-outsider in Alice Dunbar-Nelson's "M'Sieu Fortier's Violin," or the tourist-artist in Kate Chopin's "The Gentleman of Bayou Têche."

In Jewett's story, the hunter-ornithologist wants the nine-year-old Sylvy to reveal the heron's nest but cannot really "listen" to Sylvy herself. Although the ornithologist tells Sylvy he is looking for a "friend," and although she "watched the young man with loving admiration," Jewett's narrator tells us that "Sylvia would have liked him vastly better without his gun" (*AWR*, 201). The dramatic conflict in "A White Heron" concerns whether Sylvy, who has ventured out at dawn and climbed the great pine tree in order to discover the heron's nest, will actually tell the ornithologist where he can find the bird. Jewett associates Sylvy's own shyness and reticence to speak throughout the story with the "dumb life of the forest" (*AWR*, 202), but when she does not tell the heron's secret at the story's end, more is at stake than her refusal to betray the bird and create the conditions for its death. Like Murfree's Celia, Sylvy is herself in danger of being "killed," and she knows this because although she is desperate to tell her own story to sympathetic ears—and she knows that the young man "is so well worth making happy, and he waits to hear the story she can tell" (*AWR*, 204)—she intuits that the moment she has told the ornithologist what he wants to hear, she herself will cease to exist in his eyes. Like any stuffed bird, she will also become "fixed" in his representation of her as a poor country girl whose grandmother needs money and so is willing to sell herself and her knowledge of the heron. The young man has already demonstrated that he does not know how to listen, and in his appealing request that she tell him what she knows about the bird, he reveals that he cannot "read" either. Sylvy is more self-conscious than Murfree's Celia and becomes aware that, in protecting the heron from discovery, she is also protecting herself, and so Sylvy's encounter with the hunter does not, unlike Celia's, result in her own death.

In Alice Dunbar-Nelson's "M'sieu Fortier's Violin," the wealthy Courcey buys the violin but discovers that he cannot "buy" the music only M'sieu Fortier knows how to make. In this story, M'sieu Fortier, like Celia and Sylvy, occupies a social and economic class position of powerlessness with respect to the tourist-outsider Courcey, and is driven to sell his violin only after an American syndicate takes over the management of the French Opera, fires the old musicians, and replaces them with newcomers. And like Sylvy, M'sieu Fortier cannot finally go through with the sale. He returns to beg Courcey for the instrument's return: "'My heart, he is broke, I die for mon violon.'" Unlike Chevis and the ornithologist, however, Courcey learns to perceive Fortier differently—"'take your violin; it was a whim with me, a passion with you'" (*AWR*, 470)—and Dunbar-Nelson implies her own hope that the reader, as well, can learn to take a "different" perspective—on poverty, on Creoles, and on the influence of French culture in New Orleans.

And in Kate Chopin's "The Gentleman of Bayou Têche," the tourist-artist Sublet offers to pay to make a picture of the Acadian, Evariste, hoping to depict him as a stereotype of the poor, ignorant, filthy, "low-down," but picturesque inhabitants of the bayou. Intervention by Aunt Dicey, a Negro woman who occupies an equally low social position as do the Acadians on the Hallet plantation, and who recognizes Sublet's condescension and exploitation, leads Evariste's daughter Martinette to convince her father to refuse to submit to the picture. In an ambiguous ending, Evariste finally does agree to have his picture made after he saves Sublet's son from drowning in the bayou, apparently believing that he can control the way viewers from Sublet's world will "read" the portrait if he can get Sublet to agree to "put on'neat' de picture, . . . 'Dis is one picture of Mista Evariste Anatole Bonamour, a gent'man of de Bayou Têche'" (*AWR*, 426). However, what remains ambiguous for Evariste, who, we are told, cannot read, becomes clear for Chopin's own readers: Evariste lacks power over the interpretation of his own representation. We know, even if Evariste does not, that in Sublet's world, in which readers are "taught" to view persons like Evariste stereotypically, the regional character himself does not have the power to change the way he is perceived. Only the story itself, in Chopin's text, may have that power—to critique Sublet as another model of a failure to approach an "other" with respect.

The pedagogy of regionalism thus offers some examples of approaches to difference that do not allow regional characters to tell their stories in their own voices or bring into dialogue a fully enfranchised perspective; these particular stories imply, as I have suggested in my discussion, that such an approach unnecessarily inhibits reading across the lines of region, class, and gender. Stories like these provide readers with examples of cross-cultural interaction that will not work; it is as if regionalist writers want to make sure their readers can recognize the need for empathy by illustrating what happens when it is not present. In other stories, these and other writers depict more successful encounters and teach readers values of compassionate and respectful approach, of listening, of empathy, and—in some works—of the limits of empathy. In regionalist fiction, characters win by eliciting a change of heart in others—beginning with Stowe's 1834 sketch "Uncle Lot," in which James Benton first "reads" Lot Griswold's character within the rough exterior of his "chestnut burr" demeanor, then "converts" Uncle Lot's opinion of him, not by triumphing in any contest or trial but by engaging his affections. Stowe suggests an alternative approach to resolving differences between men—not an approach that would characterize nineteenth-century American cultural attitudes toward differences between white men and Indians, white men and enslaved men or women, white men and white women, white men and animals, or white men and the frontier, but nevertheless a "different" approach that Stowe believed could serve as a national model. The implicit pedagogy of Stowe's text sketches a direction for creating empathic relationships between characters within the texts of regionalism, and between the texts of regionalism and potential readers, that the following stories by Murfree, Dunbar-Nelson, Jewett, and Mary Austin further develop.

Murfree's "The 'Harnt' That Walks Chilhowee" depicts Clarsie Giles's compassion for the homeless, hunted, and crippled Reuben Crabb. One of Murfree's regional characters describes Clarsie as "a merciful critter. . . . Clarsie could tame a b'ar, ef she looked at him a time or two, she's so savin' o' the critter's feelin's" (*AWR*, 288). Taming bears rather than hunting them, feeding crippled persons rather than allowing them to starve, and having the ability to "read" value where others have dismissed it, all characterize the "different" approach regionalist texts take, and teach their readers. In Dunbar-Nelson's "The Praline Woman," an unnamed praline vendor makes her living by her success in "approaching" her customers. She compassionately "reads" their losses and points of vulnerability, and when they buy her pralines, they signify her success at human connection. In the process of "reading" her customers, she also tells her own story: "M'sieu would lak' some fo' he's lil' gal' at home? Mais non, what's dat you say? She's daid! Ah, m'sieu, 'tis my lil' gal what died long year ago. Misère, misère!'" (*AWR*, 480). Selling and telling become so intertwined in "The Praline Woman" that the story seems to lack any narrator but the praline vendor herself. "Mais oui, madame, I know you étrangér. You don' look lak dese New Orleans peop'" (*AWR*, 480). And Jewett's narrator in *The Country of the Pointed Firs* crosses class and regional lines to engage Mrs. Todd's trust; Mrs. Todd finds the younger woman so capable as an "apprentice" both in the business of selling herbal remedies and in the art of empathic listening that she not only confides in her herself, but also introduces her to others with stories to tell, stories that require a listener more interested in listening and reading than in speaking and writing.

The kind of reading that regionalist texts promote and try to teach their readers suggests that reading is more complex than it might appear, particularly when one attempts to read across cultural lines. There are skills to be learned that allow us, first, to become aware that we are in the presence of someone "other" than ourselves; second, to dismantle our own expectations about what we read so as to avoid predetermining what we will find; third, to recognize what we need to move beyond the text to learn so as to understand the text itself; and only fourth, to sufficiently learn the "language" of the text and its different approach to enable us to enter it as readers. Mary Austin's "The Basket Maker" raises these questions about reading, for her white woman narrator wants to understand and to help her reader understand the story of the Native American woman, Seyavi. But Seyavi will not be coaxed into speech; any attempt to give Seyavi voice, or to empathize with her, would violate Seyavi's privacy and fail to respect the cultural differences in which her story, like her blanket, enfolds her. Thus Austin's narrator must rely on reading Seyavi's story in its own terms, not all of which can be translated for her English-speaking readers, rather than trying to create Seyavi as a narrator of a written text. She writes, about Seyavi's baskets, that "the soul of the weather went into the wood. If you had ever owned one of Seyavi's golden russet cooking bowls with the pattern of plumed quail, you would understand all this without saying anything" (*AWR*, 574–75). The narrator can infuse her own narrative with the soul of the weather, and of the land in which Seyavi lives—and most of Austin's regionalist work is about the land, not its human inhabitants—but the cross-cultural understanding Austin hopes for, and hopes to convey to her readers, cannot itself be bridged in so many words. Austin's story "reads" Seyavi but does not "write" her story. Much involves not saying anything; or ending the sketch with an image that is meaningful to Seyavi but may or may not be meaningful to Austin's own readers: that Seyavi's life will end with the "certainty that having borne herself courageously to this end she will not be reborn a coyote" (*AWR*, 577). Austin does not tell her own readers that the coyote is a trickster in Native American culture, not an image for Seyavi to emulate; this much we need to know in order even to catch a glimpse of the "meaning" of the sketch's ending. But Austin gets only so "close" to Seyavi; and what she refuses to do is evaluate Seyavi's life by the standards of a white culture—even if she sacrifices her story's own "writing" in her fidelity to "reading" the distance that separates Seyavi from the narrator, and which she chooses to retain.

From a regionalist perspective, Austin's choice to remain faithful to her "reading" of Seyavi rather than, as she uses the term in another sketch, "The Land," to "*make* a story" (*AWR*, 590), shifts her interest from what might be believed to what can, with respect for one's subject, be said. She herself struggles in "The Land" with the difference between the two kinds of stories—stories that involve reading and stories that involve "making." One afternoon she and a friend set out to "make" a story, "testing our story for likelihood and proving it. There was an Indian woman in the tale, not pretty, for they are mostly not that in life, and the earthenware pot, of course, and a lost river bedded with precious sand." This "pot-of-gold" story takes on a life of its own after she and her friend have finished telling it because it contains the features that certain readers have been taught to expect in stories about the desert. "Then I wrote the tale for a magazine of the sort that gets taken in camps and at miners' boarding-houses, and several men were at great pains to explain to me where my version varied from the accepted one of the hills. By this time, you understand, I had begun to believe the story myself" (*AWR*, 590). In this way, she explains, stories that are "made" or written become fixed "in the body of desert myths" (*AWR*, 591). She is interested in a different kind of story, particularly a story that will not violate the privacy of her subjects: "That is why in all that follows I have set down what the Borderers thought and felt; for that you have a touchstone in your *own* heart . . ." (*AWR*, 590). Like the regionalists who preceded her, Austin wants to elicit a point of connection between her subjects and some "touchstone" in the hearts of her readers—not to "make" a story that will satisfy a reader's incredulity or justify a reader's disdain, but rather one that will teach us how to read differently.

Despite the regionalists' attempts to teach their own readers how to approach the characters in their fiction, I am not arguing that regionalism makes for easy reading. On the contrary, the sexism, racism, and classism that have come to characterize American national culture have taught us to "read" both social and natural worlds in a certain way. We might hypothesize that this particular socialization of our reading practices has obscured our ability to engage in a genuine dialogue with the social and natural world unmediated by hierarchies of gender, race, and class. The regionalists do not assume that the existence of these hierarchies is inevitable, and therefore readers, on entering the individual texts that form the mosaic of regionalism, often find themselves in uncertain territory. Through a combination of dismantling categories of gender, class, and (especially in the New Orleans and Western writers) race, regionalism both disrupts our ability to read in the ways we have been accustomed to, calling into question hierarchies of color, gender, and class value, and makes us aware of other stories that we can "enter into" but which we have not been prepared to understand. The narratives of regionalism emerge from a different social world than the one we have been taught in conventional ways to "read."

I have suggested that regionalist texts contain within them not only their own theory, but also their own pedagogy. Taking a different approach to reading involves taking a different approach to "reading" culture. I will close this essay by describing some of the responses I have received from undergraduate student readers in a course devoted solely to regionalism that would seem to confirm such an observation.

In teaching regionalism, I have discovered that for both men and women readers the unexpected immersion in stories about poor, elderly, unmarried, rural, and uneducated women, both white women and women of color, who are also often unattractive by conventional standards, or whose conflicts revolve around dilemmas of women's daily lives that students have learned to view as insignificant and uninteresting, creates an experience of reading "differently," and that students responded to the "difference" of regionalism when those texts were written both by women of color and by white women. At the same time, the very parameters within which students have been taught to read so narrow their ability to recognize an-"other's" story that some students find themselves disabled as readers and in self-defense blame the text.

Indeed, for some students, it is the immersion in gender that seems to disrupt the regionalist classroom the most: the way Rose Terry Cooke's Celia in "How Celia Changed Her Mind" gets married in order to escape the social stigma of being an old maid only to discover that marriage is oppressive and to rejoice when she has the good fortune to be left a widow and to celebrate Thanksgiving with all the "old maids" in her village; or the way Jewett's narrator in *The Country of the Pointed Firs* visits Mrs. Todd's mother's house on Green Island and discovers that an old woman can serve as a model of deity; or when Freeman's Hetty Fifield, turned down for the job of church sexton because she is a woman, moves into the meeting-house in "A Church Mouse" and preaches her own sermon on the rights of homeless women; when Sui Sin Far's Mrs. Spring Fragrance acknowledges that she would prefer her daughter, should she have one, to take as a model the suffragist character in her story "The Inferior Woman" rather than the more traditional woman in the story; the way Mary Austin's "The Walking Woman" seems to be able to live without depending on men; in short, the way character after character has some other interest than romance and text after text subordinates the stories of the lives, interests, and struggles of men to those of women. But even more, the repeated attempt to engage as central texts that depict characters otherwise marginal—and particularly women characters— created, for some students, an awareness of "difference."

This was the case for the four persons in the class who identified themselves as members of minority groups, as well as for the white students. Indeed, it was an African American woman who pointed out Mary Wilkins Freeman's sensitivity to issues of color, for the "dark woman" in her story "Sister Liddy," wanted to know whether Freeman was herself African American, and commented on her own ability to identify with various white women writers, sometimes assuming they were black. Other students reported that whenever we read works in which characters spoke in dialect, they assumed the characters themselves were African American. One of the surprises of the course was the extent to which the written transcription of various regional dialects raised the question of race. These readers responded as if anyone who speaks a different dialect of standard English must belong to a group so entirely different from themselves that it is as if they belong to a different race.

It is the regionalist text's very "difference" that makes regionalism difficult to read; but the reason for that difficulty lies outside the texts themselves. In reading regionalism, and other noncanonical literature, we thus confront two related challenges: first, the narrow parameters within which we have all been taught to read; and second, the fact that regionalism is written in some ways beyond the boundaries of those parameters. Reading regionalism immerses us in the act, and difficult art, of reading American culture. In creating representations that themselves challenge hierarchies of cultural value, regionalism indeed, at least in the sense by which we mean literary production, "makes" difference—and makes it a feature of culture as well as of literature that we can learn to approach beyond the limitations of conventional reading practices.

NOTES

1. See Shapiro for an insightful discussion of the "local color" phenomenon in late nineteenth-century America.

2. Throughout this essay, I will be referring primarily to texts Judith Fetterley and I have included in *American Women Regionalists: A Norton Anthology*, and I will cite page references in the text to *AWR*. We view this anthology as a collection that both defines a representation of regionalism and at the same time illustrates it, and we have chosen to include those texts that we believe best introduce readers unfamiliar with regionalism or with these particular writers to such representation. It is for this reason that I refer to *AWR* (where almost all of the texts I cite are readily available to readers in one volume) rather than to their original publication.

3. See Mobley for a related discussion of cross-cultural links between Jewett's Mrs. Todd and various herbal-healers in the fiction of Toni Morrison.

WORKS CITED

Austin, Mary. "Regionalism in American Fiction." *English Journal* 21 (February 1932): 97–107.

Fetterley, Judith and Marjorie Pryse. *American Women Regionalists 1850–1910: A Norton Anthology*. New York: Norton, 1992.

Kerber, Linda. "Separate Spheres, Female Worlds, Woman's Place: The Rhetoric of Women's History." *Journal of American History* 75, 1 (June 1988): 9–39.

Lerner, Gerda. "Politics and Culture in Women's History: A Symposium." *Feminist Studies* 6, 1 (Spring 1980): 49–54.

Mobley, Marilyn. *Folk Roots and Mythic Wings in Sarah Orne Jewett and Toni Morrison*. Baton Rouge: Louisiana State University Press, 1991.

Pryse, Marjorie. "'Distilling Essences': Regionalism and 'Women's Culture.'" *American Literary Realism* 25, 2 (Winter 1993): 1–15.

Shapiro, Henry D. *Appalachia on Our Mind: The Southern Mountains and Mountaineers in the American Consciousness, 1870–1920*. Charlotte: University of North Carolina Press, 1978.

Steiner, Michael, and Clarence Mondale. *Region and Regionalism in the United States: A Source Book for the Humanities and Social Sciences*. New York and London: Garland, 1988.

Rhetorics of Region in *Starry Adventure* and *Death Comes for the Archbishop*

Mark Schlenz

To attempt definitive representations of the Southwest's regional significance in American cultural history, two early twentieth-century women writers, Willa Cather and Mary Austin, employed critically distinct rhetorical strategies: Cather's *Death Comes for the Archbishop* and Austin's *Starry Adventure* illustrate what I will call a rhetoric of "symbolic regionalism" and a rhetoric of "semiotic regionalism." This distinction informs a broader theory of regionalism which suggests pragmatic contexts for emerging "green" literary and cultural studies. Adaptations of Kristevan concepts of "the symbolic" and "the semiotic" to regionalist discourse in the following analysis contrast a nomothetic disposition in representations of place—a disposition toward concrete naming in accordance with preexistent, rational, socially constructed, or abstracted structures of meaning—and a countervailing idiographic disposition toward particular, extra-rational, unmediated, or integrated expression of physical and psychological dimensions of spatial experience.[1]

In "Regionalism in American Fiction," Austin argues that Cather's insertion of a Midi-Romanesque cathedral into the unbounded spaces of the nineteenth-century American Southwest (in *Death Comes for the Archbishop*) violated essential principles of a genuine regional literature. Austin's essay articulates her definition of "genuine" regional writing and explores the significance of regional sensibilities and environmental experience for an American cultural imagination. Austin considers geography and literature as participations in a dialectical relationship—what postmodern geographer Edward Soja has called a "socio-spatial dialectic"—of culture and place.[2]

For Austin:

> [a]rt, considered as the expression of any people as a whole, is the response they make in various mediums to the impact that the totality of their experience makes upon them, and there is no sort of experience that works so constantly and subtly upon man as his regional environment. ("Regionalism," 97)

While such statements may hint at crude geographical determinism, Austin's work, particularly her representations of Indian-white relations, suggests a humanistically nuanced environmental perspective. Austin's representations of human societies in ecological contexts echoes the Boasian concept of the "culture area" that was current among her anthropologist contemporaries. Austin states that "[r]egionalism, since it is of the very nature and constitution of the planet, becomes at last part of the nature and constitution of the men who live on it" ("Regionalism," 97), but she does not conclude that cultures are merely epiphenomena of their environments. Instead, in her writing Austin approaches regions as culture areas which include both historic and biophysical legacies of human involvement with a locale.

In addition to asserting the critical significance of regional socio-spatial dialectics, Austin discriminates "between a genuine regionalism and mistaken presentiments of it." Superficial "local color" incorporations of idiographic regional settings, manners, and dialects in late nineteenth- and early-twentieth-century American literature, she argues, belie a deeper nomothetic nationalism. According to Austin, the late nineteenth-century American reading public sought "fiction shallow enough to be common to all regions, so that no special knowledge of other environments than one's own is necessary to appreciation of it." Somehow, Austin explains, faithful differentiation of regional cultures was seen as a national "disloyalty . . . and an implied criticism in one section of all the others from which it is distinguished." Through narratives of nomothetic nationalism, therefore, contributions of the geographic history of the West to democratic ideals were reduced to Turnerian figurations of a homogenizing frontier process of Americanization. In contrast to Frederick Jackson Turner's narrative transformation of the West to a figurative site of a unifying political process,[3] Austin emphasizes the idiographic integrity of western lands and peoples. Her notion of genuine regionalism resists universalizing nationalistic tendencies to focus instead on irreducible areal differences: for Austin, the true literature of a region portrays "life as it is lived there, as it unmistakably couldn't be lived anywhere else" ("Regionalism," 98–105).

To meet Austin's criteria, "the regionally interpretive book must not only be about the country, it must be of it, flower of its stalk and root, in the way that *Huckleberry Finn* is of the great river, taking its movement and rhythm, its structure and intention, or lack of it, from the scene." Though Cather's *Death Comes for the Archbishop* continues to be celebrated as a definitive literary expression of the historic American Southwest, Austin considered the novel an example of false regionalism. Austin admits that Cather "selects her backgrounds with care" and "draws them with consummate artistry," but she claims Cather perverts "the scene from historical accuracy" by omitting "the tragic implications of its most significant item, the calamity to Spanish New Mexican culture, of the coming the French priests" ("Regionalism," 105–06).

For Austin, Cather's elision of native perspectives and her celebration of imported European values "makes her story, with all its true seeming, profoundly untrue to the New Mexican event" and "removes it from the category of regionalism." Austin argues that Cather appealingly exploits the natural scene merely "by way of contrast, or to add richer harmonization to a story shaped by alien scenes." Austin concludes that as "[Cather's] hero is a missionary arriving [in the region] at an age when the major patterns of his life are set; a Frenchman by birth, a Catholic by conviction and practice, a priest by vocation, there is little New Mexico can do for him besides providing an interesting backdrop against which to play out his missionary part." Consequently, Cather's novel is "about the region rather than of it" ("Regionalism," 105–06).

In *Starry Adventure,* Austin responds to Cather's regionalism and offers her vision of architecture as a semiotic fusion of culture and environment in contrast to the symbolic separation of geographic place and human destiny signified by Latour's European cathedral inserted into the landscape of the region.

Both *Death Comes for the Archbishop* and *Starry Adventure* open with episodes of epiphany where protagonists receive spiritual experience and inspiration. Both epiphanic episodes occur during moments of heightened perception in unbounded spaces of the natural world, and both center on figures of trees. Throughout both novels, protagonists strive toward social structurations of space congruent with their visionary inspirations: both move from their epiphanies in open space to construct architectural enclosures to house their spiritual experience. But it is on exactly the point of this shared structural element that Austin's novel pivots to confront the rhetoric of region advanced by Cather's more recognized work.

In *Death Comes for the Archbishop,* Cather deploys an elaborately detailed setting as a moral testing ground with which her protagonist maintains an individual symbolic and transcendent—rather than ecologically integrated—relationship. Latour's epiphany following the prologue of *Death Comes for the Archbishop* epitomizes Cather's subordination of landscape to transcendental symbolism by projecting the image of a metaphysical icon on the vegetative world. The arc of Latour's trajectory from his vision of the cruciform tree to his interment "before the high altar in the church he had built" describes a cultural containment of the inchoate vastness of American desert wildernesses within symbolic orders of Christian civilization as the bishop's life parallels political appropriation of the region by the United States (*Death,* 299). Through superimposed templates of doctrine and faith, Latour's vision instructs him to deny his own miserable physical situation—to transcend his place—by meditating on the transcendent anguish of his metaphysical lord. Later, at Agua Secreta, he translates his wilderness vision and his salvation into symbolic terms of a "miraculous" metanarrative which continues to guide his life to its final destiny, the symbolic interment of his corpse in his Father's house. The progress of

Western history represented in this arc replaces the pastoral community and self-rule of Agua Secreta with the patriarchal order of the diocese and the political authority of the United States government.

Latour's journey from the "geometrical nightmare" of indistinguishable red hills where, parched with thirst, he prays before a likeness of the cross in the natural shape of a juniper tree, to his final burial before the crucifix in the cathedral he has constructed maps intersections of the industrial revolution with "archaic" regional cultures and sanctifies the imposition of rigid and measured—technologic—form upon the organic topography. Latour's story describes a life lived through a transformation of unmarked wilderness into a geography inscribed by patterns of an imported prescriptive social order. It is a life, like those of Cather's earlier characters, in which annihilation of identity threatened by the immensity of uncontained space—the fatal dimension of geography[4]—is transcended through symbolic acts of enclosure in which ambivalence about the overwhelming otherness of alien landscapes is resolved through assertion of familiar cultural boundaries—plowed fields, new roads, fenced prairie graves, railroad tracks, and church walls. But even more than Cather's earlier characters, Latour's life symbolizes historic progress.

Latour, as an historical figure embedded in an architectural monument, further sophisticates Cather's symbolic approach toward setting by transcending his specific place *and* time. Latour's biography and the erection of his symbolic edifice bring the terrain of his diocese within an imported mythic structure; its geographic particularity is made subordinate to a nomothetic master-narrative of Euro-American expansion; its original significance as an idiographic place gives way to its enforced position in a Western myth of progress whose authority is perennially reaffirmed by Latour's tomb.

In *Death Comes for the Archbishop,* Cather stretches her formal technique as she struggles to incorporate the regional geography of the Southwest into a single text. To subordinate vast and impersonal landscapes to the progress of human history, Cather grounds the loose episodic structure of *Death Comes for the Archbishop* within the novel's symbolic framework of the cross and the master-narrative it invokes—a master-narrative which blesses the separation of spirit and matter, which rationalizes human alienation from environments, and which sanctifies the pervasive *contemptus mundi* of Western civilization through the apotheosis of time over place.

To counter Cather's version of the definitive regional novel of the American Southwest with her own, Austin also stretched her previously successful formal technique. In *Starry Adventure*, Austin abandons the "divided narrative"[5] and short story forms which had served so successfully in her earlier regional representations, and attempts to work more fully within what was—for her—the more difficult and confining form of the novel. *Starry Adventure* falls short of Cather's work (and far short of Austin's own more structurally experimental regional work) as a formal triumph. Nonetheless, Austin continues experimenting with narrative perspective in this culminating work: the result is a semiotic alternative to Cather's symbolic regionalism. Unlike Latour's symbolic vision of the cross in the juniper, which literally signifies the Bishop's theologic and fully resolved trajectory through the text, Gard's vision, in *Starry Adventure*, of God in the aspens initiates an open-ended quest for meaning in relation to place which extends throughout—and beyond—the length of the novel.

Gard's opening epiphanic vision resists linguistic expression and leads him, ultimately, back to the land itself in a search for what might be called Austin's concept of the motherhouse. *Starry Adventure* begins with Gard and his sister sitting on the *banco* outside their parents' home preparing for their "favorite evening game of seeing things in the clouds, strange shapes and portents by which they often set the next day's entertainment" (3). But while Gard lingers over his supper, Laura, his eight-year-old elder sister, returns her dishes to the kitchen and misses the nightly moment of glory of the spectacular New Mexico sunset. Gazing past the mountain-rimmed horizon into the dome of cloud-piled sky, Gard sits alone in an instant of Wordsworthian splendor as the sun begins to drop below the edge of the world:

> Suddenly, the wonder was all about him. The edges of the banked clouds were brightly gilt, the torn films flushed

> crimson, the gleaming cumuli behind them came
> hurrying; heaping and wheeling. Great sword-like beams
> of light slashed between them ... the sword of the Lord
> and of Gideon ... the chariots and the horsemen
> thereof ... ! (4)

The "half-remembered phraseology" Gard associates with this
first phase of his vision "was from the Old Testament readings of
his grandfather, to the sound of which he so often went to sleep,"
and "the pictures which shaped for him along the upper cloud-
line were suggested by the illustrations from a book called
Classic Myths which lay on his father's table." But Gard,
enveloped in the wonder, is unaware of the connection of these
words and images to the texts of his fathers: "For him there was
no reality more real than this array of bright swords and shining
helmets and wheels dark with thunder." In the next instant, as
the vision intensifies, the imaginary scene vanishes, and Gard's
experience passes beyond the pale of linguistic conception:

> Swiftly the rain rallied and blotted out the splendor; all
> but a thin slit through which a golden wing of light flew
> toward him. Gard saw it come, grow invisible with
> nearness, and take shape again in the tops of the yellowing
> aspens in the cienaga below the house, almost on a level
> with his round-eyed staring; a golden glowing brightness
> like hot brass, like molten ends of rainbows, and in the
> midst ... in the midst ... " (4–5, Austin's ellipses)

Repetition of the unresolved prepositional phrase
interrupted by ellipses concluding her description of Gard's
vision of the ineffable allows inruption of the semiotic into the
text. The symbolic order begins to reassert itself however,
though not without some ironic undercutting, when Gard
endeavors with an ultimate term to define his experience to his
sister upon her too-late return:

> Laura came running, sharp with disappointment, "Oh,
> Gard ... !" as if he could have put off the wished-for
> moment until her arrival. "Is it over ... What did you
> see?"
>
> Gard came to out of his hushed wonder.

"I saw God," he announced, with finality. (5)

In the aspens lit by alpenglow, Gard claims direct experience of that which Latour glimpsed only a sign. But Gard's use of the term is far from final.[6] Unlike the immigrant bishop who experiences no doubt as to how to interpret and act upon his vision of the cross, Gard must struggle again and again to explain, to be believed, and even to understand the significance of his childhood epiphany in his native landscape. Readers of Austin's autobiography, *Earth Horizon*, will recognize Gard's vision in the aspens as a fictive retelling of the central epiphanic moment beside the walnut tree in Austin's own childhood which she had earlier described in *Experiences Facing Death*. Much of Austin's career in fiction can be traced to an effort on her part to, in some part, recapture, communicate, and explain the nearly mystical rapport with the natural world she experienced at that moment. Fiction became for her the most suitable vehicle for the translation of the fundamental truth of the interrelatedness of the human and natural worlds. There is perhaps some irony, then, in the situation when Gard attempts with words to share his experience and is condemned by Laura for creating fiction.

"Gard! You storied!" Laura accuses before she runs off to tattle to their mother. A juxtaposition of scenes as Gard relates his vision first to his mother and then to his grandfather, further dramatizes tension between the semiotic and the symbolic order. Having listened gently to his tale, Gard's mother answers, "I have often thought . . . that if one could see God anywhere, it would be in the alpenglow." After some moments of maternal caressing, Gard confides, "I am going down to the aspens tomorrow and *look*!" and by his mother's confirming pats along his arm, he feels "completely justified." When Gard defends his tale to his grandfather at bedtime, the family patriarch—invoking the symbolic order—responds with quoted scripture, but again, the physical contact of bodies communicates what words cannot express:

> Far over him [Gard] could hear the husky whisper, "No man hath seen the Father . . . whereas darkly . . . we shall see face to face. . . ." [B]ut he knew by the sudden tremble in the hand that stroked the covers into place that he had not been disbelieved. (6, 8)

Austin explicitly connects the semiotic with topophilia[7] when in the subsequent chapter Gard returns to the aspens in the cienaga to recover his vision, and discovers yet another ultimate term for its expression: "New Mexico"!

> A long time ago, when he supposed he had just come from the vaguely remembered "Back East," Gard had been afraid of the mountains. Sometimes still, when he had been walking near them alone, he had a frightening sense of their imminence. They had ways suddenly of swelling and threatening, of moving noiselessly about and jutting boldly out from the woods where you least expected them. But now as he took them in, inseparable from the pattern of his home, he saw that they were just earth and rocks, warm in color, with a warmth that came sensibly toward him, along with moving air that was fresh and pleasant-smelling. The slight stir of the air flicked the leaves of the aspens in bright patters of sound and set up a sudden trepidation in the straight scarlet slashes of the flowers called red rain. Quite naturally Gard found himself skipping to the same motion, as he ran toward them across the cienaga. "New Mexico! New Mexico!" he chanted happily, and, as he came down in the wet places between the grassy hummock with a pleasant splash, "God!" he shouted, "God and New Mexico!" (11)

Here Austin transforms what might be described, in romantic terms, as the terror of the awesome sublime into what Gaston Bachelard would term an experience of "intimate immensity," a "concordance of world immensity with intimate depth of being" (189). Throughout the images of this passage, the connection of Gard's experience of semiotic topophilia with what Kristeva calls the *chora*[8] resonates in inseparable patterns of landscape and home, in the sensible warmth of color, pleasant smells and movement of air, in synchronization of natural sounds with rhythmic movements of flowers, the skipping movement of the body and intoning chant, and in the delight in pleasant dampness—with all that is anterior to language and evocative of the archaic mother. In Gard's articulation into the symbolic, place and spirit—topophilia and theology—are joined even as the somewhat dissonant coupling of disparate terms reveals the inadequacy of language to express the full meaning of his emplacement in felicitous space.

A later passage strengthens resonances of Gard's semiotic topophilia with the *chora* through strategically displaced reference to the maternal—to the imagined body of the mother— when, somewhat older, Gard contemplates explanations of his experience of a spirit of place to a childhood friend:

> Often, alone, Gard would try over in his mind ways of telling David of that strange, surging warmth which came out of stars and trees and mountains and made itself felt inside you, unmistakable as a voice that called. But somehow he could never put words to it. It was most like what you felt for your mother, when, not having thought of her for a long time, suddenly the image of her floated clear in your mind. . . . Sometimes it came over Gard when the two of them were out together, walking among the pines, or riding the high ridge; but David himself never noticed. (69–70)

Though Gard never communicates his ineffable experience to his companion, Austin does express its essence for her readers through an intriguing experiment with narrative perspective. To express the topophilic experience, Austin herself struggles against patriarchal rule inherent in the symbolic order of language. According to Esther Stineman, employing the technique of filtering the second-person narrative "through the consciousness of the male protagonist . . . Austin consciously transcends her marginality as a woman writer to resist 'oppressive male authority' by appropriating the dominant discourse" (160). Kristeva writes that "entry into syntax constitutes a first victory over the mother" (*Desire*, 289). In the passage above, the second-person narrative address disrupts the conventional syntactic order between the implied narrator and readers by inviting readers to recall their own unarticulated memories of the maternal body, and again allows inruption of the semiotic disposition into the text. Eventually Gard begins to feel in his intense experience of the spirit of place the promise of a unique and exciting personal purpose or destiny—a "starry adventure"—which awaits him.

Whereas Bishop Latour's epiphany inserts a symbolic icon into the landscape which, finally, becomes concretized at the novel's conclusion in the structure of the completed cathedral, Gard's inspirational experience of the ineffable leads to an ongoing and unresolved search for the meaning of his starry adventure. Like Latour, Gard seeks architectural expression of his vision, but, in contrast to the externalized enforcement of symbolic order enacted by Cather's protagonist and the insertion of a Midi-Romanesque cathedral into the landscape of New Mexico, Gard explores a semiotic relation between social structurations of space and natural environments as expressed by the indigenous architecture of the region.

The erection of Latour's cathedral figuratively marks the end of native culture and the beginning of a dominant Eurocentric narrative in the region. Latour's body entombed in its imported European structure symbolizes the sacrifice he had made of his life to redeem the region from the rule of the native priests and the local, geographically specific communitarian adaptations of Pueblo tradition, Spanish colonial, and Mexican administration through the transcendent, salvific authority of the papal father and the centralized power of the United States government. His life story affirms the conventional plot of Euro-American manifest destiny. Austin's text, conversely, concludes with Gard's realization that his starry adventure is an ever-unfolding, internal and personal awakening to life itself, a realization which leads him, at the novel's end, to begin a search with his wife for what Austin calls "the trail of the House" in which the multicultural inner life of the region's human history inscribes intimations of its yet unrealized future. In contradistinction to Latour's imported architectural aesthetic, the "trail of the House," in the American Southwest, Austin wrote, had "been lying there, plain as script for a thousand years for anybody to read that had the wit," as an:

> open trail from the grass-lined pit to the seven-story communal heap of the pueblos and the wide-winged haciendas of the Spanish occupation, the whole open story of the building impulse, the outer shell of the inner and otherwise incommunicable life of man (414).

Latour's cathedral figures as a "house of the book" as it embodies the text of Christian scripture and the history of literate Western European civilization's dualistic opposition of spirit and matter. The story of his insertion of a distinctly European architecture in a uniquely American landscape maintains the continuity of the Judeo-Christian master-narrative of historical spiritual progress over geographical determinants. Austin, on the other hand, seeks a different continuity in her concept of "the trail of the House": hers is a search for the continuity of lived experience in a particular place and the evolution of an inhabitory ethic aesthetically expressed in the ongoing development of dwelling structures that mediate material as well as psychological interrelationships of a society's culture and environment.

At the conclusion of *Starry Adventure*, Gard and Jane Wetherill set off to discover a text of cultural continuity in what Austin figures, in contrast to Cather's completed cathedral, as a yet unfinished book of the house. Austin was not alone among contemporaries in her recognition of the possibilities of the continuity of an indigenous American architecture. Vincent Scully notes that the constructions of the Pueblo peoples— themselves imitative of mountain horizons—are among "the first skyscrapers of the North American continent" and that Mayan temples provided models for the set-back skyscraper type design in the New York skyline during the first decades of the twentieth century (16).

Austin's further contribution to a semiotics of architecture results from her emphasis on the perception of indigenous structural forms as responses to both natural earth forms and to patterns and continuities of domestic existence. Hers is a feminist search for native, matrilocal alternatives to importation of patriarchal symbolic structures in the region. Austin believed that "in New Mexico, if anywhere, the history of the house was still to be uncovered with no single link missing of its evolution, as the shell, the reliquary of the values that inhere in the lives of women" (*Adventure*, 401). Where Cather presents construction of a completed symbolic and geographically transcendent public building and culture, Austin seeks to comprehend the ongoing legacy of the interactions of people with a particular landscape and the more private significance of home and community. Where Cather places the paternal civic edifice, Austin seeks the maternal hearth. In short, the poetics of place expressed in interfaces of architecture and region in these works suggest contrasting rhetorical projects. Cather's symbolic architectural text asserts the rhetoric of the *polis*—the city or state—while Austin's quest for the semiotic of the house argues for an alternative rhetoric of the *oikos*—the household. These contrasting rhetorics draw on the discourses of feminism, environmentalism, and regionalism, and suggest an emerging rhetoric of bioregionalism that may be capable of encompassing all of these.

Of course, favorable juxtaposition of the rhetoric of the *oikos* over that of the *polis,* even for the purpose of exploring alternative approaches to issues of environmental ethics and social justice, may unfortunately re-invoke a host of problematic antimonies already familiar to feminist critics. While values of the *oikos* may indeed provide critical correctives to excesses of the *polis,* without appropriate integration of domestic and democratic political perspectives, the rhetoric of the *oikos* will ultimately prove regressive rather than liberatory.[9] Austin's attempt at what might be described as an extension of the nineteenth-century cult of "True Womanhood," which enlarges the sphere of the household to encompass the larger human community's relation to its environment, may well be read as an antecedent to contemporary ecofeminism. But, as critics of ecofeminism including Janet Biehl point out, an *oikos* expanded to global proportions could still be a world of entrapment.[10] Furthermore, since it emphasizes familial relatedness, the *oikos* provides an insufficient foundation for an international ethical structure. Kinship societies may not be properly regarded as moral inasmuch as social roles are "limited by a commitment to biological attributes, not to rational ones" (Biehl, 142). On the other hand, the *polis* extends enfranchisement to non-kin "strangers" and replaces the private blood feud with public adjudication and civil resolution of conflicts and hostilities (Biehl, 146–149).[11]

Cather's celebration of the rational ethos of the *polis* as a negotiation of cultural otherness receives dramatic figuration in her brief summary of the historic reversal of the United States government's relocation of Navajo peoples to Bosque Redondo. In her depiction of this episode, reason prevails as a determinant of civil justice and public policy: "At last the Government at Washington admitted its mistake—which governments seldom do. After five years of exile, the remnant of the Navajo people were permitted to go back to their sacred places" (296). Cather's representation of the civil resolution of this bloody cross-cultural conflict leads Latour to conclude that, contrary to what he once believed, the Indian was not destined to perish. Presumably, Cather's optimism that the fate of native peoples would be incorporated into the republic would have been encouraged by the Indian Citizenship Act of 1924. But Cather's celebration of the assimilative potential of the *polis*, especially when considered in the historic context of the actual conditions of reservation life described by the Merriam Report published in the same year as *Death Comes for the Archbishop*, fails to consider the consequences of "citizenship" for Native Americans. Since the Dawes Act of 1887, the consequences of assimilation of Native Americans into the dominant culture of the United States have been continued divestment of tribal lands, the extortion of natural resources from remaining tribal lands, and a sometimes subtle, sometimes explicit process of the termination of Native American tribal sovereignty. A reading of the ethnocidal history suppressed by Cather's text reveals that, while the *oikos* may depend on problematic definitions of difference, the rhetoric of the *polis* leans toward a potentially dangerous denial of difference altogether.

Austin's text, on the other hand, argues for a different type of assimilation. In her exploration of regional architectural theory, Austin seeks syncretic processes of cultural exchange as geographically appropriate alternatives to the dominant forces of homogenizing Americanization. Austin's rhetoric of the *oikos*, while it draws strongly on valorizations of domestic space and family connectedness, does not argue for isolation from the public sphere or withdrawal from responsibility to non-kin others. What Austin represents in *Starry Adventure* is the development of an increasingly multicultural *polis* informed and strengthened by the integrity of individual communal loyalties

and differences and their coordination within larger regional—
and even global—civic contexts.

Austin's celebration of the extra-rational ethos of the *oikos*
as a negotiation of cultural otherness receives dramatic
figuration in her brief summary of the participation of New
Mexican native peoples in the American armed forces during the
First World War. As Gard experiences ambivalence about the
war and enlistment, he puzzles over the patriotism of his non-
Anglo peers:

> Finally there was the Draft. You could settle back and take
> it as it came. You discovered that most of the native boys
> had volunteered. They kept coming in after the Draft,
> from far little placitas and prados and cienagas. And they
> didn't seem to know about the Draft, either. They just
> came. Seemed to think it was their business. . . . First
> Americans, Old American families! Funny you never
> thought of them like that. (*Adventure* 58–59)

When Gard learns of the death of his young friend Ignacio on *El
Campo del honor* and shares in the grief of his family, he wonders:

> What did they think about it, the Natives? They couldn't
> possibly know what it was about. And they had been
> among the first to volunteer. New Mexico was fifth among
> the States to get in her quota of volunteers, although one
> of the least populated—and when you thought of the
> distance, and how the Natives had to hear it by word of
> mouth! Suddenly Gard found himself moved immensely
> toward the dark, simple people in the adobe huts.
> (*Adventure*, 173)

Following the truck that bears Ignacio's body to burial after the
war, Gard experiences another epiphanic moment which reveals
to him—though still in extra-rational terms—the connections
between the concrete experience of place and home and
abstractions like patriotism:

> Crossing the wash, the chamisal was as high as the bed of
> the truck; it peered over, feeling with light finger-tips the
> folds of red and white. Gard had a quick sense of the New
> Mexican soil reaching up through the chamisal to touch
> what had been bred of New Mexico, and had been so far,
> and experienced strange things, and was come back. He

thought: That's what gives you feelings—like patriotism; it's the dust in you; the dust in the corn and the corn in you, and you in the dust again. That's what made it right, and not just sentimental to bring the bodies back. Ignacio would go back in the dust, and then, when you were old, you'd have one of those quick moments of yours, passing chamise and chaparral, and you'd know suddenly; Ignacio's dust. You'd have secret and satisfying touch with all that Ignacio knew.

Gard reached out from his own car and let the soft golden brooms of the chamisal brush his hand. It had been a long time since he had felt the earth-thrill like that; it was for him, too, a coming home. (*Adventure,* 361)

Gard, through his topophilic epiphanies, comes to understand not only that the materiality of a particular human existence is inextricable from the cyclicality of earth processes; he begins to comprehend how universal human dependency on the earth's sustenance connects diverse populations in the interdependency of a shared home. Gard's realization of how his and Ignacio's fates are joined through the land they have shared signals an ecology of cultural interaction, an expansion of the *oikos* to global proportions in which cultural differences—instead of becoming subsumed by a transcendent rational order—are recognized as repositories of immanent geographic experience and knowledge—an economy of difference—necessary to the survival of the entire human family. But Austin's global expansion of the *oikos* differs critically from problematic extensions of household hierarchy justly critiqued by Biehl and other critics of ecofeminism.

Much of Austin's fiction reeducates its male protagonists to appreciate what are too often regarded as distinctly feminine principles of interdependence. In her final fiction, Austin produces her most successfully "feminized" male in the character of Gard Sitwell. But Gard's "feminization," rather than signaling a retreat from the public to the private sphere, contributes to an enlarged sense of citizenship. The buildings and communities Gard dreams of constructing in what has become widely recognized in the twentieth-century American Southwest as the Spanish neocolonial revival architectural style combine elements of domestic spaces—structural elements uniquely evolved through a semiotic of experience of a particular place—with edifices which fulfill symbolic requirements of civic administration. In the "feminized" figure of Gard Sitwell and his architecturally expressed vision, Austin joins the immanence and practicality of the *oikos* with the transcendent idealism of the *polis* and thus joins the regional and the cosmopolitan by coordinating, rather than erasing, difference as a way of strengthening world community.

Geopolitical movement in Cather's text tends toward assimilation of the region within the rational order of a world community represented by a Euro-American metanarrative. On the other hand, Austin's text offers the semiotic integrity of the region as an antidote to the nomothetic excesses of Euro-American environmental perceptions, values, and attitudes. My concern in mapping these distinctions has been to explore a rhetoric of regionalism which endeavors toward a truly pragmatic cosmopolitanism, a world community in which universalizing humanistic desires are mediated by a corrective appreciation of the material specificity of cultural and geographic particularities.

Austin's novel is an anticipation of what environmentalist philosopher Jim Cheney has called "bioregional narrative." In an effort to develop a postmodern environmental ethic in an age of growing global limitations, Cheney argues that narratives of place provide a type of critical, geographically grounded, contextual discourse which allows us to forgo the foundationalist "coherence, continuity, and consistency insisted on by totalizing discourse" and to understand the construction of self and community "within the space of defining relations" (126). Beyond the necessary postmodern deconstruction of "[t]otalizing masculine discourse (and essentializing feminist discourse)," contextualized discourses of place allow us the reconstructive potential of achieving (as opposed to *discovering*) healthy personal and social identities through appreciative recognition of the contributions of "the various and multiple landscapes . . . which function as metaphors of self and community" (134).

As a bioregional narrative, Austin's *Starry Adventure* answers Cather's vision in *Death Comes for the Archbishop* of the erasure of regional difference in a transcendent cosmopolitanism under the theocratic sign of Western global dominance with such an ecological argument for cultural diversity. Austin's pragmatic cosmopolitanism, by asserting the values of the *oikos* within the discourse of the *polis*, contributes to a vital rhetoric of regionalism, an argument of strength through diversity, which gathers increasing urgency in the face of the increasingly rapid technocratic-monocultural degradation of human and natural resources in our shrinking planetary household.

NOTES

1. For fuller explication of "nomothetic" and "idiographic" dispositions in the history of geographic discourse, see J. Nicholas Entrikin's *The Betweenness of Place: Towards a Geography of Modernity*. The point of aligning these terms with Kristeva's concepts, as I hope will become clear in the following analysis, is to emphasize the possibility of psychoanalytic insights into dimensions of spatial cognition.

2. Soja develops his definition of this concept with a quotation from the work of the French Marxist geographer, Harve Lefebvre: "Space and the political organization of space express social relationships but also react back upon them." Soja explains, "The key notion introduced by Lefebvre in . . . [this] sentence becomes the fundamental premise of the socio-spatial dialectic: that social and spatial relations are dialectically inter-reactive, interdependent; that social relations of production are both space-forming and space-contingent (at least insofar as we maintain, to begin with, a view of organized space as socially constructed)" (81).

3. See Patricia Nelson Limerick's introduction to *The Legacy of Conquest: The Unbroken Past of the American West* for fuller development of a "New Western Historian's" critical perspective on the effects of the figurative transformation of place to process in Turner's "Frontier Hypothesis."

4. See Susan Rosowski's "Willa Cather and the Fatality of Place: *O Pioneers!*, *My Antonia*, and *A Lost Lady*."

5. See Carl Bredahl's excellent discussion of Austin for fuller development of this term and Austin's contribution of the techniques and forms it describes as means of responding to the demands and challenges of representing landscape in American literary history.

6. While Austin, in her own Emersonian mode, argued often for the possibility of the direct experience of what, in Judeo-Christian theology, is termed "God," she never rested in her search for a more adequate description of divinity: "There was no fact Mary Austin so often insisted upon as that anyone could experience the presence of God-power outside himself. She gave this force many names: not only God, but the Friend, the Friend of the Soul, the Powers, the Giver of Gifts, even the Indian term, Wakonda, used by the Sioux for the Great Spirit" (Pearce, 96).

7. According to humanistic geographer Yi-Fu Tuan, "'topophilia' is a neologism, useful in that it can be defined broadly to include all of the human being's affective ties with the material environment" (93).

8. Lechte offers a useful definition of Kristeva's term: "The *chora* is connotative of the mother's body—an unrepresentable body. The mother and the body as such in fact go together for Kristeva. The mother's body becomes the focus of the semiotic as the 'pre-symbolic'— a manifestation—especially in art, of what could be called the 'materiality' of the symbolic: the voice as rhythm and timbre, the body as movement, gesture, and rhythm" (Lechte, 129). The importance of the association of topophilia and the semiotic to the present study is suggested by Annette Kolodny's conclusion that "the mother's body, as the first ambience experienced by the infant, becomes a kind of archetypal primary landscape to which subsequent perceptual configurations of space are related" (156).

9. Biehl notes that "ecofeminist writings are remarkably bereft of references to democracy. The most common approach is simply to ignore the question of the *polis* altogether and concentrate on the presumed 'women's values' of the *oikos*. Thus, while these writings are filled with discussions of 'oneness,' 'aliveness,' 'goddesses,' and 'interconnectedness,' they provide very little vision of the democratic processes that can keep these new 'ecological' values from transforming communities into tyrannies, the way they have developed historically (as we have seen), or keep community life from deteriorating into oppressive parochialisms, as has also been the case historically. Clearly established, distinct face-to-face democratic institutions, as specifically

human 'forms of freedom' (to use Bookchin's phrase), are essential to a liberatory—rather than a repressive—community" (135).

10. "... glorification of the *oikos* and its values as a substitute for the *polis* and its politics can easily be read as an attempt to dissolve the political into the domestic, the civil into the familial, the public into the private. Just as certain bureaucratic state institutions seem to loom over us, casting a shadow over our freedom, so there is the danger that the *oikos* will loom over us, casting a shadow over our autonomy. The *oikos*, or home, is by no means the magic talisman that will provide the framework for a caring world. Not only is it often narrow-minded, self-enclosed, and incestuous; it can also produce—as it has in history—the very opposite sentiments from those that ecofeminists prize. Indeed the *oikos* has not only been women's realm, but *also men's*. It has provided a home not only for male hunters, food-gatherers, and farmers, but also warriors, kings, and patriarchal tyrants" (Biehl, 140).

11. See also Julia Kristeva's discussion of the political acceptance of foreigners in ancient Greece in *Strangers to Ourselves* for fuller development of the ascendence of the *polis* over the clan.

WORKS CITED

Austin, Mary Hunter. *Starry Adventure*. New York: Houghton Mifflin, 1931.

———. "Regionalism in American Fiction." *The English Journal* 21 (February 1931): 97–106.

———. *Experiences Facing Death*. Indianapolis: Bobbs Merrill, 1931.

———. *Earth Horizon: An Autobiography*. 1932. Albuquerque: University of New Mexico Press. 1991.

Bachelard, Gaston. *The Poetics of Space*. Trans. Maria Jolas. Boston: Beacon Press, 1969.

Biehl, Janet. *Rethinking Ecofeminist Politics*. Boston: South End, 1991.

Bredahl, Carl A. Jr. *New Ground: Western American Literature and the Literary Canon*. Chapel Hill: University of North Carolina Press, 1989.

Cather, Willa. *Death Comes for the Archbishop*. 1927. New York: Vintage, 1971.

Cheney, Jim. "Postmodern Environmental Ethics: Ethics as Bioregional Narrative." *Environmental Ethics* 11.2. (Summer 1989): 117–34.

Kolodny, Annette. *The Lay of the Land: Metaphor as Experience and History in American Life and Letters*. Chapel Hill: University of North Carolina Press, 1975.

Kristeva, Julia. *Desire in Language: A Semiotic Approach to Literature and Art*. Ed. Leon S. Roudiez. New York: Columbia University Press, 1980.

———. *Strangers to Ourselves*. Trans. Leon S. Roudiez. New York: Columbia University Press, 1991.

Lechte, John. *Julia Kristeva*. New York: Routledge, 1990.

Limerick, Patricia Nelson. *The Legacy of Conquest: The Unbroken Past of the American West*. New York: Norton, 1987.

Rosowski, Susan J. "Willa Cather and the Fatality of Place: *O Pioneers!*, *My Antonia*, and *A Lost Lady*." In *Geography and Literature: A Meeting of the Disciplines*. Eds. William E. Mallory and Paul Simpson-Housley. Syracuse, New York: Syracuse University Press, 1987. 81–94.

Soja, Edward. *Postmodern Geographies: The Reassertion of Space in Critical Social Theory*. New York: Verso, 1989.

Stineman, Esther Lanigan. *Mary Austin: Song of a Maverick*. New Haven: Yale University Press, 1989.

Tuan, Yi-Fu. *Topophilia: A Study of Environmental Perception, Attitudes, and Values*. 2nd ed. New York: Columbia University Press, 1990.

The Regionalist Community
Indigenous versus Outsider Consciousness in Deledda's La madre and Lawrence's Sea and Sardinia

Jill Franks

Regionalist literature and travel writing each seek to render the essence of place by treating the interdependence of land and culture, of geography and character, of climate and temperament. The two genres are distinguished, however, by fundamentally different approaches to the subject matter: whereas travel writing chronicles an interior or psychic journey whose lessons are derived from the contrast between one culture and another,[1] regionalist writing focuses on the lessons to be learned from long-term involvement with one community. Because the travel writer does not generally have access to a foreign community's lived history (that which we do not find in history books), he or she cannot write regionalist literature about that community. D.H. Lawrence's *Sea and Sardinia* and Grazia Deledda's *La madre*, written at the same time and about the same place, illustrate the differences between travel literature and regionalist writing. I compare them not so much to prove that the outsider cannot write a regionalist text (Lawrence didn't set out to do so, and it is perhaps unfair to judge nonfiction and fiction by the same standards), but because a comparison of the two will illustrate regionalism's oft-neglected element, the native's knowledge of community values and access to communal tragedy, that differentiates it from travel writing.

Before turning to these two texts, it will be helpful to examine existing definitions of regionalism that explore the necessity of the regionalist author's first-hand involvement with the community. The question of whether the visitor can write regionalist literature is an old one, and the position that states that s/he cannot is eloquently if somewhat sentimentally articulated by John Crowe Ransom in his 1934 essay "The Aesthetic of Regionalism," which is as much a diatribe against the ills of industrialism and personal mobility as a definition of regionalism. He defines the aesthetic of regionalism as the "natural piety" that inhabitants feel toward their native region, and regionalist art as "faithful to the regional nature and to the economic and moral patterns to which the community is committed" (297). This emphasis on the community's moral values is an important one in Ransom's definition, for it is precisely these "committed" moral values that the "philosophical regionalist," as he calls the traveler, lacks.

This moralistic tone and "we/they" attitude is carried over into the contemporary debate over what constitutes regionalism. In his 1987 article "Writer and Region," Wendell Berry responds to *The Southern Review*'s attempt to "redefine Southernness without resort to geography" with well-founded intellectual scorn: "Southernness," "blackness," and "sacredness," he retorts, cannot properly be considered "metaregions" that "achieve distinction in direct proportion to the homogenization of the physical world," as they have never been regions, and because the physical world is not subject to homogenization, even if its human inhabitants were. Imagining a map of his opponents' homogenized "metaregion," Berry objects that it is "a map without a territory," and thus impossible to "correct." He compares this intellectual territory (posited by the abolishers of geographically-based regionalism) to the "territory of art" constructed by William Matthews in which there is no inherent value in subjects, only that conferred on them by the attention of the artist. Attention, Berry asserts, is an "obligation" toward the value inherent in certain subjects, and in the case of regionalism, that subject is "the territory underfoot." The "territory of art" and the "territory of mind," according to Berry, are inseparable from the territory underfoot, and as such, are subject to the possibility of "correction" (25–6).

The term "correction" needs further explanation, and Berry's interpretation of Barry Lopez's seminal statement of the relation of mind and place suggests a possible meaning for this term. Lopez claims that there is an interior landscape (mind) that is shaped by the exterior landscape (region). Our patterns of thought, according to Lopez, are deeply influenced by the patterns of nature in the particular place we inhabit (65). To Wendell Berry, this means that the "invisible landscape" of the psyche "serves the visible as a guide and protector," while the "visible landscape must verify and correct the invisible." While this seems to place a heavy responsibility on nature, or to overestimate its powers of "correction" (can a good view cure schizophrenia?), it does derive from the well-documented subject of the symbiotic relationship between human beings and nature.

Berry next discusses "communal tragedy" as a healing element in our relationship with our place of origin. He asserts that one who leaves his or her community loses the potential for experiencing tragedy, and that only through the experience of communal tragedy can humans experience joy. Berry bases his assumption of the communal nature of tragedy, as of the tragic nature of communal life, on Aristotle's theory of the drama. The catharsis and fulfilment that are the *communal* result of tragic drama are possible because of the individual's "return to the beloved community" after the shared experience, with a "renewed awareness of our love and hope for one another" (21). Those who reject their communities cannot experience true tragedy, which for Berry is the necessary prelude to the experience of true joy.

Borrowing from Berry's theory, we can say that the non-native who writes about a region is not privy to the "tragedies" of that region because s/he lacks direct experience of them. As is the case with classical Greek drama, you have to be at the performance in order to experience the catharsis. Nor is the outsider a participant in the "conversation" of community, a term that Berry borrows from Sarah Orne Jewett to express the spoken and lived history, the shared suffering and hope of its inhabitants. The outsider, depending on his or her provenance, and the degree of cultural difference between his or her native community and his or her subject's, is to varying degrees unlikely to understand the particular community values that define such local "tragedies." Although the visitor may render tragic events or conditions in his or her writing, his or her stance as outsider tends to exoticize such events, or to call attention to details that are irrelevant to the regionalist.[2]

It is the travel writer's consciousness of culture as his or her subject that contrasts with the (unselfconscious) regionalist's subject of native community and place. The fundamental interpretive problematics of anthropology can be compared to the problem of the travel writer interpreting a regional culture. Lévi-Strauss explains the anthropological problem in terms that also apply to the situation of the travel writer:

> In choosing a subject and an object radically distant from one another, anthropology runs a risk: that the knowledge obtained from the object does not attain its intrinsic properties but is limited to expressing the relative and always shifting position of the subject in relation to the object. (44)

Lawrence's *Sea and Sardinia* is a particularly good example of this relative and shifting position of the subject (Lawrence) in relation to the object (Sardinian culture). Lawrence continually relates his mood swings to the effects that local events, scenes, and personalities have upon him, and characterizes such things accordingly. If he is angry, it is because there is something inherently wrong about Sardinia; if a Sardinian is kind to him, then all of Sardinia is lovely. His generalizations about Sardinian culture so evidently derive from his alternately irascible and inspired moods during his stay that they must be suspect as representations of "intrinsic properties."

Whether moody or stable, all travel writers are primarily concerned with cultural difference. Their automatic comparisons of aspects of the "new" culture to those of their own culture deeply influence and shape their projects in more or less explicit ways. In the regionalist's writing, on the other hand, comparisons to other cultures are incidental or subliminal, as when the characters wish to escape to some idealized other location, usually perceived as a better way of life, a comparison that tends to underscore the particularities of their well-known community and place rather than the unknown Other. In this, the traveler and the regionalist have opposite priorities; the traveler's agenda, whether implied or stated, is always one of comparison, and as such, it emphasizes the place of origin and the effects of the native place on the writer's psychic development, rather than the new, exotic place, which provides an occasion and a framework for such analysis. But the regionalist's agenda is not primarily one of comparison; it is one of story-making, in which the particular land and community form both a particular human spirit and a spirit of place. Another way of illustrating this difference is by noting that, whereas the "stories" of many travel books could feasibly be placed in different settings because the author's psychic process is more focal than place (as in *Sea and Sardinia*), the regionalist's story is made possible exclusively by a particular place (as with Deledda's *La madre*).

Grazia Deledda was born in Nuoro, a small Sardinian village, in 1871; she lived there until 1900, when she moved to Rome with her husband; she published *La madre* in 1922, won the Nobel Prize for literature in 1926, and died in 1936. She was a prolific novelist whose attention was almost exclusively devoted to stories of her native Sardinia. Through failed experiments with an almost Gothically romantic style, Deledda learned to replace its artificiality with something more natural; returning to her soil for inspiration, she found most of her plot material in the recollection of stories and gossip told by the servants in front of the fire when she was a girl, and from stories told by her brother's friends as they gathered in the oil press (Miccinesi, 29). These stories accentuated and celebrated the pride taken by the Nuorese in their autochthonous tradition, and in particular, two aspects of it: they were shepherds, and they were resistant to all external influence because it threatened their ancient way of life.

The community values of the Sardinians who inhabit Nuoro emanate from a distinct local history. The island of Sardinia, being strategically positioned and endowed with raw materials (salt, metals, and men), was a prime target of the invasions of early imperialists. In the ninth century B.C.,

Phoenicians invaded Sardinia and enslaved its native inhabitants, imposing harsh laws on them. The Romans took over during their centuries of ascendancy, adding to the disgrace of the conquest by shipping all of their "undesirables" (delinquents, convicts, Jews, dissidents, and others who threatened the political and social order) to work in the Sardinian salt and metal mines. These pariahs, however, had the right qualities for becoming members of the native resistance movement, called *brigantaggio*, or brigandage. They fled to the mountains of the central island, where Nuoro lies, which were difficult for the enemy to penetrate; they lived in rustic stone dome-shaped dwellings called *nuraghi*. They made their living by goat and sheep herding and, though Rome of course did penetrate the hills and impose foreign law upon them, the *Barbagie* (Barbarians), as they were scornfully named, maintained their own laws, handed down orally from generation to generation, while stubbornly resisting the foreign imposition. It was a matter of pride for *Barbagie* to be called *vendicatori* (avengers) or *banditi d'onore* (honorable bandits). They had their own strong sense of justice that was often opposed to what imperial law dictated (Giacobbe, 31).

The alternation of foreign dominators during the next 1,500 years (Vandals, Goths, Greeks, Arabs, Pisans, Genoese, Aragonese, Austrians) didn't change the *Barbagie*'s resistance to the injustice of outside control. But that resistance became more passive over the centuries. Instilled in Sardinians was what Giacobbe calls "a deep mistrust of the consequences that European affairs would have on them," which "was transformed in the popular subconscious into a rooted apoliticalness, a dark sense of extraneity, of nonparticipation, even abstractly, emotionally or intellectually, in any event that occurred outside the confines of the village or the zone"(34)[3]. It must have seemed, in fact, that their village history was the one thing they could be sure of, as the foreign dominators tried to purge them of a consciousness of their ethnic and national history; even after Rome's recognition of Sardinia as an autonomous Italian region, Sardinian history was not taught in the schools (Giacobbe, 34). Yet the *Barbagie* still passed down their own laws and maxims orally from generation to generation.

Maintaining a strict ethical code of their own and yet having to appear to follow the state's laws resulted in a complex duplicity that only a native-born Nuorese is likely to understand:

> The persistence of their ancient code, unwritten but well-articulated and ruled by precise juridical norms, as well as the conflict which this persistence caused them with the government, and the duplicity that they were constrained to employ out of loyalty to one and the duty of obedience to the other, together with a very original and functional popular culture, formed the special substratum of the Nuorese world that Grazia Deledda knew as a child, and that she reproduced with almost documentary faithfulness, particularly in the pronouncements and maxims that occur so frequently in the dialogues between her Sardinian characters. (Giacobbe, 32)

A related aspect of Sardinian culture that may be difficult for the outsider to understand or to recognize the signs of, is the vestiges of matriarchy. It was women's role to pass down the oral tradition which included the special local code of laws. Giacobbe tells us that because of this, even in Deledda's time, the women were like "queens" invested with prestige and dignity inside the domestic walls, while they were "pariahs" outside in the male world (19). Although it is difficult to imagine how the parameters could be so strictly drawn (wouldn't a woman at times carry out this matriarchal role in the community?), Deledda's female characters bear witness to the fact of female superiority and of their obedience to the code; they are generally stronger morally than the male characters. The title character of *La madre* and her son are prime examples of this phenomenon.

This is the unique social world that D.H. Lawrence stepped into for a week's tour in January 1921. Taking no notes, he collected impressions that were to become the book *Sea and Sardinia* in six weeks' time, one which many critics have praised as the best of his four travel books. Its popularity depends largely on his comically cranky personality. He plays the main character of the story, and is always center-stage. But readers still believe that he, in the words of Anthony Burgess, "extracted the very essence of the island and its people" (ix). Lawrence's motivations for his journey help explain his disillusionment with

Sardinia; he left his residence in Taormina, Sicily, to get away from the dwellers-under-Etna, "the most stupid people on earth," who "never knew what truth was and have long lost all notion of what a human being is" (2, 3), hoping to find in Sardinia a people "unsubdued" by civilization, with an untainted consciousness. Complaining that whereas Sicilians suffer divided consciousness (one part for every race that ever ruled them), Sardinians were never subdued by their invaders, and never learned to think like them, Lawrence compares the two:

> [the Sicilian] is an over-cultured, sensitive ancient soul, and he has so many sides to his mind that he hasn't got any definite one mind at all. . . . The Sardinian, on the other hand, still seems to have one downright mind. I bump up against a downright, smack-out belief in socialism, for example. (80)

"Seems" is a good qualification here, if we remember the duplicity which Sardinians have to engage in to live by two differing standards of conduct, foreign and native.

Putting aside the problematic theoretical issues created by Lawrence's binary oppositions of stereotypical Sardinians and Sicilians (one mind/many-sided mind, outside of culture/over-cultured, pure/corrupted, truthful/false), we can still anticipate the letdown he will experience when individuals that he meets while traveling don't match his expectations of them. The difference between his impossible idealization of the Sardinians and the reality that he experiences, as limited as that experience is, provides the main element of comedy in the book, as both the reader and, at times, the author, are aware of an inherently ironic situation, the gawking foreigner who turns everyday habits and customs of a strange population into farce (if he is disgusted) and romance (when he is admiring).

These comic elements, farce and romance, so typical of travel literature, are not present in the kind of regionalist writing that concerns me here (I qualify the term because a regionalist like Mark Twain is a notable exception). Instead, the basic ingredients of regionalism are tragic, both in Wendell Berry's sense of the losses borne together by a community, and in the literary-generic sense of fatedness or environmental determinism. In regionalist literature, the interdependence of plot and place typically results in characters' inability to escape fates which are in part determined by environment. Conversely, to escape would deprive them of the consolations of community experience that Berry holds to be essential for the experience of tragedy and joy.

La madre's triangle of characters are stuck in such a predicament; each one wants to escape from the village. That they cannot leave their consciences behind by leaving their village is implicit from the beginning of the story. Their lives are circumscribed by their community's values, and their adherence to those values is so powerfully inbred that neither love nor the desire for exiled isolation can break it. The story is as follows: the Mother has worked hard to support the career of her son as a priest. Once he is ordained, they return to her native village, Aar (presumably based on Deledda's village, Nuoro), so that he can assume the long-vacant post of village priest. Paul is content, if not happy, until he falls in love with the orphaned parishioner Agnes. His love is not blissful but tormenting, as it conflicts with his religious beliefs and duties. But he is alternately overcome by the need to be with Agnes and the need to obey his mother. Curiously, his mother's disapproval of the relationship is a greater factor in his final renunciation of Agnes than his own relationship with God.[4] His moral weakness is evident in the interior monologues of his sleepless nights and in the final, climactic scene where he quakes with fear while delivering the Mass, for he is certain that Agnes will denounce him to the congregation, as he has finally decided to forsake her. Agnes does not in fact reveal his sin, but paradoxically, Paul's mother, for whom he had made this sacrifice, dies of shock from her own anticipation of the scene.

Paul's fatedness, then, is in part determined by his weak character, in part by the rigid code of his community, and in great part by his submission to the matriarch—a feature as much cultural as it is personal. Deledda does not, in the end, limit Paul's conflict to spiritual versus material desires, but to the duty of obedience to his mother, whom we have seen is the conduit of autochthonous culture in the *Barbagie*, versus his responsibility to himself and his lover, who begs him to take her away from the village. That Deledda is on the side of the love choice is clear enough: her affectionate portrait of the ghost of the ex-parish priest, who gave up the sober habits of the cloth to drink and socialize with the village rascals, leaves little doubt of her scorn for those who use the church to hide from the pleasures of life. The priest-ghost calls Paul's attraction to Agnes his "destiny" and exhorts the mother to let Paul follow it instead of forcing him to make the same mistakes that he did, learning too late what God had intended man to do with His creation: "God sent us into the world to enjoy it. He sends suffering to punish us for not having understood how to enjoy, and that is the truth, you fool of a woman!" (52)

In Paul's relationship with his mother, Deledda has created a paradigm of place: as proud as the Nuorese are of their indomitability vis-à-vis the foreign conquerors, they rebel only at their spiritual peril (witness Paul's intense anguish and subsequent tragedy) against the inside order of the house, represented by the mother, who is the honored keeper of the oral, autochthonous tradition. An outsider to Nuoro might attempt to write this classic plot, of the priest's temptation by carnal love, with no appreciation of the subtleties born of place, in particular, of the fact that Paul's real conflict was between himself and his mother, not himself and the church. And how does the outsider render that rare (to Western eyes) phenomenon, the matriarchy, in which the mother's authority represents a social order so delicate and threatened that it must be rigidly enforced, even at the expense of the personal happiness of her son? It may seem that Paul's mother aligns herself not with any autochthonous tradition, but instead with the Catholic church, but careful reading indicates that she is more concerned with her and Paul's acceptance by the community, and with their powerful standing there, than with the ethical questions inherent in Paul's choice. The necessity of obedience to maternal authority, then, is more compelling than the rightness or wrongness of the mother's desire to stifle her son's love life.

Lawrence certainly perceives the flavor of female superiority in Sardinia, but he also perceives male superiority, and simply does not address the question of the matriarchal heritage. His observations of relations between the sexes are as stylized here as they are throughout his canon: the important thing to Lawrence about these relations is the power struggle, in Cagliari, Sardinia, as in Nottingham, England. In Sardinia, he admires "the defiant, splendid split between the sexes, each absolutely determined to defend his side, her side, from assault. So the meeting has a certain wild, salty savour, each the deadly unknown to the other" (67). Of such meetings he knows nothing. Of men and women's bearing, he knows only what he sees around him while traveling. He interprets the posture of local females as a statement of their (gendered) independence:

> They are amusing, these peasant girls and women: so brisk and defiant. They have straight backs like little walls, and decided, well-drawn brows. And they are amusingly on the alert. There is no eastern creeping. Like sharp, brisk birds they dart along the street, and you feel they would fetch you a bang over the head leave as look at you. Tenderness, thank heaven, does not seem to be a Sardinian quality. (66)

This is entertaining as caricature, but renders nothing characteristic of the region: Lawrence describes Sicilians, North Italians, and "the modern European woman" in similar terms elsewhere.

His portrait of the males is similarly beyond regionalist concerns. In a central passage, his distaste for them, mixed with his admiration, incites him to characterize them as animals: at one moment they are "half-wild dogs that will love and obey, but which won't be handled," then their stocking caps remind him of lizards' crests, next their coarseness is compared to a goat's, and finally he works himself up to the inevitable conclusion that they are unknowably Other, which he expresses in terms of the Christian myth of crucifixion: "They have no inkling of our crucifixion, our universal consciousness. Each of them is pivoted and limited to himself, as the wild animals are" (90). Their stocking caps are a sign to Lawrence of their tenacity in rejecting the civilized world. He pretends to speak for them when he calls their way of life a "hell": "Coarse, vigorous, determined, they will stick to their own coarse dark stupidity and let the big world find its own way to its own enlightened hell. Their hell is their own hell, they prefer it unenlightened" (91). Lawrence probably does not intend to sound mean and superior here, for it is a tenet of his personal faith that primitive religions have more truth and beauty to offer than Christianity, and that the pagan "me-consciousness" is superior to the Christian "thou-consciousness" (see "The Theater" chapter of his *Twilight in Italy*). But nevertheless, he does hierarchize two different ways of behaving, and imposes his own cultural standards on another race of people. Deledda may be speaking through Paul when the character condemns the villagers for their blind faith in him, but the villagers are never "them" to Paul (or Deledda) in the same way that Sardinians are to Lawrence.

In a similar way, the landscape itself takes on alienating shapes and meanings for Lawrence, while Deledda, who belongs to it, integrates it with the thoughts, actions, and personalities of her characters. It is at the same time more and less of a phenomenon for her than it is for Lawrence: more because she understands how the natural world influences the interior landscapes of her fellow Nuorese, and less because it is not an alien presence which one must seek to understand by comparison (Lawrence begins to appreciate the stark hills of northern Sardinia only when he equates them with the "Celtic spirit" found in Cornwall, Ireland, and Derbyshire). There is nothing sinister or meaningless in the land for Deledda, even though the wind of Aar is imbued with a powerful character. Nor is there an attempt to describe the land like a picture. Lawrence's reaction to the Sardinian landscape alternates between an appreciation of the picturesque, a reverence for the "savage" beauty, and a feeling of emptiness.

The following passage is Lawrence's description of Nuoro, and I quote it at length because it provides a good contrast to Deledda's description of what is likely to be the same scene of her home village:

> We came to the end of the houses and looked over the road-wall at the hollow, deep, interesting valley below. Away on the other side rose a blue mountain, a steep but stumpy cone. High land reared up, dusky and dark-blue, all around. Somewhere far off the sun was setting with a bit of crimson. It was a wild, unusual landscape, of

> unusual shape. The hills seemed so untouched, dark-blue,
> virgin-wild, the hollow cradle of the valley was cultivated
> like a tapestry away below. And there seemed so little
> outlying life: nothing. No castles even. In Italy and Sicily
> castles perching everywhere. In Sardinia none—the
> remote, ungrappled hills rising darkly, standing outside of
> life. (143)

The passage is marked by references to emptiness or absence: the "hollow" valley, the "untouched" "virgin-wild" hills, the "hollow cradle," "nothing," "no castles," just "remote" hills standing "outside of life." Alternatively, the landscape is "interesting" and "unusual," the epithets of the uninspired tourist. But for Deledda, the landscape is full of meaning, and she has none of the detachment of the touristic stance.

The first Deledda passage that I quote describes how the mother sees the village piazza and the valley below on the night she secretly follows Paul to Agnes's house:

> The gleam, now blue, now yellow, of the moon as it was
> traversed by large racing clouds, illuminated the grassy
> field, the levelled piazza in front of the church and the
> presbytery, and the two lines of cottages winding down
> the two sides of a steep road that lost itself among the
> thickets of the valley. And in the middle of the valley
> appeared, like another grey and windy road, the river that
> in its turn merged among the rivers and the roads of the
> fantastic landscape that the clouds, pushed by the wind,
> alternately created and destroyed on the horizon at the
> edge of the valley.... In the village you could no longer
> see a light or a thread of smoke. All the poor houses slept,
> clinging like two rows of sheep to the grassy slope, in the
> shadow of the little church that with its slender belltower,
> itself protected by the mountain ridge, seemed like a
> shepherd leaning on his staff.(6)

In this passage, Deledda's metaphorical images are simple, almost fairy-tale-like. They evoke the mother's love of her small native village and her sense of her son's role there, as protector of the poor sheep clinging tenaciously to a difficult pasture. The mountain does not stand "outside of life" but actually protects the village life. The images also mirror the anxious mental state of the mother, in which she sees shadows created and then destroyed on the landscape of her mind as she contemplates the meaning of Paul's actions and of her doubts. The power of the wind to create and take away, as well as the tendency of the rivers to "lose themselves," reflect her fears about losing her ascendancy over Paul and thus over her own future.

To Deledda, unlike Lawrence, the landscape is almost too full of meaning, as the wind seems to voice not only hers, but all the sorrows of the world:

> The row of alder trees before the piazza wall shook furiously in the wind, black and twisted like monsters; to their rustle responded the lament of the poplars and the reeds in the valley: and into all that nocturnal dolour, with the gasping of the wind and the drowning of the moon in the clouds, merged the agitated anguish of the mother pursuing her son. (7)

Perhaps to an exaggerated degree Deledda "merges" the destiny of the mother with the landscape, unlike Lawrence, who separates himself from the place by various methods: creating the picturesque, straining toward an expression of collective unconsciousness in the feel of granite underfoot (83), or by the more mundane comments that the quoted passage contains: the judgment of the land as without interest (the word "interesting" often suggests its opposite when it is not explained), or, worse, as empty or meaningless: "there is nothing to see in Nuoro" (150).

Similarly, while Deledda again imparted mythical significance to a scene in which the villagers stoke their evening bonfires in the piazza to welcome Paul back and celebrate his "miracle" of exorcising the devil out of a village girl, Lawrence, describing an evening bonfire on a ledge above the piazza, comments incidentally on its lack of meaning for him: "Why were these folk at the town-end making this fire alone?" (143). Neither did he understand the social activity taking place in the main piazza of Nuoro that night; there were dancers, still dressed up in their carnival disguises, "doing a sort of intense jigging waltz. Why do they look so intense? Perhaps because they were so tight all together, like too many fish in a globe slipping through one another" (143). Lawrence doesn't understand the intensity of the characters, nor the reason why they would dance so closely together, whereas Deledda, through Paul, understands only too well the intensity and the reason of the community ceremony with bonfires, even from the far vantage point of the mountain road. Lawrence in fact tends to deflate the intensity of his Sardinians with moralizing or belittling aphorisms, whereas Deledda celebrates their intensity, endowing it with mythical and metaphorical meaning.

The preceding is clearly only a small part of a potential comparison of how Lawrence's outsider status and Deledda's insider status affect their respective renderings of Sardinia. Lawrence goes to Sardinia to find cultural relief from over-cultured (but "stupid") Sicilians, hoping to find a "primitive" culture that will teach him something pure and simple about living. Instead he finds substandard plumbing and dining, "coarse, stupid" men who resemble goats, and a feeling of emptiness or absence in the scenery. He omits any discussion of the historical matriarchy and finds instead the universal battle of the sexes. He doesn't understand certain local customs or behaviors, and he feels a "gulf" between himself and the Sardinians. Deledda, on the other hand, is not overtly critical of her Sardinians; she is empathic in the way that only a native can be: the hidden restrictions on their behavior, and their secret motivations, are known to her. The community's code by which her characters live is clear to her (she spent her first twenty-nine years accommodating that code, which stipulated that she should not write). She witnessed the "community tragedies" that bind one to a particular place. She followed the first lesson in writing fiction: write about what you know.

NOTES

1. Norman Douglas emphasized that the reader takes a special interest in the psychic ingredient of travel writing: "It seems to me that the reader of a good travel book is entitled not only to an exterior voyage, to descriptions of scenery, and so forth, but to an interior, a

sentimental or temperamental voyage, which takes place side by side with the outer one" (9).

2. See Carlos Alonso's Introduction to *The Spanish American Regional Novel* for an amusing and informative discussion of the exoticizing tendencies of the foreigner as well as the "ardent cultural nationalist" who "produces" the autochthonous experience of his or her native region with an emphasis on the uniqueness of the local culture.

3. This is my own translation from the Italian, as are the rest of the quotations from the works of Deledda and Giacobbe.

4. Anna Dolfi discusses the "maternal principle" as the ruling force of Paul's life. She combines both psychoanalytical and regionalist observations when stating that Paul's general suffering arises from "the tension of detaching himself from the nurturing principle of the mother, while his specific pain develops when this vague inclination to be tied to mother's apron materializes into the necessity for a personal, rapid, and contradictory choice between his mother and Agnes" (114, my translation). To Dolfi, the mother represents the social order, which always prevails in Deledda's works: "[Paul's] sacrifice is an attempt to prevent a distancing from his mother and the death that she offers as a continuing pledge of loyalty and of prohibition, as an eternal immutable proof, beyond any biological fact, of the triumph of the order represented by the apotheosis of the maternal principle" (115).

WORKS CITED

Alonso, Carlos. *The Spanish American Regional Novel: Modernity and Autochthony*. Cambridge: Cambridge University Press, 1990.

Berry, Wendell. "Writer and Region." *Hudson Review* 40 (1987): 15–30.

Burgess, Anthony. Introduction. *D.H. Lawrence and Italy*. New York: Penguin Books, 1972.

Deledda, Grazia. *La madre*. Milan: Fratelli Treves, 1929.

Dolfi, Anna. *Grazia Deledda*. Milan: Mursia, 1979.

Douglas, Norman. "Arabia Deserta." *Experiments*. New York: Robert M. McBride, 1925. 1–22.

Giacobbe, Maria. *Grazia Deledda: Introduzione alla Sardegna*. Milan: Bompiani, 1974.

Lawrence, D.H. *Sea and Sardinia: D.H. Lawrence and Italy*. New York: Penguin Books, 1972.

Lévi-Strauss, Claude. *The Scope of Anthropology*. Trans. Sherry Ortner Paul and Robert A. Paul. London: Jonathan Cape, 1974.

Lopez, Barry. *Crossing Open Ground*. New York: Charles Scribner's Sons, 1978.

Miccinesi, Mario. *Grazia Deledda*. Florence: La Nuova Italia, 1981.

Ransom, John Crowe. "The Aesthetic of Regionalism." *American Review* 2 (January 1934): 290–310.

Regionalism and Value Structure in Erckmann-Chatrian

Warren Johnson

Regionalism would seem to be the converse of exoticism. The depiction of the foreign and exotic frequently seeks to evoke what is repressed in the dominant culture for being extreme or excessive and thus constitutes a zone of freedom beyond normative constraints. By contrast, regionalism—the representation of an area subsumed within the dominant culture—often attempts to capture the sense of a defined space through the evocation of detail that will appear to the readers both typical of their own experience and stereotypical of a given place. Exoticism thus can function as a tool in the service of cultural criticism, directed at the dominant culture, a foreign one, or both (such as in Montesquieu's *Lettres persanes*), whereas regionalism, sometimes reduced to "local color," appears essentially conservative, nostalgic, valorizing the quaintness of the rural or provincial landscape and society. While exoticism appeals to the transgressive imagination (or imaginary), regionalism tends to rely on recognition of the familiar and remembrance of the *déjà vu*, and to reinforce conventional value structures.

This conception of the split between exoticism and regionalism has much to do with the current interest in travel narrative and the image of the Other in literary texts, while at the same time suggesting a reason for the eclipse of the once immensely popular team of Alsacian writers, Erckmann-Chatrian. As Pierre-Pascal Furth notes, the accusation of regionalism is in itself a way of dismissing an author. Furth attempts to salvage the reputation of Erckmann-Chatrian by denying the importance of regionalism in their work, arguing, truthfully enough, that they neither confine the action of their writings to Alsace-Lorraine nor present enough in the way of details of customs or food to distinguish this region.

Yet just as exoticism has ulterior motives behind its evocation of the distant and unpronounceable, the regionalism of Erckmann-Chatrian transcends the enumeration of what is rightly or wrongly considered particular to a certain locale. Their regionalism operates through a similar opposition between the familiar and the Other as in exoticism, with all the potential for ambivalence and complexity that underlies the exotic in Montesquieu, Flaubert, Mérimée and others. In Erckmann-Chatrian, region becomes a metonym for a complex of value systems that has much more to do with the preservation of certain ideals of individual liberty and justice than with local pastries and sausages.

Their Alsace-Lorraine stands out as a region distinct from, say, George Sand's Berry, less on account of the occasional specialized terms such as *schlitteur* (sleigh maker, a word of obviously Franco-German origin), and references to a more inhospitable climate than in the rest of the Hexagon than because of the insistence on the region as the sphere of work and commerce, war and peace—at the time, of course, specifically masculine pursuits. The love interest in their work is purely conventional and incidental to the characters' greater goals of forging a more equitable political system and making a comfortable living.

Alsace-Lorraine represents for Erckmann-Chatrian not only a physical space but more importantly a site of numerous conflicting ideological forces whose resolution requires negotiating the pulls of the French and Prussian states, region and capital, and even Prussia and other German-speaking regions. Interlayered into the tensions associated with geography are conflicts between the bourgeois-dominated Second Empire and republican or revolutionary ideals as well as the growing culture of *Gesellschaft* that sapped away at traditional values of family and work. Erckmann-Chatrian see in the Alsace-Lorraine region the possibility of a synthesis of these opposing tendencies in ways that offer an instructive example to the French nation as a whole. The value system they advocate, a combination of French revolutionary ideals and traditional Teutonic beliefs in the value of family and labor, along with a muting of class conflict, seeks to reverse much of the direction France was taking in the nineteenth century. But even that wish needs to be seen in the light of their awareness of the influences of historical factors on ideology. While condemning a simplistic, reactionary clinging to whatever is old-fashioned, Erckmann-Chatrian claim the moment was ripe in the France of the 1860s and 1870s to recuperate values preserved among the common folk of the northeast provinces.

Erckmann-Chatrian's adherence to the goals of liberty, equality, and fraternity needs little elaboration here, thanks notably to the analysis of Colette Dimic. These revolutionary ideals are linked, as Dimic points out, to traditional values that include the love of God (though not of the clergy), country, and family through an opposition between the capital and the provinces:

> Compared with the Parisian, the inhabitant of Alsace-Lorraine displays all the bourgeois virtues: love of solidity and of the money that guarantees it, sense of utility, order, measure, prudence, wisdom, resignation due to the awareness of his strength, love of work, practical and peaceful mind. (Dimic, 331)

Erckmann-Chatrian see their mission as essentially didactic, according to Armand Roth, as committed to the goals of universal and secular education that would provide equal chances for social advancement, the foundation of liberty. This essay will explore the interconnections between the representation of region and the elaboration of a system of values that Erckmann-Chatrian implicitly offer as an ideal synthesis of two national cultures.

Alsace-Lorraine is obviously in a unique position to contain within its ideological frontiers elements of both the Other and the domestic. Ceded to France by the Peace of Westphalia in 1648, the area bitterly resented (according to our novelists) the loss of autonomy it enjoyed under the Holy Roman

Empire. French domination, in Erckmann-Chatrian's eyes, meant the exploitation of the region through the innumerable indirect taxes of the ancien régime and the drain on human and material resources on account of the imperialistic wars of the two empires. Yet the republican Erckmann-Chatrian, as critics often point out, look to the Revolution as a crystallization of their desires for the abolition of arbitrary barriers to individual social advancement and prosperity. Just as Paris is both oppressor and source of an ideology that will liberate the region, Prussia and the other German states likewise are ambiguously the source of the work ethic and the characteristic love of comfort that still appears in guidebook descriptions of Alsace as well as the fatherland of a rapacious and brutal army of occupation during the Napoleonic period and Second Empire. The forced annexation of these regions with the newly unified Germany after the Franco-Prussian War of 1870 led, in fact, to a renewal of local identity, so that, according to Daniel Faucher in his historical account of the area, the desire to be Alsacian was a way of becoming once again French (378).

While the novels and tales express conflicting and contradictory attitudes toward the two national cultures for which Alsace-Lorraine served as the literal and ideological battleground, the image that emerges of the region has definite tendencies. Erckmann-Chatrian present the northeastern provinces as embodying a synthesis of the ideal of a society where class conflict is muted, yet where an every-man-for-himself attitude becomes the key to economic development and social harmony. By choosing to focus on preindustrial, small-scale communities, they idealize a vanishing socioeconomic structure linked by association to this borderland region.

Since Erckmann-Chatrian constantly define what is most laudable in the French character by what the Prussians try to repress, and what is most reprehensible in the Teutonic people by what the French would not deign to do, attempting to discuss either in isolation would obscure the dynamics of their representation by essentializing the division. Further complicating the ambiguities is the general shift in Erckmann-Chatrian's attitude toward Germans that critics have discerned after the Franco-Prussian War. In "Annette et Jean-Claude," set during the Restoration and published as part of the *Contes vosgiens* in 1877, revolutionary ideals, symbolized by the use of the French language, are suspect in the eyes of the parish priest, Fischer, who dismisses it as the "language of Voltaire." (By contrast, the narrator remarks that the hermit Yéri-Hans, who tries to assault the young Annette, "let out a horrible oath: one of those endless German oaths that no civilized language could translate . . ." [12: 325]). The imposition of the German language, a much more pressing concern after the loss of the territory from French control, becomes an instrument of power through cultural indoctrination in religion as well as autocratic principles. The association of Germans and the German language with barbarism, while on the surface merely an unfortunate xenophobic reaction, reveals how the general tendency to associate region and value operates through a metonymic shift that translates ideology in terms of particular cultural manifestations.

While Fischer looks back regretfully to the time before the Westphalia treaty to when the region was under German control, a similar nostalgia informs the views of the sympathetic narrator of *Histoire d'un paysan* (whose first part appeared in 1868), where Alsace-Lorraine before the French monarchy gained hegemony over it is seen as an idyllic territory that attracted settlers because of its free land and absence of serfdom. In the work of Erckmann-Chatrian, the same region is invested with contradictory associations depending on the historical moment of the observer and his own *Weltanschauung*.

Both before and after the war of 1870, Erckmann-Chatrian distinguish—though never consistently—between the Prussian military structure and the simple German soldiers who carry out orders. "The Lord God made the Prussians to command, and the other Germans to obey," says the narrator of *Histoire du plébiscite* (11:152). The same narrator claims that for the Prussians, war is "a means to get rich, to seize the possessions of inoffensive natives" (11:218). By contrast, the Frenchman, Pinto, in *Histoire d'un conscrit de 1813* reminds a soldier who is about to steal a pipe from a wounded Prussian soldier that the Gallic sense of honor prohibits such acts. Yet the narrator of *Histoire du plébiscite* notes that the German soldiers steal and commit unspeakable horrors (i.e., rape), regarding which he says, "That's what you call good old German morals" (11:126) and toward the end he gives vent to bitter anger at the self-satisfaction of the enemy that is specifically identified with the German nation:

> Ah! the French people, without being as pious, as educated, as wise as the *good German people*, have yet a different sort of heart and mettle; they have less of the Gospel on their lips, but they have it in the depths of their souls. They are not hypocritical; and that's why we, inhabitants of Alsace and Lorraine, prefer being French to belonging to the *good German people* and to resembling them. . . . (11:233, emphasis in the original)

Paradoxically, the narrator elsewhere vaunts the discipline of the Prussian army, which he attributes to the unquestioning acceptance of a hierarchy of authority in the German character, while advocating that military obedience should be inculcated in French schools and military service should be obligatory for all Frenchmen. The disorder in the French ranks during both the wars of 1812–14 and 1870, due in large part to the incompetence of their commanders, would have been rectified had the French systematized their military organization. That such a disciplined organization is at odds not only with French "individualism," usually criticized in Erckmann-Chatrian as lusting after money or glory, but with the egalitarianism of the ideal community as well, suggests once again that in their world, ideology ought to be a function of circumstance rather than absolute, a response to historical conditions and not inflexible. Just as the moment defines the race and milieu (to recall the elements of Taine's historical determinism), it dictates the ideology appropriate at a given historical juncture. National identity has thus a shifting and unstable relationship with values attributable to it.

Further evidence of Erckmann-Chatrian's conflicting attitudes toward the Germans can be seen in the pre-1870 *Un conscrit de 1813*. Joseph Bertha, the narrator, expresses shock at the ferocity of the Prussian military, saying, "You would have thought that they wanted to eat us. . . . They are a vile race" (4:197), yet he also remarks, "God forbid I should say anything bad about the Germans; they were fighting for the independence of their homeland . . ." (4:202). The German postmaster remarks that during the Revolution, the average German soldier, despite his superiors, supported the same ideal of liberty as the French infantryman he fought, but during the Napoleonic invasion, the German nation now is the champion of freedom in the face of French imperialistic designs.

Region, as signifier of an ideological structure, cannot be divorced from the historical moment, from the complex of economic and social forces that shape attitudes of the individual and the group. "German," "Prussian," or "French" function less as fixed stereotypes than as provisional Others against which to develop a self-definition and identity for the self or collectivity by the rejection of what violates characters' growing sense of the ideal moral order. That ethical sense remains inarticulate or unperceived until it collides with an alien complex of values or the disastrous effects on others of unbridled individual ambition.

Clearly, much of the characters' hatred against the occupying Prussian armies derives from their incessant requisitioning and simple theft of private property. The increasing concern with stability and property rights in the early nineteenth century, which Foucault describes as underlying the increased regimentation of institutional structures, in Erckmann-Chatrian is valorized as the foundation of peace and the community as well as, implicitly, individual liberty. For Joseph Bertha in *Waterloo*, the sequel to *Un conscrit de 1813*, "After the good fortune of marrying Catherine, my greatest joy was to think that I was going to become a bourgeois . . ." (4:265). To Erckmann-Chatrian, the middle class represents not the growing monied and predominant social group, by opposition to the dispossessed workers, but simply those who mind their own business, in both senses of the phrase. The bourgeois is the inhabitant of the *bourg*, the urban entrepreneur who creates wealth and prosperity. In this etymological and medieval sense, *bourgeois* designates the motive force behind a productive and progressive economic structure, an outsider to the *cité* dominated by the parasitic nobility and clergy who come to represent the collective interests of the Third Estate without regard to class distinctions as they intruded themselves in nineteenth-century France.

The economic well-being of Alsace-Lorraine is threatened not only by the Prussians who bleed the region to supply their war effort during both the Napoleonic and Franco-Prussian wars, but by the ambitions of certain individuals and their love of glory, a peculiarly French preoccupation. Glory, the obsession with one's own image especially identified in the novel with Napoleon, is the antithesis of communal values, as Joseph Bertha remarks: "I am well aware that that is called glory; but common folk [*les peuples*] are very stupid to glorify such people. . . . Yes, you would have to have lost all common sense, heart, and religion" (*Waterloo*, 4:424). This understanding of the futility of glory comes to him only through the disillusionment at war, though he started like many others, complicitous in the desire to exalt the emperor, and in the process tried to give value to his own life as he imagined the response of his beloved upon hearing of his death in combat. The narrator of *Histoire du plébiscite*, Christian Wéber, resentful of the French abandonment of Alsace-Lorraine in 1870, especially after the approval of the plebiscite that was supposed to guarantee its security, claims that the concession was not motivated so much by the protestant complexion of the region as the mismanagement brought on by the greed of highly placed individuals in the Second Empire. (It was this corruption that Erckmann-Chatrian's contemporary, Zola, whose concerns and politics were so radically opposed to the Alsacian writers,' considered exemplary of the putrefaction of the Second Empire and made the centerpiece of several of the Rougon-Macquart novels, particularly in the figure of the financier Saccard in *La curée*.) Individual ambition contrasts with attending to one's own affairs, as the narrator Michel Bastien notes in *Histoire d'un paysan*: "The main thing is to keep a good eye on your own business; what you've seen yourself, you know well; you have to take advantage of it" (1:5). This valorization of first-hand experience underlies the predilection in Erckmann-Chatrian for first-person narrators, but also reinforces the dual structure of reader participation in the text, to draw on the familiar in order to evoke the readers' recognition of the novelistic world, but also to transmit the values his narrators assign to that world to their (French) readers.[1] That the "what you've seen yourself" for readers is in fact second-hand information suggests that the recollection of a place on which regionalism traditionally relies is at least here as much a textual construct as an actual remembrance.

Wars of aggression on Alsacian soil destroy the economic framework, while the role of the government, in the eyes of Joseph in *Waterloo*, should be to encourage and facilitate trade. The anger at the settlement of the Franco-Prussian War amounts to stripping the inhabitants of Alsace-Lorraine of their national identity: ". . . we have paid," says the narrator of *Histoire du plébiscite*:

> we have given our hay, our straw, our grain, our flour, our cattle; and that still wasn't enough! Finally, they gave us away; they told us:
>
> "You are no longer French, you're Prussians!" (11:1)

Both the French and the Germans constitute alien forces that disrupt the harmoniousness and commonweal of the region by entangling it in vain disputes. The nostalgia, the wish to return to an era when outside intervention was rare and each member of the community could pursue his own interests unhindered, is equivalent to a wish to subtract the individual from the historical forces that shaped Alsace-Lorraine throughout the nineteenth century. This removal, Erckmann-Chatrian make clear, does not imply a physical isolation, as the peasants in *Les deux frères* who reject the proposal to improve the roads in the region (in order to facilitate trade) are seen as so encrusted in their old ways as not to realize what is in their own interest. Rather, the nostalgia of Erckmann-Chatrian emerges from a sense of the powerlessness both on the part of the individual and of the local community. The dominant chord in the twin novels about the Napoleonic period, *Un conscrit de 1813* and *Waterloo*, is the desire to return home from war. Similarly, the entrapment of the collectivity as well as the subject by exterior historical forces provokes an impossible wish to go back to the pre-seventeenth-century status of the provinces. This desire can be characterized as conservative in the sense of needing to hold onto not only domestic comfort— summarized in the remark of Michel Bastien, "When you have it good, you have to hold onto it" (*Histoire d'un paysan*, 1:25)—but an equitably structured economic network that balances individual demands with the needs of the collective.

Whereas exoticism can provide, at least imaginatively, a space for the expenditure of excess energy that in the view of Georges Bataille is intrinsic to culture, the outside beyond Alsace-Lorraine is frequently seen in Erckmann-Chatrian as exhausting not only superfluous but vital energies. Their "conservatism" thus takes on an additional meaning, a vision of the region as a space in which to conserve, manage, and replenish these forces. The difficulty of this position lies not only in the impossibility of escaping historical determinism, but the dependence discussed before of ideology on the historical moment. Even the values of individual liberty and communal harmony, at least in the manifestations preconized by these texts, are the result of certain historical influences, responses to untenable situations. The very fact that Erckmann-Chatrian's characters experience moral development calls into question the ahistorical nature of the values that they come to champion.

If Erckmann-Chatrian's idealization of the Alsace-Lorraine region envisages shielding the individual from being buffeted by larger historical forces, the notion of community that constitutes the foundation of the region's role as ethical model requires the abstraction of workers from the large-scale modes of production of the late nineteenth century. The intimate *ateliers* in which Erckmann-Chatrian's characters labor (associated particularly with the northeast provinces)[2] do not give rise to the alienation of the worker that aggravated the economic gap between social classes. As Furth notes, few peasants or descriptions of agricultural work appear in Erckmann-Chatrian. The goal of their "outrageous paternalism," according to Giuliana Mannarelli (84), is to establish ethical norms for each social class that will work to efface those hierarchical distinctions. Artisans and *petits bourgeois* appear as the homogeneous group that guarantees a coherent system of values centering on the importance of labor. Work can be a moral value only when the individual has a sense of the purpose of toil, which implies a pride in the production of a utilitarian manufactured object or a personal relation between worker or shopkeeper and consumer. Property, the source of anger at the pillaging Prussians and the greed of French speculators and profiteers, includes for Erckmann-Chatrian not only material things viewed as objects of consumption but as products of manual labor. Human relations should be defined by equitable economic ties—"good accounts make good friends," as the French proverb goes—which can only take place in a community united by personalized commercial links. Economic advancement rewards those, like Michel Bastien in *Histoire d'un paysan*, who hold proper values. In naming Michel master blacksmith, the old master says he deserves the promotion "by your good behavior . . . by your work and your attachment to your family" (1:383). In contrast to Zola, who thought Erckmann-Chatrian naive and in whose works the individual is subsumed under a barrage of material objects and impersonal forces, everything in Erckmann-Chatrian is reduced to a human scale and a small cast of characters blends with its surroundings instead of being at the mercy of them. The nostalgia for a return of Alsace-Lorraine to a time when outside interference was minimal and the common man's life uninterrupted by reckless and futile imperialistic ventures goes hand in hand with a wish to escape the historical forces shaping modern economic structures. The idealized community is founded on the denial of the reality of modern industrial France, including the Alsace-Lorraine region.

While the desire to be ensconced in bourgeois comfort, the espousal of the values of religion, patriotism, and love of the family which form an indissoluble unity, may strike the modern reader as precisely what Matthew Arnold attacked in the English as Philistinism, in fact this emphasis on the return to indigenous beliefs in Erckmann-Chatrian serves as a model for the spiritual regeneration of the French nation as a whole. The rest of France, and particularly Paris, shaken by the class warfare of 1848 and oppressed by the reaction under Napoleon III, often heedless of moral values under the mask of a cynical anticlericalism, had become infected with the a lust after personal ambition and glory at the expense of others. Alsace-Lorraine, through its peculiar liminal position as the melting pot of the Teutonic emphasis on hard work and the revolutionary French exaltation of individual liberty, could act as a guide toward the moral regeneration of the rest of France. The regionalism of Erckmann-Chatrian suggests this role for the area, without articulating it as such, by maintaining in tension values from the two cultural Others from which it is formed. Clearly, the balance between the two is unequal, and the continual address to the French nation— through texts written, of course, in French—arises out of a belief that the greatest potential for the conservation of the traditional values of religion, family, and especially community lies in a return of Alsace-Lorraine to France and a return of France to the ideals that guided the Revolution.

The novels and tales of Erckmann-Chatrian resemble the scenes of country life at the Louvre seen by the apprentice cabinetmaker, Clavel, who experiences a desire to imitate the rustic life depicted there, saying, "you would have wanted to join them," that is, the honest folk who populate the countryside (*Histoire d'un homme du peuple*, 9:139). The ineluctability of historical influences on the individual suggests that a just appraisal of Erckmann-Chatrian's association of region and values should not be divorced from a recollection of the need to restore individual rights neglected by the Second Empire and to allow for a time of healing and social reconciliation as well as economic reconstruction after 1870. The viability of the idyllic society as moral guide itself must be historicized.

Nevertheless, Erckmann-Chatrian repeatedly call into question a sentimental nostalgia that ignores the real and potential moral evolution in the French people during the nineteenth century. The narrator of "Annette et Jean-Claude," for instance, rejects "certain minds, encrusted in old memories like snails in their shells" who "regret what they call the good old days" (12:283). This ethical development toward greater individual freedom represents not a rupture with the ancien régime so much as a return to a prelapsarian time before the imposition of a decaying feudal structure that tended to oppress the common people. Erckmann-Chatrian's desire for a spiraling back of history to a natural order centered on family (though not the rearing of small children, generally missing from their texts), work (conceived as a unalienated bond between producer and consumer), and religion (once the nefarious influence of the clergy on education has been eliminated) shows their essentially optimistic faith in the possibility of a renewal in the rest of

France. While choosing to ignore the effects of industrialization to focus on the ideal of community, Erckmann-Chatrian advocate through their depiction of Alsace-Lorraine what might be called a positivistic nostalgia. The apparent paradox of that formulation lies at the crux of their value system and representational practice. Sustained by the suspension of Alsace-Lorraine between the ideological and military forces of France and Germany, their regionalism shares a common fundamental structure with nineteenth-century exoticism in opposing the familiar and Other in order to forefront cultural criticism. Though the works that fall under the rubric of the *Contes et romans nationaux* are ostensibly realistic, the notable absence in many texts of interpersonal conflict further serves to direct attention toward the model of mutual dependence and economic well-being made possible through a shared ideological framework. Their Alsace-Lorraine is an ideological construct, where a commitment to republican ideals of justice and equality combines with the love of peace and hard work characteristic of the region in a synthesis of new ideas tempered by the common sense of the average person. The simplicity of this bourgeois work ethic should not blind us to the subtleties of its elaboration through the representation of this region.

NOTES

1. Another function of the first-person narrators is to limit severely the dialogical interaction or "heteroglossia," in Bakhtin's term, that might be expected when two languages, conceived as systems of values, intermix. The fact that the synthesis of belief systems is filtered most often through the consciousness of a French narrator who is either the principal *raisonneur* or in close agreement with him means that the image of the Other is tinctured and refracted by a narrating consciousness expressing sincere conviction, however problematic at times those beliefs may be. For this reason it is difficult to discern irony in Erckmann-Chatrian except at those moments when the narrator

unambiguously ridicules another's discourse or points to his own moral
development.

2.   A notable exception occurs in *Histoire d'un homme du peuple*,
though the Paris to which Clavel moves in order to find work bears
little resemblance to the alienated city of Baudelaire and in fact has
almost the appearance of a small Alsacian village.

WORKS CITED

Dimic, Colette A.M. "Erckmann-Chatrian, progrès social et valeurs
     traditionnelles," *Neohelicon* 13.1 (1986): 321–49.

Erckmann, Emile, and Alexandre Chatrian. *Contes et romans nationaux et
     populaires*. 14 vols. Paris: Jean-Jacques Pauvert, 1962–63.

Faucher, Daniel. *La France: géographie, tourisme*. Vol 2 of 2 vols. Paris:
     Larousse, 1952.

Furth, Pierre-Pascal. "Erckmann-Chatrian, écrivain alsacien?" *Europe*
     53.549–50 (1975): 34–55.

Mannarelli, Giuliana. "Un projet de normalisation et d'intégration du
     peuple: les *Romans nationaux et populaires* d'Erckmann-Chatrian,"
     Romantisme 16 (1986): 83–95.

Roth, Armand. "Erckmann-Chatrian, écrivains du peuple," *Europe*
     53.549–50 (1975): 8–26.

Reconstructing Reconstruction
Region and Nation in the Work of Albion Tourgee

Peter Caccavari

Reconstruction as a domestic policy following the American Civil War was an attempt to expunge sectionalism and create a unified nation. The division of the South into military departments that transcended state boundaries was part of this policy, an attempt to rearrange sectional loyalties in such a way as to subordinate regional and sectional identities to a national identity.[1] However, despite the devastation of the war and the loyalty oaths which former Confederates pledged to the Union, the majority of white Southerners continued to believe in and advocate states' rights, viewing the nation from a sectional and regional perspective. After "Redemption" and the return of "home rule" when federal troops evacuated the South as a result of the Compromise of 1877, widespread lynching and disfranchisement convinced many African Americans that the nation's commitment to civil rights was waning and that regional control meant their marginalization.

Albion Tourgee was an active and provocative participant in the debate over how to reconstruct the nation and what the relationship between region and nation ought to be. While unknown to most critics and readers today, Tourgee was relatively famous in his own day as a novelist and civil rights activist. Born in the Western Reserve region of Ohio, he fought in the Civil War for the Union. After the war, he moved to Greensboro, North Carolina, where he briefly operated a freedmen's school, became involved in local Republican politics,

and became a state Supreme Court justice before returning to the
North in 1879. Tourgee also wrote fiction, and his two most
important novels, *A Fool's Errand* (1879) and *Bricks Without Straw*
(1880), chronicle local and national events of Reconstruction. As
a "carpetbagger" or Northerner who had relocated to the South
and become active in Republican politics, Tourgee was an
emblem of the complex relationship between region and nation.
Was he a Northerner because of birth? Was he a Southerner,
having spent fourteen very active years in public life in North
Carolina? As a Union soldier, had he fought for the North or for
the United States? As a novelist, was he recreating a region from
within, or was he observing it from without for nationalist or
universalist purposes?

In his writings, Tourgee explored different ways of
understanding regionalism and nationalism. In *A Fool's Errand*,
he proposed means to replace regionalism with nationalism, but
in *Bricks Without Straw*, he allowed a positive role for
regionalism, seeing it as dynamic and cognitive, rather than
static and organic. As a carpetbagger, Tourgee saw himself as
being both of two regions and of none. By using his own life as a
model, he argued that a nation composed of fragmented regions
could find unity in experiencing more than one region. This is
accomplished by learning both what makes a region unique and
what makes it connected to other regions. For Tourgee, a
unifying tolerance would arise from such an experience of
multiple identities.

Before I begin to address in greater detail Tourgee's
understanding of the forces of regionalism and nationalism, it
will be useful to outline some past theories concerning these
forces. These theories fall into two categories: one examines the
relationship between region and nation; the other examines the
relationship between individual and region (and ultimately,
nation).

Critics have noted that the concepts of regionalism and
nationalism are inextricably bound, constituting both an
aesthetic and political tension between decentralization and
centralization. Hamlin Garland wrote in 1894 that the process of
interior cities wresting away control from literary centers "is one

of decentralization, together with one of unification" (154). Donald Davidson had a similar observation in 1938:

> We cannot define regionalism unless at the same time we define nationalism. The two are supplementary aspects of the same thing. Regionalism is a name for a condition under which the national American literature exists as a literature: that is, its constant tendency to decentralize rather than to centralize; or to correct overcentralization by conscious decentralization. (232)

Given that there will always be this tension, that region and nation must co-exist in some fashion, we must ask what kind of Reconstruction will be forged to accommodate and manage this tension.

Emerson had proposed at the end of his "American Scholar" address in 1837 a bloodless Reconstruction that would not require a civil war:

> Is it not the chief disgrace of the world, not to be a unit;— not to be reckoned one character;—not yield that peculiar fruit which each man was created to bear, but to be reckoned in the gross, in the hundred, or the thousand, of the party, the section, to which we belong; and our opinion predicted geographically, as the north, or the south? Not so, brothers and friends,—please God, ours shall not be so. We will walk on our own feet; we will work with our own hands; we will speak our own minds. . . . A nation of men will for the first time exist, because each believes himself inspired by the Divine Soul which also inspires all men. (71)

Emerson's solution to the regional/national dichotomy was to shift discussion to a different dichotomy, that of individual and nation, abolishing regionalism, or rather, creating a regionalism of one. But within this utter fragmentation would come an utter unity. If sectionalism were reduced to individualism, "a nation of men" could be created because each man would be inspired by the same "Divine Soul."

Emerson hoped to wish away all collective identities other than a national one. Nonetheless, he did express the need for a critical federalism, not of nation and region, but of nation and individual, using an imagined spiritual homogeneity as a balance against the potential anarchy of individualism. The political reality of Emerson's day, however, was that regionalism was not vanishing but gaining strength. A century later, Davidson pointed out not only the mysticism of Emerson's idea of union, but also the masking of his own regionalism as a transcendent nationalism. For Davidson, Emerson's "was not the voice of America, but of New England, and his plan of salvation was to result not in peaceful unification but in bloody disunion" (237). After the war, the sectional division was not resolved by mere victory. Instead, a nation had to be not *re*constructed, but constructed for the first time. Emerson's dreams of unity did not materialize. Reconstruction would have to take place on other grounds and have other goals.

Emerson had wanted not only to dissolve regional loyalties by bonding the individual to the nation, but to do so by reworking the very logic of regionalism for nationalist purposes, for it had been the relationship between individual and region which had formed the strength of regional identity. Whereas a nation is generally perceived as an abstract ideal and ideology which unite disparate groups of people, a region is usually seen in terms of a fairly well-defined group of people, sharing a more or less homogenous culture and inhabiting land dominated by a particular terrain. Because of this relation to a place, especially between people and the land, regionalism is often thought of in "organic" terms. Garland viewed regionalism in such a way:

> Local color in a novel means that it has such quality of texture and back-ground that it could not have been written in any other place or by any one else than a native.
>
> It means that a statement of life as indigenous as the plant-growth. . . . the tourist cannot write the local novel. (64)

Garland's organicism expresses a kind of nativism which is meant to validate a marginalized regional identity rather than an imagined and coercive national homogeneity and ethnic/racial purity, but it remains subject to the sort of exclusivity that the national version invokes.[2] Davidson invokes Allen Tate regarding the organic nature of regionalism, saying that "a good regional literature needs only (to quote Allen Tate) 'the immediate, organic sense of life in which a fine artist works'"

(232). Like Garland's indigenous plant-growth, Davidson uses an organic metaphor, this time to show the link between region and nation: "The national literature is the compound of the regional impulses, not antithetical to them, but embracing them and living in them as the roots, branch, and flower of its being" (232–33).

More recently, Wendell Berry has indicated how regionalism might move away from organicism. He replaces an indigenous connection between place and observer with a cognitive connection. In contrast to Garland's sense of regionalism, Berry defines regionalism as "local life aware of itself," linking the observer to place by conscious choice, a will to indigenousness. Berry's regionalism involves "a particular knowledge of the life of the *place* one lives in. . . ." This "local knowledge" is "complex" rather than instinctually simplistic. But knowledge is not enough. In conjunction with this complex knowledge is "the faithfulness to one's place on which such knowledge depends . . ." (67–68). Knowledge and faithfulness (in both the sense of fidelity and faith) must go hand in hand.

Like Garland and Davidson, Tourgee saw regionalism and nationalism as a tension between decentralization and centralization. In his political treatise on education, *An Appeal to Caesar* (1884), Tourgee claims that because so many officials were appointed by Southern county and state governments rather than elected, the "one important feature common to all Southern States" is that "they are the best examples of centralized power to be found in our Federal Union. Their governments are centripetal in all their tendencies" (326).

Drawing from Tocqueville, Tourgee's solution to this problem is the township system. Speaking to Congressman Washington Goodspeed, Hesden Le Moyne, the reconstructed Southerner of *Bricks Without Straw*, argues for greater individualism, not less, in the South. Tourgee situates this individualism in a political hierarchy, culminating in a centralized national power. "Each township is in itself a miniature republic, every citizen of which exercises in its affairs equal power with every other citizen." But unlike Emerson's individualism which jumps straight from individual to nation via Divine Soul, these "miniature republics" are situated within a highly defined structure: "Each of these miniature republics becomes a constituent element of the higher representative republic—namely, a county, which is itself a component of the still larger representative republic, the State" (508). In this way, these miniature republics are prevented from becoming the divisive and disintegrating force that sectionalism became. Tourgee's model funnels up, rather than down, as Southerners conceived sectional/national relations. Tourgee saw this same divisive regionalism in the operation of the Ku Klux Klan, which he referred to as "an imperium imperio," or an empire within an empire (*Fool* 257).

But there is ambivalence in Tourgee's mixture of classical images. He calls regions "republics" to indicate a positive localization and terms an extralegal and treasonous regional organization like the Klan an "imperium." However, the Klan is an imperium *within* an imperium, the larger empire being the Union itself. In his *An Appeal to Caesar*, the Caesar of the title is the President of the United States, and Caesar of Rome was himself the "imperator." Davidson said that "our provinces are more like nations than provinces" (236), but if the ambivalence in Tourgee's imagery here is played out, regions resemble provinces of the Roman Empire, independent-minded tribes subjugated to a central bureaucracy. In some ways, Tourgee's ideal Reconstruction, especially in *A Fool's Errand*, is a "pax Americana," a peace and unity achieved by force.

In his treatise on the Klan, *The Invisible Empire*, which accompanied *A Fool's Errand*, Tourgee invokes a religious rather than classical paradigm that reveals another ambivalence concerning the tension between individuals and collectivities which separates the North from the South: "The strong individualism which marked the Northern colonist, and which was ever at war with that Puritanism which was its parent, was almost entirely lacking in the Southern colonies" (118). Tourgee conceives of Puritanism as anti-individual, whereas, if anything, the township system is *more* centralized and *less* individualistic than congregationalism because it is more hierarchical. Rather than being anti-individual, Puritanism would have been *too* individualistic for Tourgee's tastes, had he understood it fully. But it is the Puritans' conception of regionalism that makes them most resemble Southerners. Sacvan Bercovitch says that the Puritans' notion of "covenant" was "the sense of the importance of *this* people in *this* locale . . ." (50).[3] The increasing individualism to which Puritanism logically gave rise (antinomianism, Unitarianism, even secularism itself) and their regional perspective writ large into a national one—and Emerson's Puritan/Unitarian roots in his individualism and his New England nationalism are important here—was the source of both Tourgee's hopes and fears for the nation in terms of democracy and disintegration.

Angela Miller has said of nineteenth-century nationalists, "The creators of the national landscape—painters, writers, and critics—steered a course threatened by the anarchy of localism, on the one hand, and the tyranny of the imperial center on the other hand" (208). Through townships, Tourgee sought to find a balance between the anarchy of localism and the tyranny of the imperial center, a middle ground between the utter decentralization of such forces as congregationalism and the devouring centralization of a federal empire. Townships could accomplish this, in Tourgee's view, through an acknowledgment of the depth of regionalism and, using Berry's logic, by replacing an organic connection between this people and this locale with a cognitive connection, rendering regionalism less divisive.

The protagonist of *A Fool's Errand* is Colonel Comfort Servosse, a "carpetbagger," like Tourgee himself, who came to the South after the Civil War. According to Garland's nativist definition of regionalism, Tourgee should not have been able to write the local novel (although Tourgee could hardly be called a "tourist" after living in North Carolina for fourteen years) and Servosse should not be able to truly understand the region. For Tourgee, however, the carpetbagger is of two regions and of no region. Having lived in the North and the South, Servosse tries to stand outside both so as to understand them in a way that natives of either cannot see themselves or others. The narrator gives the perspective of both Southern and Northern whites, devoting a paragraph to each of the following antebellum ideologies: "Northern Idea of Slavery," "Southern Idea of Slavery," "Northern Idea of the Southern Idea," and "Southern Idea of the Northern Idea." The post-bellum categories include:

"The Northern Idea of the Situation," "The Southern Idea of the Situation," "The Northern Idea of the Southern Idea," and "The Southern Idea of the Northern Idea" (138–39). It is not that Tourgee is trying to transcend his regionalism; rather he is trying to juxtapose his regional experiences so as to understand each better. Reconstruction failed, according to Tourgee, because the North did not understand the South any better than the South understood the North. Like Emerson, the North did not see either how deeply regionalism divided the nation, or how that regionalism operated.

The solution offered in *A Fool's Errand* is to destroy regionalism and replace it with nationalism by force, but by an informed force, one which understands the natures of both region and nation. Servosse tells Dr. Enos Martin, a fellow Northerner, near the end of the book:

> These two [Northern and Southern "civilization"] must always be in conflict until the one prevails, and the other falls. To uproot the one, and plant the other in its stead, is not the work of a moment or a day. That was our mistake. We tried to superimpose the civilization, the idea of the North upon the South at a moment's warning. We presumed, that, by the suppression of rebellion, the Southern white man had become identical with the Caucasian of the North in thought and sentiment; and that the slave, by emancipation, had become a saint and Solomon at once. So we tried to build up communities there which would be identical in thought, sentiment, growth, and development, with those of the North. It was A FOOL'S ERRAND. (381)

Tourgee emphasizes the imperial center and worries little about its potential tyranny, but he does not believe the imperial center to be omnipotent. The failure of Reconstruction to actually create an imperial center had shown that. The purpose of Reconstruction should be, according to Servosse, "to secure a development homogenous with that of the North, so as to render the country what it has never been heretofore—a nation" (166). To do this, the narrator suggests that

> the region they [the Confederate states] once embraced should be divided up into Territories without regard to

> former statal lines, and so remain for a score of years under national control, but without power to mold or fashion the national legislation—until time should naturally and thoroughly have healed the breaches of the past, till commerce had become reestablished, and the crude ideas of the present had been clarified by the light of experience. (132)

Such a move is clearly unconstitutional,[4] and the narrator admits that certain actions that would result in a true reconstruction of the nation cannot occur "without violating some of the *traditions* of our Federal republic, but *not* its principles, and especially not its spirit" (236). Given how much the framers of the Constitution feared the tyranny of the imperial center, it is difficult to understand how destruction of states is consistent with the Constitution's "spirit." But Tourgee felt that the federal government had assumed a false nationalism (a homogeneity that did not exist) and a false regionalism (a superficial sense that denied how deep sectionalism ran), rendering Reconstruction legislation and policy ineffective. Instead, Tourgee sought to destroy regionalism and establish nationalism by breaking the link between land and people that constituted regional attachment. Destroy the states that had claimed sovereignty for themselves politically, and loyalty for themselves ideologically, Tourgee argued, and *this* people would become *we* the people.

In *Bricks Without Straw*, a book most critics find inferior to *A Fool's Errand*, Tourgee develops a much more complicated sense of region and nation. Whereas the intent of *A Fool's Errand* is to destroy regionalism by informed force and replace it with nationalism, Tourgee's proposition in *Bricks Without Straw* is to make regionalism dynamic rather than static, experiential rather than essential, and thereby not only less destructive to the nation, but also constitutive of it. I have already drawn attention to the discussion of townships in terms of the tension between centralization and decentralization, but Tourgee also used townships as another way to break the connection between the people and the land. As Le Moyne tells Goodspeed about the township system, Goodspeed assumes that Le Moyne is referring to the physical aspect of townships as parcels of land, wondering if Le Moyne is suggesting "that the Government should send an army of surveyors to the South to lay off the land in sections and quarter-sections, establish parallel roads, and enforce topographic uniformity upon the nation?" Instead, Le Moyne calls for a political and cultural uniformity: "It is the *people* that require to be laid off in townships, not the land" (509– 10). For if the people are laid off in townships ideologically, then *this* locale becomes irrelevant.

The Puritan model which Tourgee invoked in analyzing North-South relations in *The Invisible Empire* had ramifications for replacing an organic regionalism with a cognitive one. According to Perry Miller, the congregational church covenant was based on the idea that "a church was not just any number of people thrown together by chance or birth within the geographical confines of a parish, it was a deliberate creation of the regenerate acknowledging their faith to each other" (442). A congregation is not a physical collectivity but a mental one, the result of a "deliberate" choice of identity rather than an organic or automatic one. In this way a congregation acts like a region in Berry's terms. Furthermore, the relationship between "acknowledging" and "faith" is similar to Berry's regionalism that relies on a connection between "knowledge" and "faithfulness." The congregational idea of a parish is much like Tourgee's understanding of a township. The land does not need to be laid off in parishes; the people do. A people's identity is the result of "deliberate creation" rather than an organic outgrowth of a nativist relation to the land, and this is Tourgee's ideal method of Reconstruction.

With the break of the organic connection of people to the land, Tourgee validates carpetbaggers, causing them to be seen not as intruders but as immigrants who can be naturalized, or rather "regionalized." Suzi Jones has written that "the process whereby folklore makes itself at home in a new geographical environment, that is, the regionalization of folklore, is a rhetorical strategy" (110). Philip Fisher speaks of rhetoric in an almost regional sense, suggesting that rhetoric is both a matter of place and movement, of location and relocation: "Rhetoric is the mark of temporary location and justification" (xxii). Jones's concept of regionalization and Fisher's regional sense of rhetoric can be useful for understanding Tourgee's project as well. Jones emphasizes that folklore, the local knowledge of a people, is not necessarily indigenous but migratory, capable of being naturalized and assimilated. Fisher makes this connection between migration and immigration explicit. Speaking of "[t]he right to 'move on' or 'head out west'" within the nation, he asserts that "individual mobility was historically profound because it was the means of renewing the act of immigration—leaving behind and moving on—which was each individual's first drop of American identity" (xxi). Furthermore, Jones emphasizes that regionalization is rhetorical. Tourgee, through the image of the carpetbagger, is showing how regionalization occurs, that it is not organic but an act of will (and in Berry's terms, a combination of local knowledge and faithfulness), and he does this through a rhetorical process, through fiction. Fisher shows that the very act of rhetorical representation is itself a kind of regionalization, of locational and cognitive mobility.

Bricks Without Straw has a number of characters who bring into focus the problems of region and nation. Mollie Ainslie is a white New England schoolteacher who moves to Red Wing, North Carolina after the Civil War to teach freedmen. Despite her good intentions, she still cannot understand the freedmen because of perceived racial differences:

> She had never once thought of making companions, in the ordinary sense, of those for whom she labored. They had been so entirely foreign to her early life that, while she labored unremittingly for their advancement, and entertained for many of them the most affectionate regard, there was never any inclination to that friendly intimacy which would have been sure to arise if her pupils had been of the same race as herself. (218)

The narrator makes it clear that Ainslie is wrong for feeling this way, but he is also sympathetic to her as someone who has good qualities despite her limitations. His attempt to both criticize and sympathize with a character is the kind of carpetbagger's multiple perspective that Tourgee developed in *A Fool's Errand*. It is also a criticism of the North as unable to understand not only the white South but the black South whom it was supposedly committed to aid and protect. Ainslie moves to

Kansas where, because of a railroad that is built nearby and develops the small town of Eupolia, the value of her land holdings increases, making her quite wealthy. She bought the land originally with money saved from teaching the freedmen at Red Wing, and she overcomes her race prejudice, encouraging many of the freedmen to follow her to Kansas where they can make a new start without the racial violence of the Ku Klux Klan. She discovers that Mulberry Hill, a plantation near Red Wing belonging to Le Moyne's mother, is legally hers, but she had been defrauded of it. She refuses to accept the plantation, and stays in Kansas until Le Moyne marries her and brings her back to live at Mulberry Hill. Ainslie has been the supreme carpetbagger, living not in two regions but in three. All three places give her different perspectives, and ultimately two identities: that of living in a region and that of living in a nation. Ainslie's marriage to Le Moyne is a common fictional trope of reconciliation between North and South in Reconstruction literature, but Tourgee substantially revises this trope. Ainslie has gone west by herself and made her own fortune, an unusual portrayal of a woman in nineteenth-century fiction (as opposed to the more acceptable role of wife or even schoolteacher). Her belonging to three regions is an expansion of the usual two-region heroine, making her representative of a broader concept of nation than is typical in such scenarios. Her husband is a Southerner who has accepted a Reconstructionist interpretation of both his own region and the nation. Her return to the South is an act of will, a regionalization with nationalist purposes, and Le Moyne's reconstruction is a re-regionalization of the indigenous, becoming a native carpetbagger, creating an evolving sense of this place and this people.

What makes Tourgee's vision of the South, North, and the nation different from his contemporaries[1] is how fragmented it is, and how this can still be subsumed into a national unity. But that fragmentation does not end with Ainslie and Le Moyne. Jordan Jackson is a poor white Southerner who is active in Republican politics, otherwise known by the pejorative term "scalawag." Tourgee shows the fragmentation of the "solid South" not only in regard to region, but also class. Jackson thinks of himself as a Southerner, calling it "our country" in a letter to

the formerly aristocratic but now reconstructed Le Moyne (451),
but Jackson has been threatened by the Klan and has gone to
Eupolia to start a new life. He is impressed by how birth and
heredity do not have any standing in the West. The regionalism
of the West is dynamic rather than static, as in the South. In other
words, regionalization can occur in the West, but not the South:
"The West takes right hold of every one that comes into it and
makes him a part of itself, instead of keeping him outside in the
cold to all eternity, as the South does the strangers who go there"
(452). Jackson feels not that one can escape regionalism entirely,
but that it can be mobile and not merely an accident of birth (and
therefore not organic or nativist). "Nobody stops to ask where
you come from" in the West, and in this way the West becomes
the ideal microcosm of the nation, naturalizing immigrants,
domestic- and foreign-born. If a person comes to the West,
Jackson says, "he'll think he's been born over again, or I'm
mistaken" (452). The West becomes the hope of an itinerant
indigenousness, not of the tourist's superficialness, but of Berry's
regionalist who combines local knowledge and faithfulness.

Besides fragmentation along regional and class lines,
Tourgee also devotes much more narrative energy in *Bricks
Without Straw* than in *A Fool's Errand* to showing the divisiveness
along racial lines in the South as well. Eliab Hill, a freedman and
preacher who has been crippled since childhood, becomes
educated and leaves Red Wing to attend college in the North,
financed by Le Moyne. After college, Hill has the opportunity to
teach at a black school in the North, which he is inclined to take,
but when Le Moyne writes to him asking him to return to Red
Wing to teach, Hill accepts. Like Ainslie, Hill has gone to another
region, lived there, and returned to settle with a new
perspective. Like Le Moyne, he comes to see the region of his
birth in a different way (which he achieved, unlike Le Moyne, by
leaving it), resulting in a new indigenousness.

We can see Tourgee's purposes in the portrayal of Hill
more clearly by comparing him to his historical counterpart.
Tourgee based Eliab Hill on a freedman of South Carolina
named Elias Hill. Like Eliab, Elias Hill was attacked by the Klan.
Unlike Eliab, Elias's response was not to remain in the place of
his birth, although he had a strong sense of connection to the

land there, as indicated when he told a joint congressional committee investigating the Ku Klux Klan in 1871: "I was born belonging to the Hills . . ." (1406). Elias became involved in a plan to emigrate to Liberia's "North Carolina Colony" along with sixty to eighty black families. Hill told the committee that he and others were willing to leave because "we do not believe it possible . . . for our people to live in this country peaceably, and educate and elevate their children to that degree which they desire. They do not believe it possible—neither do I" (1410). He was asked by the committee if emigration to the West might not solve the problems of blacks. But Hill did not believe the West to be the promised land that Tourgee made it out to be: ". . . I found that in Liberia there was greater encouragement and hope of finding peaceful living and free schools and rich land than in any place in the United States that I had read of." In fact, Hill does not really think of himself as an American, and using an organic model of regionalism, he hearkens back to an earlier indigenous identity. Of moving to Africa, he says: "That is where my father came from" (1412). Tourgee rewrites Elias Hill's life into a different kind of regionalism that better fits his regionalist, nationalist, and racial purposes.

Tourgee kept Eliab Hill in North Carolina to do his fictional/cultural work of indigenous carpetbagging and used Berry Lawson to further rewrite the historical Elias Hill, making Lawson a black counterpart to Jordan Jackson who finds a West not only of economic opportunity and social harmony, but racial equality as well. Lawson, formerly one of the freedmen of Red Wing, meets up with Hesden and Mollie Le Moyne on their way back to Mulberry Hill from Eupolia. Hesden asks Lawson, "Where are you from?" Jackson has already said that Westerners do not ask this question, and because Hesden does not intend to reassert class and racial hierarchies, his question contrasts sharply from its earlier context. Lawson replies,

> Whar's I frum? Ebbery place on de green yairth, Marse Hesden, 'ceptin' dis one, whar dey hez ter shoe de goats fer ter help 'em climb de bluffs; an' please de Lo'd I'll be from h'yer jest es soon ez de train come's 'long dat's 'boun' fer de happy land of Canaan. (490)

The chapter in which this scene appears is titled, "The Exodian," and the difference between the white characters and the black characters is that the black characters are more often exiles than the whites, and the result is a different sense of multi-regionalism than for characters such as Mollie Ainslie or even Jordan Jackson. Hesden and Mollie send Lawson, the "exodian," to Jackson, who is now administering their Kansas lands, and the narrator links Lawson and Jackson by region and circumstance, transcending race, referring to Jackson as Lawson's "white fellow-fugitive from the evils which a dark past has bequeathed to the South . . ." (500–01).

Tourgee has used these characters in such a way as to break the organic bond between people and the land to create a nation through the instrument of tolerance. In *A Fool's Errand* Tourgee says that the South was characterized by intolerance because of its history of slavery: "The terrible suppressive power which slavery had exercised over liberty of thought and speech had grown into a habit of mind" (147). Southerners "were harsh masters, and did not permit dissent from their political views to be entertained or expressed with impunity" (143). The exchange of ideas through migration could help lessen this intolerance. Regionalization could weaken the organic foundation of intolerant nativism and unite the heterogenous nation by sanctioning dissent and localism within a larger framework. Whether Tourgee's ideas for Reconstruction were any less mystical than Emerson's perhaps remains to be seen, for in some ways we are still in an era of reconstruction as we struggle with tolerance, multiculturalism, and identity politics.

In trying to understand our own epoch, Fisher also identifies regionalism with intolerance, but he tries to locate American studies, rather than the nation, as the site of tolerance:

> The new American studies has grown up alongside but also as an alternative or aftermath to this regionalism that tore apart the various unifying and singular myths of America. The key limitations to this new regionalism, as well as of all earlier regionalisms [the latter which Fisher identifies as "geographical" and "ethnic" regionalisms], were its need to define itself and its ability to thrive only within a highly politicized atmosphere. Regionalism is always, in America, part of a civil war within

> representation. It is seldom or nèver a matter of tolerance,
> the blooming of a thousand, or even of three, flowers. In
> the regionalism of the past decades, identity is formed by
> opposition: black/white, female/male, Native
> American/settler, gay/heterosexual. . . .
>
> The new American studies has stood outside this
> regionalism by locating a set of underlying but
> permanently open national facts around which all
> identities are shaped and with which the many rhetorics of
> our culture are engaged. (xiv)

Fisher sees the United States as characterized not by a totalizing
ideology but a multiplicity of rhetorics (xxii), and it is the
analysis of these rhetorics in American studies that he believes
enables one to stand "outside" regionalism, maintaining
diversity and creating tolerance. As immensely useful as Fisher's
essay is for the study of regionalism, I do not think that
American studies is an "alternative" to regionalism any more
than nationalism is. I like Thomas J. Schlereth's cumbersome but
helpful term "Regional and American Culture Studies" which
indicates that this is not an issue of alternatives but of
ambivalence.[5] Fisher's characterization of today's American
studies sounds too much like a newer version of the "literary
nationalists" whom Garland, Davidson and Tate have criticized.
Instead, Fisher has given us a more satisfying conceptualization
of American studies' role in the relationship between region and
nation than the one he seems to profess here. Rather than "a set
of permanently open national facts" which American studies
identifies and transcends, we need to go back to his assertion
that rhetoric is "the mark of temporary location and
justification," seeing American studies as *inside* this
impermanent location, an intellectual regionalism within an
ambivalent dynamic of rhetorics and ideology, of partiality and
totalization.

      Although hailed as an important writer in his day,
Tourgee has become relatively obscure to contemporary readers
and scholars. His importance, when noted at all today, is usually
qualified as "historical" or "sociological." A sort of false
disciplinary regionalism (in the sense of a trivialization by a self-
proclaimed center) marginalizes his writing within literature and

literary criticism because it is "ideological" or "propagandistic" rather than "aesthetic." Furthermore, a false regionalism of literary history ignores him because Reconstruction is a period generally deemed less productive of "Literature" than the American Renaissance, canonical Realism, Naturalism, or Modernism. In a time when we are faced with the tensions of multiculturalism and diversity within our classrooms and our society, Reconstruction and Tourgee's reconstruction of it can become a useful reference point for understanding the intersection of the margin and the center, the regional and the national, the local and the global.

NOTES

1. "Section" and "region" are not interchangeable terms, but neither are they unrelated. "The South" is a section, while "Appalachia" is a region. However, even this distinction belies the difficulty of identifying a region. Is all of Appalachia one region? Where does Appalachia begin and end, as a geographical entity? As a cultural one? For my purposes here, a section is a hybrid of region and nation in that it has a regional perception of a people connected by geography and culture combined with a nationalist conviction (and the Latin root here of "vincere" or "to conquer" is important) that creates loyalty to a transcendent and more abstract collectivity. Despite these differences, however, both sectionalism and regionalism share crucial qualities, including reactions to nationalism which range from antagonistic to counterbalancing in their geographical identification and their tendency towards fragmentation. Tourgee virtually always refers to section rather than region, but I will be reframing his argument in more regionalist terms.

2. Eric Sundquist has explored the complicated relationship between regionalism and nativism in Garland's day:

> The narrative strategies by which the alien is made either brutish or exotic reflect in literature the imperatives of foreign colonialism and Progressive reform observable in the social and political thought

of the period, which stressed the homogenization of American life through a process of economic control and cultural improvement. One result, increasingly evident in the realism of both city and country, is an anthropological dimension in which new "regions" are opened to fictional or journalistic exploration and analysis. The country's continued spirit of Manifest Destiny, peaking in imperial adventurism at the turn of the century, along with a sudden rise in anxiety about immigration, is not unrelated to the developments of capitalism but rather is its engine of power. For this reason, economic or political power can itself be seen to be definitive of a realist aesthetic, in that those in power (say, white urban males) have more often been judged "realists," while those removed from the seats of power (say, Midwesterners, blacks, immigrants, or women) have been categorized as regionalists. (502–503)

The relative powerlessness of the regionalists allowed their organicism to be coopted, feeding into the national and international ambitions of the United States regarding immigration and colonialism. For the purposes of my discussion, "organic" regionalism does not necessarily lead to nationalist "nativism." Organicism is the inner logic of nativism, and organic regionalism always resonates with nativist nationalism and its agenda as part of a historical context, but the two terms are not identical.

3. Bercovitch claims that Protestantism began as a protest against the Catholic Church's emphasis on "geographic locale," but by that he means a *single* locale, "the Holy Roman Empire" (47). Thus, Protestantism is in its roots a regional movement—politically, culturally, and rhetorically—as is indicated further by the use of vernacular translations of the Bible.

4. Article IV, Section 3, Paragraph 1 reads: ". . . no new State shall be formed or erected within the Jurisdiction of any other State; nor any State be formed by the Junction of two or more States, or Parts of States, without the consent of the Legislatures of the States concerned as well as of the Congress."

5. In his introduction to *Nation and Narration*, Homi K. Bhabha quotes Tom Nairn's characterization of the nation as "the modern Janus" wherein he claims that "it is an exact (not a rhetorical) statement about nationalism to say that it is by nature ambivalent" (*The Break-up of Britain, London*: Verso, 1981, p. 348, quoted in Bhabha, p. 2). Bhabha

explains this idea of the ambivalent nation in terms corresponding to many of the issues which I have tried to address in this essay:

> The "locality" of national culture is neither unified nor unitary in relation to itself, nor must it be seen simply as "other" in relation to what is outside or beyond it. The boundary is Janus-faced and the problem of outside/inside must always itself be a process of hybridity, incorporating new "people" in relation to the body politic, generating other sites of meaning and, inevitably, in the political process, producing unmanned sites of political antagonism and unpredictable forces for political representation. (4)

WORKS CITED

Bercovitch, Sacvan. "The Modernity of American Puritan Rhetoric." *American Letters and the Historical Consciousness: Essays in Honor of Lewis P. Simpson.* Ed. J. Gerald Kennedy and Daniel Mark Fogel. Baton Rouge: Louisiana State University Press, 1987. 42–66.

Berry, Wendell. "The Regional Motive." *A Continuous Harmony: Essays Cultural and Agricultural.* New York: Harcourt, 1972. 63–70.

Bhabha, Homi K. "Introduction: Narrating the Nation." *Nation and Narration.* Ed. Homi K. Bhabha. London: Routledge, 1990. 1–7.

Davidson, Donald. *The Attack on Leviathan: Regionalism and Nationalism in the United States.* 1938. Gloucester, MA: Peter Smith, 1962.

Emerson, Ralph Waldo. "The American Scholar." *Essays and Lectures.* Ed. Joel Porte. New York: Library of America, 1983. 53–71.

Fisher, Philip. "Introduction: The New American Studies." *The New American Studies: Essays from Representations.* Ed. Philip Fisher. Berkeley: University of California Press, 1991. vii–xxii.

Garland, Hamlin. *Crumbling Idols: Twelve Essays on Art and Literature.* Ed. Robert E. Spiller. 1894; Gainesville, FL: Scholars' Facsimiles and Reprints, 1952.

Jones, Suzi. "Regionalization: A Rhetorical Strategy." *Journal of the Folklore Institute* 13 (1976): 105–20.

Miller, Angela. "Everywhere and Nowhere: The Making of the National Landscape." *American Literary History* 4 (1992): 207–29.

Miller, Perry. *The New England Mind: The Seventeenth Century.* Boston: Beacon Press, 1954.

Schlereth, Thomas J. ""Regional Culture Studies and American Culture." *Sense of Place: American Regional Cultures.* Ed. Barbara Allen and Thomas J. Schlereth. Lexington: University Press of Kentucky, 1990. 164–83.

Tourgee, Albion W. *An Appeal to Caesar.* New York: Fords, Howard, & Hulbert, 1884.

———. *Bricks Without Straw.* Americans in Fiction Series. 1880. Ridgewood, NJ: Gregg, 1967.

———. *A Fool's Errand.* Ed. John Hope Franklin. 1879. Cambridge: Belknap-Harvard University Press, 1961.

———. *The Invisible Empire.* Ed. Otto H. Olsen. 1880. Baton Rouge: Louisiana State University Press, 1989.

U.S. Congress. *The Ku Klux Conspiracy: Report of the Joint Select Committee Appointed to Inquire into the Condition of Affairs in the Late Insurrectionary States. . . .* Vol. 5. Washington, DC: U.S. Government Printing Office, 1872. 1406–15.

Buenos Aires in the 1920s
A Center within the Margin

Rosa Sarabia
Translated by Laurence de Looze

Buenos Aires has a unique culture because of its complexity and heterogeneity within the Latin American context. This uniqueness is the result of a gradual gestation beginning with economic and political independence from Spain (1810), which led to an opening to other centers of influence, above all England, France, and the United States.[1] The 1920s were the culmination of a postcolonial period in Buenos Aires marked by a questioning and analysis of a truly Argentine culture in terms of its own interests.[2] At the time, Buenos Aires was only one of several urban centers that led the avant-garde, including Mexico City, Santiago, Montevideo, and Lima, yet each center responded differently to its particular history and topography. In a comparative study of the cultural milieu prior to the advent of the new avant-garde aesthetic, Angel Rama argues that the intellectual circle of Argentina had greater plasticity than the Mexican intelligentsia; for Rama this is evident in an openness to modern and national ideas that permitted Argentines to sketch a vision of what their society was to be, albeit a vision based on European models (153–54).

The culture of Buenos Aires in the first decades of this century has a regional dimension to the extent that the use of a particular type of Spanish is deeply involved with the concept of national identity. "Regional" is therefore seen as designating unique cultural patterns and an identity distinctive to a particular place. This identity is, in turn, conceived as a physical space which is both central and peripheral. Given the concentration of economic and cultural goods that pass through the capital city and maritime port, Buenos Aires is necessarily anti-federalist. However, in respect to Europe and Spain, the city is subsidiary, not only because of its historic past as a colony, but also because of its geographic distance and the youthful state of its economic development. Buenos Aires constitutes, therefore, a healthy challenge to an oversimplified cultural mapping that unthinkingly sets "center" and "margin" in diametric opposition, namely by creating a third alternative, one that simultaneously occupies both poles. This proposal, put forth by the discourses and sociocultural practices of the avant-garde in the 1920s, results in a "universalization" of the region.[3] This new regionalism is endowed with a wider dimension, for it breaks the confines of previous limits. It also posits the possibility of an autonomous culture which has been blended with the most recent international trends. Finally, Buenos Aires reconstructs itself as a center of modernity within the periphery of a vast and diverse region—Latin America. In this sense, Buenos Aires was unrivalled by any other city in South America.

To analyze this process, I will use a series of writings, manifestoes, and letters that appeared in issue No. 42 (1927) of the most popular avant-garde literary journal in Argentina: *Martín Fierro*.[4] These texts were themselves a response to a provocative Spanish editorial in the Madrid journal, *La Gaceta Literaria* (April 1927, No. 8), directed by Ernesto Giménez Caballero and Guillermo de Torre.

Alarmed by the decrease in Spain's prestige among young intellectuals of the New World, de Torre in his editorial put forth Madrid as the "intellectual meridian of Spanish America." Faced with the attraction that radiated from France and Italy in the Hispanic world, he called for the reestablishment of a symbolic line drawn across the map between America and Spain. One passage of the editorial reads as follows:

> Let's establish Madrid as the definitive meridian point of
> our mental geography and as the most authentic line of
> intersection between America and Spain. Madrid: the

point of convergence for a Spanish America in balance, neither limiting nor coercive, generous and European, and ranged against Paris, which stands for a narrowly reduced "latinism" and contemptuous of anything that does not revolve around its axis.[5]

This text, at times confusing and ambiguous, proposes the erasing of frontiers between Spanish America and Spain as a vital question but at the same time puts forth a call that "the legitimate interests we [the Spanish] have and from which we have deviated" be recovered by Spain. This double discourse exhibits both an international desire for an exchange of cultural goods and an intranational one that Madrid might be able to avoid giving up her dominant position. Nevertheless, it would be a mistake to see Spanish intellectuals as uniformly propagating colonialism. *La Gaceta Literaria*, which according to the front page was the critical organ of the *Generación del 27*, put forth a triple program: Iberian, American, and international. And although it was primarily a Spanish-language publication, it nevertheless accorded a certain amount of space to things Portuguese, Catalan, and Galician. This inclusiveness formed part of a national effort to legalize and revalorize peripheral languages that in their turn were represented in the Spanish Royal Academy prior to the *coup d'état* of Primo de Rivera in 1923. Given these factors and considering that these avant-garde writers share areas of interest and literary tastes with those on the opposite side of the Atlantic (Río de la Plata), it is worth wondering, therefore, why this editorial sought to ring a death knell for colonial culture with its wish to recover the hegemony of the center, if the periphery was already moving toward other cultural meridians or else sought to be its own center for the construction of an American identity. There are a variety of possible responses, and it may well be that the polemic unleashed against Buenos Aires was a reflection of the marginal position of Spain itself within Europe, an isolation that was aggravated by the internal situation and the failure of democratic institutions.

The pages of *Martín Fierro* published by the Argentine avant-garde offered an arena for the point of view opposing the authoritarian lines laid down in the Spanish editorial. The

Argentine response attempted to give the *coup de grace* to the
cultural map still held by the Old World, despite its already
having been unsettled by Rubén Darío and the "modernismo"
movement. To the single and singular Spanish editorial, a
plurality of manifesto-responses opened the debate, at once both
cartographical and ideological, under a title that was also a
question: "Is Madrid the intellectual meridian of Spanish
America?" The literary "guerilla war" of the *porteños* (the name
given to the inhabitants of Buenos Aires because of their port)
not only questioned but indeed rejected Madrid's patronizing
stance. Pablo Rojas Paz, Ricardo E. Molinari, Ildefonso Pereda
Valdés, Nicolás Olivari, Jorge Luis Borges, Santiago Ganduglia,
B. Scalabrini Ortiz, Lisardo Zia, and Roberto Ortelli (whose
pseudonym Ortelli y Gasset parodied the name of the Spanish
philosopher José Ortega y Gasset) were among those who
claimed cultural independence. The debate did not end there. In
La Gaceta Literaria (No. 17) a large number of Spaniards (among
them, Gómez de la Serna, Gerardo Diego, Antonio Espina,
Francisco Ayala, Guillermo de Torre, Ernesto Giménez
Caballero, Jarnés, etc.) responded to the Argentine challenge in a
series of articles entitled, "An Impassioned Debate: The
Intellectual Meridian World Championship." Moreover, a
subsequent Spanish editorial, "The Meridian Verbena" (issue
No. 18), was very different in tone from the first one, and
declared with considerable humor that an argument was
preferable to indifference.

Finally, the dispute for cultural dominion carried out in
the context of literary, or more generally intellectual, journalism
came to be articulated as a characterization of groups—that is, as
"us" versus "them" (Altamirano and Sarlo, *Ensayos*, 97).
Nevertheless, one has to emphasize that both *La Gaceta Literaria*
and *Martín Fierro* were avant-garde publications of similar
nature, that they shared contributors, and that they provided a
forum for a common corps of writers, artists, and intellectuals
from both continents. The result is that the tone, except in the
case of the provocative Spanish editorial, is of the biting and
acerbic style to which the avant-garde is usually drawn.[6] But the
series of editorials and manifestoes is more than a playful
exchange between young writers of the two continents. A second

reading reveals the deep structure of the Argentines' discourse as an epilogue to a long-standing debate about national culture, identity, and language, which opens up a wide range of plans regarding authority and subalterns; neocolonial and postcolonial discourses are caught between the phallic mother country and her satellites. Underlying the debate was the desire of the Buenos Aires writers to develop a voice of their own. Francine Masiello describes the writing in Argentine journals of the period as a struggle for power:

> It always describes the modern writer with dogmatism, and his authority turns out to be central to every discursive event. This presentation of the literary subject becomes the central focus of the little literary review as it manipulates specific proposals regarding art so as to coincide with the auto-affirmation of the authors. (66)

The discourse of young Argentines strives for the legitimization of a language and national character in a context that goes well beyond a simple confrontation of center and margin. The pliability of the Spanish language spoken in Argentina, including indicative expressions, accent, and syntax, is one of the forms this legitimacy acquires and is very much present in literary works of the 1920s. These manifestations should be seen not as the mere representation of a particular social group or as an expression of rebellion by means of an anti-poetic register, but rather as the first signs of security and confidence that Argentine writers had regarding their own language.[7]

With good reason, the very name of the literary journal *Martín Fierro* alludes to an Argentine tradition of independence, one which the avant-garde took up again in their zeal to create a national culture alongside all that modern international culture provided.[8] The director of *Martín Fierro*, Evar Méndez, envisioned as part of the project he called "newspaper-group-action" the establishment of the coordinates for creating a new sensibility that would replace the time-honored, now-defunct aesthetics and make possible plans for the construction of a new canon. A print run of 20,000 copies of one issue was a symptom of the new receptivity toward whatever was novel and permitted people to keep up with both domestic and foreign events.

Nevertheless, this also indicated the necessity for laying the basis for a national culture. As Sarlo points out, "the new" is at the same time a rereading of the tradition (105). *Martín Fierro* evokes both a rupture with and a renewal of a tradition rooted in the language. "*Martín Fierro* has faith in our phonetics," states the periodical's manifesto, written by Oliverio Girondo and published in the fourth issue. This reflects the mixture of an "urban creole," to use Sarlo's term (105) and the universal cosmopolitanism that the young intellectuals of this camp were anxious to fuse. Paradoxical though this reality may seem, it formed the basis of the Argentine avant-garde and established the points of reference for subsequent literature.[9] According to Rama, the avant-garde or "experimentalist modernization" is a return to and restoration of an older project of "independence, originality, and representativity" that began in the latter half of the eighteenth century (18). As the center of the periphery in cultural terms, Buenos Aires is consistent with the most defining trait of the avant-garde: cosmopolitanism blended with creole in a process whose hallmarks are continuity and conflict. To be a "center"—or to wish to be one—implies on the one hand a cosmopolitan compromise and a desire to place one's own city on a par with Paris, Rome, New York, and ultimately Madrid. On the other hand, for Buenos Aires to remain on the periphery signifies a turning inward toward the intranational and a search for identity. I want to stress that these traits do not exist independently of each other. On the contrary, Buenos Aires defies pigeonholing since its complexity results in a cultural hybrid in which to be marginal with respect to other centers permits it at the same time to create a place for itself in the world. Symbolically, the avant-garde made Buenos Aires the center of modern authority for the continent.[10]

In effect, these traits are present in the letters, discourses, and manifestoes of the nine Argentine avant-garde writers determined to cut the umbilical cord with the hegemonic center, to paraphrase the manifesto of Oliverio Girondo in *Martín Fierro*. Almost immediately the question arises, however, as to how to express this untying of the cultural knots with Spain and avoid at the same time the colonizing language. The responses to this quandary are responsible for many of the attempts, with varying success, to establish a truly Argentine Spanish in the 1920s. That is, a language was formed of marginal influences: typically Argentine elements and Galicisms mixed with influences from immigrant tongues and the oral speech of the rural areas. Literature was no longer the sacred province of pure-blooded Castilians and it demanded the right to mix freely with "gaucho" literature, the theatrical forms of the grotesque (*grotesco* or *sainete*), as well as with the lyrics of the tango. In the last analysis this amounted to an attack on the center of *logos*, in the form of the dominating Castilian, from a periphery dressed up in jargon, slang, and local expressions.

Rojas Paz, the most political and programmatic of the group, expresses matters as follows in "Untilled Imperialism," his contribution to *Martín Fierro*:

> We should try to spoil Castilian Spanish so much that a Spaniard who happens by won't understand a word of what we say. That's what the French, the Italians, and the Spanish did with Latin. . . . Why should we want to attach ourselves to a completely artificial tradition that is found only in congressional declamations? We are founding a language for ourselves alone which will give us freedom. . . . Language is a richness like any other which can only be brought to life by being transformed.

Rojas Paz is aware of the cultural imperialism of the great hegemonic centers that, in their desire to extend their dominion, coin names that reinforce relations of dependence: "Pan-America" by the Americans, "Latin America" by the French, and "Spanish America" by the Spanish.

Olivari, in turn, follows a line similar to Rojas Paz's in his response to Madrid: "By chance we happen to speak Spain's language, but we do this so badly that in our disrespect we end up creating an Argentine language. After a few more years they'll have to translate us if they want to appreciate our lyric flow." On the subject of a national idiom, Ganduglia, who was less systematic but more conscious of the new centers of influence that reside in Buenos Aires, had this to say: "It is impossible to speak of a linguistic identity because we are all somewhat polyglot and accustomed to write in our own language. . . . We are modern . . . and idiosyncratic: half French and half Yankee. Soon we will be speaking English as much as any other language that we are used to."

The language problem was a constant preoccupation ever since independence and especially during the romantic movement. Domingo F. Sarmiento, Eduardo Gutiérrez, and Juan Bautista Alberdi all had theories on this.[11] Some writers turned theory into practice as, for example, in the case of "gaucho" literature, of which Hernández's *Martín Fierro* stands out, in which the oral speech of rural peoples was reproduced by writers who were from the city. Jorge Luis Borges, González Lanuza, and other avant-garde writers of the 1920s continued this practice by deleting final *d*'s, writing *i* for *y* and even *j* for *g*. Far from being mere games, these orthographical alterations obeyed both an aesthetic and an ideology of oral and urban writing that captured a particular stage in the evolution of a national literature. Likewise, a characteristically Argentine lexicon was put forward, as well as a certain form of inflection and a style devoid of "rhetorical petticoats," as Leopoldo Marechal put it. Roberto Arlt, Scalabrini Ortiz, and Borges all made contributions to this meditation on the question of a national language. *Idioma nacional de los argentinos* [*The Argentine National Language*] (1900) by Luciano Abeille, *El tamaño de mi esperanza* [*The Breadth of my Hope*] (1926), and "El idioma de los argentinos" ["The Argentine Tongue"] (1927), by Borges are examples of this preoccupation. Nevertheless, Borges deliberately avoided slang as well as anything that might smack of new creole or the speech of recent immigrants.[12] By contrast, for the author of *Don Segundo Sombra*, Ricardo Güiraldes, father figure of avant-garde writers, as well as their collaborator, it is old creole speech that merits attention. Borges's contribution to the debate with *La Gaceta Literaria* is interesting not so much for the critical position adopted as for the political weight of his words. Indeed, Borges recognizes his debt to Madrid (and we would do well to remember that it is in Spain that he founded "Ultraism" [*el ultraísmo*] with de la Torre, whence he later imported it into Buenos Aires in 1921). Despite his debt to Spain, Borges describes the immense cultural gap separating Europeans from the reality of daily life in South America:

Madrid simply doesn't understand us. In a city in which an orchestra can't strike up a tango without robbing it of its soul, in a city whose Irigoyen is Primo de Rivera, in a city whose actors can't tell a Mexican from an Uruguayan, in a city whose only invention is the "galicism" (*galicismo*)—for no one else ever talks so much about it— and in a city where people say something is "enviable" to praise it, how are they possibly going to understand us and how can they possibly get a glimpse of the terrible hope that we, the people of the Americas, live with daily?[13]

Without doubt, the most extreme essay in the polemic between *Martín Fierro* and *La Gaceta Literaria* is Ortelli y Gasset's. This extremity is due less to what Ortelli y Gasset actually proposes, albeit in a sarcastic tone that deliberately belittles and insults Spain, than to the use of slang (*lunfardo*), a particular suburban dialect that is full of loanwords and the residues of other linguistic entities. Moreover, to express oneself in slang in defense of a national culture is to legitimize the language that a hegemonic idiom sees as peripheral.[14] This text provoked a reaction in *La Gaceta Literaria* from Jarnes (3), who ironically declared that he agreed with the Argentines that they needed their own language and suggested they go to the flea market (*Rastro*) to look for debris.

Argentina knew that as a new country if it was going to be incorporated into the continuum of international culture it would have to do so as a nation, not as a colony. "Uncolonizing" itself became the necessary first step toward the sort of cosmopolitan interaction to which the avant-garde aspired. In Latin America modernity brought with it a concept of the nation and of democracy. But Argentina saw its process of modernization interrupted in 1930 by the military coup that replaced President Irigoyen with Uriburu. Thereafter, Argentina, like many countries in South America, has known a long succession of military governments, economic dependence, and deep political crises. In this sense one could say that modernity still has not fully arrived.[15]

The foundation of modernity consists in appropriating intellectual goods as well as cultural goods in general (Collazos, 10). The Argentine avant-garde, as part of a cosmopolitan appropriation, needed to acquire that which it found in its own culture while at the same time getting out from under the vestiges of Spanish dominion.[16] This need for independence is evident in Olivari's answer to *La Gaceta Literaria*:

> Spain is of no intellectual interest for us. To be fair, France and Italy have more to offer than Spain. We, the Argentine avant-garde, claim the right to be unsullied [*vírgenes*] by any influence and to marvel daily at our own qualities, our creoles and our national riches that we are busy describing in our cities and our countryside. We may be aboriginals, we may be Italian as well, and we are always French, but never Spanish!"

Here are the two positions typically taken by the Argentine avant-garde. First is the passion for all that is new, as in the insistence on expressions such as "unsullied" [*vírgenes*] and "to marvel daily." This attitude was summed up by Oliverio in *Martín Fierro*: "'everything is new under the sun' if it is seen with the eyes of today and expressed in a contemporary way" (No. 4, 1924). Second is this contestatory spirit of the counter-debate. Olivari's pronouncements constitute the opposite side of the *Gaceta Literaria* editorial's argument that "it can be openly affirmed that all the greatest values of high cultural significance, both of the past and the present, both historical and artistic, are either Spanish or, if not, are either indigenous, aboriginal, but by no means French, Italian, or British."

Nevertheless, Argentine national culture in the twenties was a project in the process of becoming. The writers of the centennial, and I am referring here to Ricardo Rojas, Leopoldo Lugones, and Manuel Gálvez (though each holds a distinct opinion), laid the basis of what the new avant-garde generation subsequently saw a possibility of making concrete. Indeed, this is the sense the totality of writings about the intellectual meridian has: not only are they testimonials to the independence from the double-edged Spanish protectorate, but they are also part of an internal debate regarding the formation of a national identity. *Martín Fierro*, like much of the intellectual production of those years, reflects the changing energies as the cultural task of superimposed aspects, both autochthonous and cosmopolitan, was formed and comes forth with nationalist values of the avant-garde already inserted in it.

Along with language, the city is also an object of debate along ideological and aesthetic lines. This is not simply a confrontation between Buenos Aires and Madrid, but is a more complex relationship. Not only does Buenos Aires feel that it is a force that is "adjacent not convergent" to/with Madrid, as Zia put it in his rebuttal to *La Gaceta Literaria,* but it wishes to be the central city in South America. Its marginality has not only a desire to end with being marginal but also to gather around it other peripheral forces. In addition to the insolence and irreverence that comes through the irony and sarcasm of these young avant-garde writers, their arrogance and towering pride are evident in their proclamation of Buenos Aires as the spiritual midpoint of the new Latin American world, capital of South America and "lookout for American problems." Pereda Valdés said it succinctly in his rejoinder to the Spanish: "The intellectual meridian of America is not Madrid, it's Buenos Aires. . . . We are busy constructing our own art, part Aztec, part *inkaiko,* and part pure creole, and these patronizing gestures of those who would claim to be our tutors do us violence." Naturally, Pereda Valdés in turn creates an authoritarian and hegemonic discourse. This is repetition with difference: the desire is to be the center within a peripheral conscience.

It is worth asking why Buenos Aires felt justified in seeing itself as a center of attraction not only on the American continent but also in Europe. In effect, the twenties brought together economic affluence and political stability. Once the economic crisis that began before the First World War and continued during it was safely in the past, Buenos Aires was as active as it ever had been.[17] Foreign money flowed in. There were few social conflicts in the government of Alvear.[18] An ethnic mosaic was formed out of the immigration that had accelerated the growth of the city since the end of the nineteenth century.[19] As an example of its cosmopolitanism one might bear in mind that Buenos Aires was the twelfth city in the world, and the first one in South America, to have a subway system (Korn, 135). In sum, Buenos Aires presented a landscape of European-inspired modern architecture that made it stand out from other cities on the continent.

Unlike Mexico City, however, with its thousand-year history, Buenos Aires had almost no past. This suggests why so many poets and writers of the twenties took it upon themselves to reinvent a mythic Buenos Aires. Borges creates an illusory past in his famous poem, "The Mythological Founding of Buenos Aires" (*Cuadernos de San Martín*, 1929). Consider, for example, the final verses:

> Hard thing to believe Buenos Aires had any beginning.
> I feel it to be as eternal as air and water.[20]

Architecture developed in a similar fashion. If a modern European aesthetic was quickly digested by the people of Buenos Aires, it is also true that they borrowed from pasts that had never been theirs. Buildings inspired by Greco-Roman styles or by the Italian Renaissance or eighteenth- and nineteenth-century French architecture coexisted with long-standing colonial Spanish structures, the totality of styles contributing to the eclectic look Buenos Aires has to this day.[21] One might say à la Derrida, that *porteño* culture of the twenties is one of "supplementarity," and indeed both the creation of a mythic past (in literature) and the borrowing of foreign pasts (in architecture and sculpture) bear witness to the logic of the supplement which is haunted by emptiness and absence.

Scalabrini Ortiz, in his response to Madrid in the argument about the meridian, notes as much when he says, "We speak in Spanish, we conduct affairs in English, we take our pleasures in French, and we think . . . well, do we really think?" The question looks like a joke, and it still crops up as a witty saying supposed to show how idiosyncratic the *porteños* are. Nevertheless, it poses the fundamental question of the Argentine national identity. To be sure, the writings of the twenties neither define nor give us a definitive picture of what it means to be Argentine. What they do give us is a confrontation with Spain as a center that has been imposed on Argentina and a realization that there are other centers to choose from as well: the United States, France, and England.

These texts disputing cultural cartography which both manifest a desire for a language of their own and the security that they can count on a modern, cosmopolitan, urban setting comprise what Michel Pêcheux has called a discourse of counter-identification.[22] The subjects of enunciation that announce themselves through their own language try to displace Spanish culture, imposed since colonial times, by appropriating other influences—that is, centers—and creating a new type of culture in the end.

In confronting the Spanish intellectual meridian and rejecting the proffered model, the avant-garde created a counter-discourse. Although rebellious and argumentative, this group of *porteños* proposed practices that were reforming, though hardly radical. What limited them was the implicit danger of reproducing the very model they rejected, though with themselves as the center point now, and because they created a subject that counter-determined itself when choosing other centers of influence. Paris, that "City of Lights," was the cultural nucleus adopted not only by the avant-garde but also by subsequent generations. (Oliverio Girondo, Victoria Ocampo, Julio Cortázar, Manuel Puig, Juan José Saer, Osvaldo Soriano, Luisa Futoransky, and Juan Gelman are among those who opted for Paris, either voluntarily or because of necessary exile.)

The *porteño* city of Buenos Aires put itself forth, in effect, as a center within the marginal world of South America which no longer had a single, monopolizing center but rather only disparate and heterogenous points of reference. The result is a postcolonial discourse of the avant-garde in this series of manifestoes that concerns a crisis of authority and a need to redefine one's culture according to the given lines of modernity.

NOTES

1. James R. Scobie points out that from independence on, the position of Buenos Aires as a principal port grew beyond what the other

factors that favored it, such as being the largest city and the provincial capital, would necessarily lead one to expect. Scobie notes the underlying dilemma and helps clarify Buenos Aires's position in a passage that concurs with my own study: "[The] virtual monopoly of Atlantic and, therefore, European commerce [by Buenos Aires] continued to fuel its population growth, but failed to resolve Buenos Aires's political dilemma: how to legitimize and make acceptable to all of Argentina a political authority acquired by royal fiat in 1776 and reimposed by local *porteño* activism in 1810. . . . To mix metaphors, the door became an appendage without attachment to the Argentine body politic" (43).

2. This construction of identity which permits individuality is a process that integrates different articulations at the sociopolitical and cultural level. The formation of union organizations of anarchist or socialist origin that carry out strikes and demand better salaries and working conditions joins with new procedures and political groups such as feminist parties, new industrial centers, and university reform. For an analysis of each of these phenomena, see Romero and Romero.

3. I am using here the term "universalization" of the region differently from Coutinho's, for whom this is the last stage of regionalism in Latin American fiction in the 1940s. In using the term "regionalism" I am not referring to the generalized concept of a literary representation of the rural or provincial tradition. I use the term "regionalism" in a broader sense that includes sociocultural and political marginality.

4. The variety of avant-garde publications from this period is explained not only by a desire to touch many aspects of the culture but also to bring forth new modes of reading and reinstill a concept of reception in the literary tradition. An incomplete list might read as follows: the mural review *Prisma* (1921–22), the first publication in which Borges, among others, initiates the "ultraist" movement; the three unfoldable pages of *Proa* (1922–23, 1924–25); *Inicial* (1923–27); and perhaps most revealing of all, the *Revista oral* (1926) which, given its purely vocal form, has left no trace apart from the testimonials of its former contributors. *Martín Fierro* is the best known and most discussed review from the period. The daring nature of this publication is evident in comments such as that of avant-garde writer González Lanuza, who described the newspaper as "a bibliographical curiosity," or of Beatriz Sarlo and Carlos Altamirano, who have called it an "adventure" (*Ensayos argentinos*).

5. All references to *La Gaceta Literaria* are to the 1980 edition, with a prologue by Gímenez Caballero. As for *Martín Fierro*, I refer to the facsimile edition of 1982, which, like the original, has no page numbers.

6. Ortega y Gasset was the principal ideologue behind this jocular attitude. But even he agitated, with considerable success, among both Latin American and Spanish young people for a new art that would be "pure" and "dehumanized": "Even if a pure art is impossible, there is without a doubt a tendency toward a progressive elimination of the human, all too human, elements that were dominant in romantic and naturalistic writing" (*Obras*, 359). The Peruvian thinker of the period, José Carlos Mariátegui, severely criticized Ortega y Gasset and what he considered to be the fallacy of a dehumanizing art in the Latin American context.

7. Angel Rama points out that language came up as a kind of defensive reduct and as a proof of independence beginning with the period between the two world wars, a period Rama sees as characterized by a second modernizing impact. What began as clearly regional features—dialects, glossaries, the phonology of popular speech, etc.—later writers (among them, for example, Cortázar in the '40s) associate with a concept of a more modern organic artistic process in which a linguistic unity of the literary text resides in the confidence or faith in the truly American Spanish, defined as that which the writer uses daily.

8. *Martín Fierro*, written by José Hernández in 1872, is considered the national epic from the "gaucho" tradition in Argentine literature.

9. Adolfo Prieto comes to a similar conclusion: "It is easy to find in the most representative books of this group abundant evidence of this somewhat paradoxical—and frequently snobbish—inclination, but their books represent only a small part of the mania for creole. The other part got dispersed and petered out in collective excursions to *porteño* neighborhoods and in café discussions . . . and in the erudite register of the oldest tangos and *milongas*" (38).

10. In Latin America the avant-garde movements shared European symbolic practices that situated them in a universal space, while at the same time they brought with them historical baggage and literary practices that gave rise to differentiation. Both the nationalist romantic current of the nineteenth century and the "modernismo" at the end of the 1800s—still in force in avant-garde irruptions—are the two axes that come together in the avant-garde. For a study of the cosmopolitan value in Latin America, see Salomon.

11. For a list of publications on the problematic of language generally in Latin America from the mid-1800s to 1922, see Ernesto Quesada (34–40); for more recent publications, see Cambours Ocampo (19).

12. Sarlo writes: "Language is one of the central problems for the Argentinean avant-garde. . . . The language appears insecure not for reasons of chastising purity but because of the open port and the many immigrants the city took in in earlier decades. Even the intellectual camp is controlled by voices that do not belong to the register slowly acquired from the old creole speech. . . . The debate against the purists has an ironic collaborator in Borges who is opposed, at the same time, to slang, considering it a hybrid brought on by the suburbs and immigration" (118).

13. The language debate between Argentines and the Spanish returns later with the appearance of *La peculiaridad lingüística ríoplatense y su sentido histórico (The Linguistic Peculiarity of Argentina and Its Historical Meaning* (1941) by the purist, Américo Castro. The Spanish critic speaks here of the corruption of Castilian in Argentina through the use of regional expressions. Borges responds in his article, "Las alarmas del doctor Américo Castro" ("The alarms of Américo Castro") (*Obras Completas*, 653–57) and accuses Castro of "conventional superstitions."

14. As an illustration, consider the following lines from Ortelli: "No hay minga caso de meridiano a la valenciana, mientras la barra cadenera se surta en la perfumería del Riachuelo: vero meridiano senza Alfonsito y al uso nosotro." A rough translation would be: "The devil take the meridian of Valencia! While we will nourish ourselves on our own waters, the true meridian is that one which has no King Alfonse and which subscribes to our habits."

15. Jean Franco says with respect to the novel that "because pluralism of style is not equivalent to democratic participation, those texts which open up to the multiple and often antagonistic discourses of the continent represent a political as well as an aesthetic choice, a Utopia glimpsed beyond the nightmare of an as yet unfinished modernity" (212). Cf. also Picón Garfield and Schulman.

16. I follow Weimann in the use of the term "appropriation."

17. Cortés Conde: "After the First World War, Buenos Aires returns to the dynamic business climate of previous decades. Each day thousands of people arrive in its port, thousands of tons of grains and meat are exported, and many manufactured goods enter the country. . . . A new influx of money, most of it short term and from the United

States, reactivates commerce. The years of Alvear's presidency constitute the high point of this extraordinary period" (42).

18. Luis Alberto Romero points out that the type of literature published during these years, whether translations of European classics, novels about love and adventure, or scientific studies—is all directed toward the formation of a "cult of man" within a society that experienced its conflicts less keenly, perhaps because they were simply less virulent or because people had become accustomed to them (18).

19. The last census taken prior to the 1920s was in 1914. It showed that foreigners accounted for 49.4 percent of the population in the city and 47.7 percent for the greater metropolitan area. Although by 1936 the percentage had dropped to 36.1 percent, it is still a significant part of the cosmopolitan configuration of Buenos Aires. To this one might add the data Richard Walter pulled together: "Between the first national census of 1869 and the third national census of 1914, the population of the city of Buenos Aires increased ninefold, from 177,787 persons to 1,576,597. This phenomenal demographic growth has continued to characterize the metropolitan area. Between 1914 and 1936, the population of the city, or federal capital, grew by almost a million to 2,413,829 persons" (67–8).

20. The translation of Borges is by Alistair Reid, as cited in Foster (133), who also provides an analysis of the poem in which he sees as a necessity the fact that the poets of this period "formulate an ancient lineage and an appropriate mythology for their beloved city" (130).

21. Francis Korn records the observations of one foreigner on the period: "How, we ask ourselves, how and by what miracle has a population that began to throw away all its money on the macaroni style of *art nouveau* and the *modern style* managed to protect itself from the influence of Belgium, Germany, and Catalonia? . . . Here everything is discrete, clear, and done right. You say everything is vulgar, a copy, and a transplantation of French and Italian styles from other centuries? . . . You are probably right. But given that we have to choose between beautiful copies and ugly inventions, the great virtue of the "arriviste" *porteños* has been to avoid the temptation to *épater les bourgeois* and to have been content to construct edifices with noble classical lines in the gardens of the great avenues" (47–8).

In addition to the decor, visits of international importance finished the work of widening the cultural spectrum, as for example those of Lévy-Bruhl, the Prince of Wales, Albert Einstein, the Maharaja of Kapurtala, Eugene O'Neill, Saint-Exupery, Le Corbusier, the Prince of Savoy, the Count of Keiserling, Waldo Frank, Benavente, Gómez de la Serna, Marinetti, and Ortega y Gasset.

22. Pêcheux argues that there are three modalities in which subjects are constructed. The first mode consists of a superimposition of subject of enunciation and the universal subject. This superimposition characterizes the discourse of the "good subject" that spontaneously reflects the Subject. The second modality "characterizes the discourse of the 'bad subject' in which the *subject of enunciation* 'turns against' *the universal subject* by 'taking up a position' which now consists of a *separation* (distantiation, doubt, interrogation, challenge, revolt . . .) *with respect to what the 'universal Subject' gives him to think*: a struggle against ideological evidentness on the terrain of the evidentness. . . . In short, the subject . . . *counteridentifies* with the discursive formation imposed on him by 'interdiscourse' as external determination of his subjective interiority, which produces the philosophical and political forms of *the discourse-against* . . ." (156–7). But later he adds that this modality is finally limited. The danger of "counterdetermination" is that it may inadvertently support what it seeks to oppose by confirming a "symmetry" between the two (164–6). The third modality, which Pêcheux characterizes as "disidentification," constitutes a *working* (transformation-displacement) of the subject form and not just its abolition (169).

WORKS CITED

Altamirano, Carlos, y Beatriz Sarlo. *Ensayos argentinos: De Sarmiento a la vanguardia*. Buenos Aires: Centro Editor de América Latina, 1983.

———. *Literatura/Sociedad*. Buenos Aires: Hachette, 1983.

Borges, Jorge Luis. *Obras completas*. Buenos Aires: Emecé, 1974.

Cambours Ocampo, Arturo. *Lenguaje y nación*. Buenos Aires: Marymar, 1983.

Castro, Américo. *La peculiaridad lingüística rioplatense y su sentido histórico*. Buenos Aires: Losada, 1941.

Collazos, Oscar. *Los vanguardismos en la América Latina*. Barcelona: Península, 1977.

Cortés Conde, Roberto. "Riqueza y especulación." *Buenos Aires: Historia de cuatro siglos*. Eds. José Luis Romero and Luis Alberto Romero. Buenos Aires: April, 1983. 31–43.

Coutinho, Eduardo F. "Regionalsm and Universalism." *Proceedings of the XIIth Congress of the International Comparative Literature Association.* Eds. Roger Bauer and Douwe Fokkema. Vol. 4. Munich: Iudicium verlag, 1990. 191–195.

Foster, Merlin H. "Buenos Aires: Culture and Poetry in the Modern City." *Buenos Aires: 400 Years.* Eds. Stanley R. Ross and Thomas F. McGann. Austin: University of Texas Press, 1982. 127–141.

Franco, Jean. "The Nation as Imagined Community." *The New Historicism.* Ed. H. Aram Veeser. New York: Routledge, 1989. 204–212.

González Lanuza, Eduardo. *Los Martinfierristas.* Buenos Aires: Ediciones Culturales Argentinas, 1961.

Korn, Francis. *Buenos Aires: los huéspedes del 20.* Buenos Aires: Sudamericana, 1974.

La Gaceta Literaria. Vol.1. Vaduz/Liechtenstein: Topos Verlag A.G., 1980.

Martín Fierro. Buenos Aires: Centro Editor de América Latina, 1982.

Masiello, Francine. *Lenguaje e Ideología: Escuelas argentinas de vanguardia.* Buenos Aires: Hachette, 1986.

Ortega y Gasset, José. *Obras completas.* Vol.3. Madrid: Revista de Occidente, 1966.

Pêcheux, Michel. *Language, Semantics and Ideology.* New York: St. Martin's Press, 1982.

Picón Garfield, Evelyn, and Iván A. Schulman. *"Las entrañas del vacío": Ensayos sobre la modernidad hispanoamericana.* México: Cuadernos Americanos, 1984.

Prieto, Adolfo. *Estudios de literatura argentina.* Buenos Aires: Galerna, 1969.

Quesada, Ernesto. *La evolución del idioma nacional.* Buenos Aires: Mercatali, 1922.

Rama, Angel. *La ciudad letrada.* Hanover: Ediciones del Norte, 1984.

———. *Transculturación narrativa en América Latina.* 3rd ed. Mexico: Siglo XXI, 1987.

Romero, José Luis, and Luis Alberto Romero. *Buenos Aires: Historia de cuatro siglos.* Buenos Aires: April, 1983.

Romero, Luis Alberto. *Buenos Aires en la entreguerra: Libros baratos y cultura de los sectores populares.* Buenos Aires: Cisea, 1986.

Salomon, Noël. "Cosmopolitism and Internationalism in the History of Ideas in Latin America." *Cultures* 6.1 (1979): 83–108.

Sarlo, Beatriz. *Una modernidad periférica: Buenos Aires 1920 y 1930*. Buenos Aires: Nueva Visión, 1988.

Scobie, James R. "The Argentine Capital in the Nineteenth Century." *Buenos Aires: 400 Years*. Eds. Stanley R. Ross and Thomas F. McGann. Austin: University of Texas Press, 1982. 40–52.

Walter, Richard J. "The Socioeconomic Growth of Buenos Aires in the Twentieth Century." *Buenos Aires: 400 Years*. Eds. Stanley R. Ross and Thomas F. McGann. Austin: University of Texas Press, 1982. 67–126.

Weimann, Robert. "History, Appropriation, and the Uses of Representation in Modern Narrative." *The Aims of Representation, Subject/Text/History*. New York: Columbia University Press, 1987. 175–215.

Unseen Systems
Avant-garde Indigenism in the Central Andes[1]

Ricardo J. Kaliman

Once assumed that regions may be defined in terms of social practices, one might yet be tempted to discern between the space referred to in the literary text and the social space at which the text aims, the *community* of readers where "mutual anticipations" hold. A familiar concept of "regional" or "regionalist" literature could be phrased on the basis of this distinction: strictly speaking, regionalist writers would be those talking about a given region, to be understood by people of that region (be it either elite or popular classes). A measure of the greatness of a regional writer would be to be able to reach a "universal" dimension while at the same time satisfying the two previous requirements. Nowadays we could hardly seriously accept this pattern. It would seem quite naive after we have gained deep suspicions about supposed universal values (and, concomitantly, about universal literature), and some consciousness about the typically hegemonic incidence of the center-periphery structure in literary considerations.

I want to take the problem from the core of the distinction itself, namely its implicit claim of ontological independence for the referred space. In writing, it could be argued, the subject represents itself and therefore cannot help bringing with it the whole of its context, "real" or imaginary. Its image of the reader community implies the image of the represented space. Referential space (together with its connotations of exoticism, colorfulness, or realism, etc.) is just another feature of the target

159

community. In identifying the represented space, we would be doing nothing else than describing the imaginary spatial configuration governing the act of reading. What would then be the sense of making the distinction? I want to bring here a case study to support the claim that even though shared expectations involved in the literary speech act carry some sort of spatial configuration, there is still a conceptual need for a second term for it: region as experienced by social groups different from the ones dominant in the literary institution.

To be sure, to conceive region as a social experience brings about new problems, not the least of which are the difficulties that any attempt to abstract from the experience of social groups must face. I will assume here that some notion in the line of Raymond Williams's "structures of feeling" will prove operative in confronting this problem. If I insist on exploring this notion of region, it is because it may be a key concept in relation to a theoretical threat posed to us by contemporary interest on regionalist studies. This interest was born from an increasing concern about difference, but for this very reason it may lead us either, logically, to a turmoil of atoms randomly connected to each other or, ideologically, to a new discursive reordering of space. Region as experience, grounded on a social base of shared interpretation, offers itself as a better alternative, since it is conceptually able to provide empirical support and to be articulated in models with explanatory power, as I will try to show in my analysis of avant-garde indigenism in (referred to hereafter as AvInd) in the South Central Andes.[2]

AvInd may seem too particular to Latin American states, which, although they imitated the European model, were the offspring of a somewhat chancy sequence of political episodes that took place with little or no regard for common heritage, autochthonous cultures, or any other circumstance of the type alleged in Europe for legitimizing the equation of nation to state. Consequently, indigenous peoples (whose interests, at any rate, had no influence at all over these processes, and who became socially and economically more and more marginal) found their territories arbitrarily sectioned by the new national frontiers, giving room to social experiences of the type considered here. However, the literary phenomenon of AvInd may turn out to be a specific case of a more general concept: region as a social experience of a counter-hegemonic nature. In another dimension of abstraction, we should be led to think that it is not the case that literature is something occurring in a given region, nor that an institutionalized region occurs in literature, two traditional ways of characterizing the concept of "regional literature." It would rather be that literature is one way of doing and undoing region, the process where different conceptualizations and evaluations of surrounding space collide, complement, or compromise to each other. I do not plan to pursue all these consequences here, although the concepts proposed for the analysis are aimed at allowing them to be explored in the long term.

The paper is in two parts. The first one is mainly narrative, both because it is the best way to put together the relevant facts, which, as far as I know, have not been previously pictured in the way I am doing here; and also because most of the readers are probably unfamiliar with the texts and practices introduced here (which perhaps has something to do with what regionalism is all about). As Sayer pointed out, there is no theoretically neutral narrative in social sciences. In the second section, I will discuss some conceptualizations implicit in the first section, in order to clarify my understanding of the theoretical import of avant-garde indigenism in the South Central Andes in the 1920s and '30s.

Some Facts and Texts of AvInd

In 1926, Arturo Peralta-Miranda, whose pen name was Gamaliel Churata, founded the *Boletín Titikaka*, which would endure until 1930. Although closely related to Marxist intellectual José Carlos Mariátegui and his journal *Amauta*, the *Boletín* was less obviously socialist in its orientation, and more directly in contact with the concrete forms of indigenous cultures. For instance, Churata published poems written in quechua, some of which would later be incorporated into his *El pez de oro*, a poligeneric and multilingual text written in the late '20s but published only in 1957. In this environment, a textual practice embodying an apparent confluence of avant-garde literary techniques and indigenist material, which has been known as AvInd at least since the work of Monguió on so-called *post-modernista* Peruvian poetry (Monguió, 1954), was born in the writings of Alejandro Peralta (younger brother of Churata) and of Luis de Rodrigo. In 1926, Alejandro Peralta published *Ande*, the first properly AvInd book, followed in 1934 by *Kollao*. Only in 1968 would both books be published again, in a single volume under the name of *Poesía de entretiempo*. Peralta would yet send to print a very different book, called *Tierra-Aire*, in 1971, and after his death (1973), his posthumous poems were collected under the title *Al filo del tránsito*. Already far from AvInd, in 1969 he received the National Poetry Award of Peru.

The poems which are of interest here are those of Alejandro Peralta's first two books, which take their subject matter from the landscape and indigenous people of the Titikaka region. Particularly in *Kollao*, a definite political standing emerges clearly, denouncing the miserable situation of the Indians and proclaiming the need for a revolutionary change. In a couple of poems ("El indio Pako"), it links these social urges with those of other marginal groups. However, most of the poems are restricted to introducing the human and natural landscape, with many poems dedicated to the everyday life, especially the work habits, of indigenous people of the Titikaka. As Palau de Nemes remarked, characters are surrounded by a heroic and solar image, which is relevant in opposition to an archetypal image of melancholy and lassitude which was accorded to Indians by previous forms of indigenism. For those who do not know these poems, this introduction to them may suggest a somewhat clear reference, a sort of descriptive poetry. But this is not the case. On the contrary, what we are calling avant-garde (which shows up also in the use of the blanks of the page, capitalization of scattered sentences, and lack of punctuation) rather blurs the contour of the reference through an explosion of metaphors.

The following excerpt of the first five stanzas of "La pastora florida" ("The flowery shepherdess") may serve as a small illustration of Peralta's AvInd language:

Los ojos golondrinas de la Antuca
se van a brincar sobre las quinuas.
Un cielo de petróleo echa a volar 100 globos de humo.

Picoteando el aire caramelo
evoluciona una escuadrilla
de aviones orfeónidas.

Hacia las basílicas rojas
sube el sol a rezar el novenario.
Sale el lago a mirar las sementeras.
El croar de las ranas se punza en las espigas.

Los ojos de la Antuca
se empolvan al pasar por los galpones.[3]

Creacionista features are the futurist images (petroleum, aircraft), the strange metaphors, and the unusual perspective from which facts are presented. However, it is important to remember that for Vicente Huidobro, the major theorist of this modernist school, this language is aimed at creating a world with its own laws, completely independent from those of nature. If only for his isotopic referential stance, it is clear that this is not Peralta's attitude, but that he rather engages in *creacionista* rhetoric in order to refer to an admittedly independent reality.

The third major AvInd book is *Luna Muerta*, by Manuel J. Castilla (1918–1980), who was born and died in the province of Salta, Argentina, where he always had his residence. From there, Castilla would undertake long trips which covered especially Salta, the neighboring province of Jujuy, and Bolivia, particularly the miner cities of Oruro and Potosí. These trips supplied him with most of the material for his poetry, which was honored with the National Poetry Award in 1974. By then, he had already become a representative of the telluric line within neo-romanticism, the dominant trend among the poets of his generation. Among Argentine neo-romantics, tellurism was opposed to an introspective poetry, one characteristically homesick for some kind of lost paradise, embodied often in the symbol of childhood. The cult of nature, as a way of escaping from an ominous environment, was another topic to which they were sensitive, and in this context Castilla's landscape and characters were well received. A number of poets emerging from the interior of the country were acknowledged by the neo-romantic institution. In 1944, a group of poets from northwestern Argentina, among them Castilla, came together under the name of "La Carpa," declaring their explicit aim of "rescuing" regional values. Their poem shows their enrollment in the general bases of neo-romantic practices. A year before, however, Castilla had published something very different, *Luna Muerta*.

The book takes its name from a *lote,* one of the divisions of the plantations of sugar cane owned and exploited by one of the big sugar mills which had been for half a century the most important industrial plants of the region. During the period of sugar cane harvesting (the *zafra*), the *lote* Luna Muerta was inhabited by Chaguanco and Mataco Indian workers.[4] Castilla's book portrays their lives and denounces the exploitation they suffer.

Each poem usually begins with a denotative declaration of a work or other everyday situation of Chaguancos and Matacos in Luna Muerta. In the following description, some other, quite prosaic, statements alternate with metaphorical ones, thus clearly signaling what is talked about, but transferring it at the same time into an imprecise atmosphere. The *creacionista* rhetoric is almost out of sight, but the strangeness of the perspective chosen and the unusual character of the analogies reveal the avant-garde attitude, closer to the imagery of the *ultraísta* poets. As illustration, I include here "Milagro de la luna" ("Miracle of the moon"):

> Trenzan lazos de chaguar los Matacos
> y fajas amarillas.
> Corren ríos de sol y me parece
> que tejieran la siesta de cuclillas.
>
> ¡Qué derroche de luz desparramada
> y qué ardiente la selva!
> El agudo silencio de los indios
> se nos viene de punta como flechas.
>
> ¡Oh, qué duro el silencio de las chinas
> y qué blandas las manos!
> Si les cayera lluvia, de morenas,
> serían chinas de barro.
>
> Sobre los urundeles a la luna
> querrán verla bien ancha;

y cuando caiga el agua de la lluvia
sobre la arena blanca,
tendremos el milagro cristalino
de la luna pintada.[5]

Copajira (1949) is the culminating point of AvInd, devoted to the life in the mines of Oruro and Potosí, which Castilla had been visiting since the beginning of the decade. For the Bolivian Plate and Argentine Puna, the mines represented an economical pole with similar consequences to those of the sugar mills for the rest of northwestern Argentina.[6] Generally speaking, *Copajira* follows the pattern of *Luna Muerta*, alternating prosaic statements and original metaphors. This book, however, presents us with much octosyllabic verse, as opposed to the free verse dominant in the previous cases. Formally, it also takes from the *romancero* stanza the assonant rhyme, which contrasts with the completely blank verse of the rest of AvInd text. None of these is really systematic, as illustrated by the following brief poem, entitled "Coca":

Como tu propia sombra deshojada
sube a tu boca para que la exprimas.
Entonces crece sobre tu esperanza
un poco de ceniza.

Tu sed es quien la busca
para su arena seca y amarilla,
pero al final, el sueño,
en tus ojos de lacre ya no tiene cabida.

Yo pienso que la quieres
porque todo en ella arde,
y si le echas ceniza
para tornarla suave
ello es únicamente
para que se te apague
y se convierta en musgo
donde se duerma tu hambre.[7]

AvInd as a System

The assumption implicit in this narrative is that of the systemic character of AvInd. I must point out that the notion of literary systems, although to a lesser degree than its ancestors "movement," "school," and the like, has not been defined rigorously by literary historians and theoreticians. The obvious advantages of applying models originated in the theory of systems cast healthy light upon the relationships of literary systems to other social systems, but does not seem to have affected the relatively silent admission of already established generalizations over literary practices of given periods. Systems have usually been taken as objects available to study, not as objects to be built on the basis of criteria emerging from the theory of systems itself.[8]

I will be presenting the AvInd system as a hypothesis, although I expect it to be self-evident, that, at any rate, its validity is at least as well grounded as that of any other literary system so far proposed. In the introduction to this section I will follow a general framework of social systems, which lend themselves to the articulation of literary systems within social systems in general.[9] In the following subsections, the case for systematicity will be reinforced, as I discuss some of the reasons why AvInd, as a system, has not shown up in literary histories in which it could have been taken under consideration (namely, accounts of Peruvian, Bolivian, Argentine, and global Latin American literature).

There is something in the notion "institution," understood as a set of "mutual anticipations" that is appealing for our interests. It carries the assumption of the text as a process, particularly pointing to the pragmatic rules governing this process. One can conceive of mutual anticipations as constituting a sort of particular competence, ideally shared by a community of readers. By "literary system," I mean the set of discursive practices institutionalized within one such community. If, following the guidelines of the structuration theory of social systems, we assume that literary systems are both constituted by and the output of social practices, we may take the processes of production and reproduction of texts as the fundamental social practices relevant to literary systems.

Some "literary" properties—in the strictest sense of the term—of AvInd poems allow us to identify features of the community within which they take place: the novelty of metaphors with unusual second terms which create an atmosphere of un-realism. AvInd poems are structured as a collection of somewhat isolated complex images, which can rarely be easily traced to any tradition, calling the reader to engage in this originality. Thus lacking a framework of *a priori* fixed aesthetic values, AvInd seems to invite a process of either watching things in unusual ways or concentrating in the linguistic realm of the image itself.

On the other hand, these poems evolve isotopically around characters (often identified with their proper names) and situations drawn from an explicit environment, that of living indigenous cultures, articulated in socioeconomic subordination. This is exactly the reason for the name of "indigenism": not only because of the chronological and ideological coincidence (in both the "realist" attitude and an obvious will for denunciation of exploitation) with the political and literary (mainly narrative) movement which spread throughout these countries of Latin America during the second and third decade of the present century, but also because the target community is not the depicted one. To be more precise, the community of illustrated readers of AvInd will recognize themselves as "other" with respect to the indigenous people portrayed in the poems. Similarly, the indigenist political discourse was directed to dominant white society, mainly by lower middle-class intellectuals who appropriated the voice of indigenous cultures in the classical manner in which subordinated social groups try to adhere to the claims of other marginal groups in order to strengthen their own position when beginning a struggle for a better place in the distribution of power (cf. Rama, 1974; Cornejo-Polar, 1980; Barré).

Perhaps it is this seeming contradiction between derealization in modernist style and a political quest for bringing reality to the eyes that makes the idiosyncrasy of AvInd. There are many alternative interpretations to this phenomena, and I will briefly discuss below some important lines regarding their consideration. However, one important point is the identity it renders to their work considered as a whole, a fact that seems to demand some kind of explanation and, in any case, which strongly supports the hypothesis of its systematic nature.

Region and nation

The AvInd system has remained invisible for literary studies. Peruvian literary historians have acknowledged the peculiarity of that poetry, but it has been accorded a marginal status, reduced to the Orkopata group of Puno, and mainly the two first books of Alejandro Peralta. On the other hand, Manuel J. Castilla's *Luna Muerta* and *Copajira* are mentioned only as part of the early production of this poet in national histories and anthologies of Argentine literature, and this only with the kind of prehistoric connotation usually accorded early works of authors whose mature work only is accorded some merit.

Of course, one could argue that AvInd's absence from canonical anthologies follows from the marginal nature of AvInd. Even if one could come to prove that it worked properly as a literary system, it has not generated a global movement of social practices that could make it deserve careful study. Even the most advanced project of Latin American literary history, sustained by scholars from many countries in a couple of conferences (see Pizarro), insisted on a model then proposed and later brilliantly developed by Angel Rama, in his book *La ciudad letrada*, which centered around the role of the cities throughout the history of Latin America, as poles of power controlling and subordinating the discursive practices. No doubt, urban-centered models like this may capture the hegemonic structure involved, since rural voices can only be heard when they manage to get into the urban apparatuses where they might join other subordinated discursive practices struggling to gain positions. In such a framework, AvInd would turn out to be a tiny piece with no real significance for the whole, prevailing, as it was, among relatively small groups of poets from minor cities, with low levels or no industrialization at all, located in the political and economical periphery of their respective countries, and talking about indigenous peasants and miners.

The multiple perspectives that recent historiography has been recognizing offers a response to this argument. Society seems to comprise an *a priori* unordered crowd of little systems rather than an organized set with an "objective" preestablished hierarchy between them. In order to reduce the risk of hegemonic modelization, we should concentrate on the assumptions of models themselves, rather than taking them as a stable framework for evaluation and analysis. Given the responsibilities of the institution of literary studies in establishing canon and valid representations of tradition, this very institution becomes part of our subject. The models proposed can be seen as discursive self-reflections of implicit views of history and tradition, which they, at the same time, reassess and develop. We can make explicit those assumptions, discussing them and overtly accepting or refusing them, on the most independent grounds we can find.

I find at least two such assumptions at work behind the devaluation of AvInd. A major one is implicit in the concept of national literature, which implies that juridical national frontiers define the closure of literary systems. In the case of Latin American countries, at least, this usually carries with it a hierarchical structure, with its top in the capital city, and/or the most economically powerful ones. A concept of regional literature as minor practices, subsidiary to those of the center of the system, follows from this conception and, in fact, it has been pervasive in literary studies in Latin America. For a model based on such an assumption, when taken too literally, AvInd is not only invisible, but it cannot exist at all. However, even if some flexibility is allowed so that literary practices may cross national boundaries, AvInd would still remain invisible as long as the political administration is seen as the definitive model for the determination of literary communities.

Obviously, we should not underestimate the importance of national structures in literary practices. We have seen that the mature work of Alejandro Peralta and Manuel J. Castilla was oriented along the national coordinates (both of them even received respective official recognition in the national context), witnessing to the strength of the field of force that state apparatuses create. However, on the one hand, AvInd happens to be relevant for understanding the ways in which these writers operate within their respective national literary institutions. Castilla's mature poetry, for instance, satisfies neo-romantic aesthetic requirements by introducing structures taken from indigenous cultures, basically through the concept of *tierra*, which is, in his poetry, a convincing form of the Andean *Pachamama*. In a way, this is a renewal of the attitude of AvInd, in that it inserts into the dominant discourse cosmological concepts inspired by the socially marginal indigenous cultures.

On the other hand, the very invisibility of AvInd casts doubts over the validity of a national literature pattern which is unable to see it. Since the centrifugal forces of the "nation" are responsible for the disappearance of a system, one cannot help thinking that some other similar centripetal systems may have vanished in the same way. The way of thinking of which that pattern is an instance (namely, making literary practices depend directly upon structures that are, in the strictest sense of the term, "political") reveals itself as building social systems, rather than loyally representing them. For those willing to elude such a sort of solipsism, it is necessary to admit at least some other sorts of "nations" as valid ground for literary systems. In this respect, it is worth remembering that we can find poems in Castilla's late work where his Bolivian experience is included in enumerations, obviously aiming at an idea of global unity together with his Argentinian sources. Literary critics, however, have barely mentioned this extension of the region, while they quite often classify Castilla's poetry as "regionalist" with explicit reference to northwestern Argentina. Thus, the Andean "nation," as Castilla may have conceived it, is as out of sight for national literature conceptions as AvInd is. Let me simply conclude, for the time being, that, at least, these different kinds of "nations" have to be taken into account when representing literary systems.

Polysystemic structures

The other major postulate that seems to me to be responsible for the invisibility of AvInd is the unilateral way in which literary practices spread from the center to the periphery. In the strongest form—indeed, an idealized form, not easily found—of the models I am trying to challenge, this is the only way in which influence may go across national frontiers, now arriving from international prestigious centers to the peripheral centers, which in turn distribute them to their respective area of influence.

This assumption of unilaterality partially explains the invisibility of AvInd. As mentioned above, the name of this system implies a contradiction in terms, since the avant-garde line taken connotes some way of anti-realism while indigenism is basically realist. Nelson Osorio has lucidly reviewed the critical views around the opposition between avant-garde (stressing, for this matter, its cosmopolitanism) and indigenism (which is concerned with local problems and linked, in many cases, to nationalism), finally pointing out in a footnote a caveat against taking this opposition too far, given the case of Alejandro Peralta's *Ande*. Incisive as this observation is, it nevertheless reveals the precritical way in which AvInd would be dealt with if it is perceived at all: as a mere instance of two broader systems at the same time, each of them respectively well rooted in the central discursive formations. Since this view fulfills the requirements of the unilaterality model, no questions will be asked about the peculiar way in which the subjacent contradiction has been solved, and whether the synthetic resulting discourse does not imply an abandonment of the foundational tenets of any or both of those systems.

However, not only will the peculiar features of AvInd remain invisible for such a framework, but so will the system itself, because of the above-mentioned "softening" of avant-garde language in its later manifestations. It is commonplace among poets, friends of Castilla, and some scholars to point to the almost simultaneous visit of Nicolás Guillén to northern Argentina and the publication of Castilla's *Luna Muerta*, in order to conclude that this book was written under the influence of the

Cuban poet. This has been for some time the only explanation available for such a strange token as that book represents. This hypothesis followed the principle of unilaterality from consecrated literary practices down, inasmuch as Guillén himself was assigned to a line born in the *Romancero gitano* by Spaniard Federico García Lorca. However, Castilla's book lacks the tropical musicality and the constant displays of onomatopoeia which are characteristic of Guillén's neo-popularism, and, on the other hand, the language and form of *Luna Muerta* cannot be traced back to the forms of literary practices of the Chaguanco Indians, as it is the case of many poems by Guillén in relation to Afro-Cuban culture, and García Lorca, inspired by southern Spanish gypsy and *romancero* traditions (in one of the poems, Castilla declares explicitly that he cannot even understand the Chaguanco language). The aforementioned absence of a proper avant-garde environment in northwestern Argentina and of the conspicuous typographical and futurist elements in the book itself did not allow the unilaterality model to identify a better source. The postulation of an AvInd system and its internal dynamics was all the time offering the right framework, but it was impossible to see it.[10]

As with the national literature model, the unilaterality model is a way in which critical institutions read themselves, and portrays quite adequately the distribution of power within literary practices. An alternative was suggested by Even Zohar's polysystemic conception (see his "Polysystem Theory"). Rejecting the monolithic nature of traditional literary formations, even Zohar proposed instead a structure in which many systems coexist, taking it to be a duty of empirical research to determine the relationships between them. Among these relationships, he concentrates on the dominance of given systems, and sets out to conceptualize the process by which different systems gain and lose control of the polysystem. His proposals rely on "defamiliarization," but allow me to speculate about some other perspectives of polysystem dynamics.

A polysystemic model seems to be able to capture the relevant phenomena of which unilaterality was a manifestation, but without getting stuck on unilaterality itself as a principle, allowing, in consequence, systems like AvInd. On the other hand, if we take polysystems as idealized versions of the set of systems available in the poetic "market," it is possible to establish a conceptual base on which to ground rich analysis of empirical data.

Taking our case at hand, it is worth observing that Alejandro Peralta, before he got into the AvInd practice, wrote poems which were clearly *modernista*, in the sense this term receives in Spanish-speaking literary studies, naming a movement simultaneous and similar to French symbolism and Parnaso. Peralta's *modernista* poems, published under the very medieval Spaniard pen name of Goy de Hernández, can be found in the first issues of *Gesta Bárbara*, which is itself a *modernista* journal. The "impersonality" of literary systems can also be found in the case of Castilla. Between his two AvInd books, *Luna Muerta* and *Copajira*, he published *La niebla y el árbol* in 1946, full of baroquism and a lyrical atmosphere which remind us of Neruda (there are even many allusions to the sea, which is far away from Castilla's countryside), to simplify things to classical unilaterality for the sake of exposition.

It would not be difficult to ground the claim that this Nerudian line was part of the dominant systems among Argentine poets of those years, as was Spanish-speaking *modernismo* among Bolivian ones during the second decade of the century. Roughly speaking, AvInd would have been located in the periphery of the polysystem all through this period. The fact that both Peralta and Castilla were able to engage distinctly in both the dominant systems and AvInd speaks for the autonomy of the second one, given that there seems to be no trouble recognizing the autonomy of the former one. Now, of course, we should not hope that systems will always show up in such "chemically pure" forms. Rather, what is to be expected is that concrete literary practices will be fed in different degrees by the different systems, as poets, to express it in Goldmanian terms, go across a number of *trans-individual* subjects alongside their discursive careers.

I will introduce a modelization of some Bolivian poetry belonging to the AvInd system in some degree but not completely, which I will assume might be explained by postulating some kind of interaction between it and some other systems. One case is a group of poets (the Vizcarra brothers, Oscar Cerruto, and others. See Bedregal), who, while explicitly calling themselves avant-garde poets, adopted a language close in metaphorical preferences to AvInd. Another case is that of the book *Brújula* by Omar Estrella, from La Paz, later politically exiled in Argentina and a member of the aforementioned group "La Carpa" from northwestern Argentina, to which Castilla also belonged. The poems in this book present us with capital letters, some quasi-futurist images, and many allusions to Indian culture, although it was written in a period previous to the Chaco War, the historic experience that properly brought about indigenism to Bolivian discourse (cf. Gómez Martínez).

Being AvInd on the periphery of the polysystem, this Bolivian poetry ought to attract discursive practices from the left of the ideological formation, which, together with the only partial articulation of the mentioned poems in the system, can explain why it was not taken into account in conservative Bolivian literary histories, given also that it has not been recognized as a valid system in any other known literary history. I am not only trying to illustrate how I consider we might relate a polysystem model to the complexities of real practices. Coexistence, compromise, and eventual contradiction between different systems, as I have merely suggested, are quite similar to the subjective engagement in ideological formations that Raymond Williams called "structures of feeling" and whose theoretical implications have been recently underlined by Terry Eagleton. The parallel holds an aspect relevant enough to map it onto the proposal that this unstable mixture may play a crucial role in later developments within the formation, as long as it begins to take more definite shape and gain acceptance within given social groups. Under this projection, we could conceive of interaction of systems in given textual practices as symptoms of movements inside the polysystem which are relevant for the direction it could take in the near future.[11]

How literary systems spread

Turning again to our main subject, the question arises whether AvInd is a system or merely a transitory confluence of two broader systems. In order to justify my predilection for the first option, we need to examine the way in which avant-garde and indigenism in AvInd are related to avant-garde and indigenism in the broader sense, which extreme "unilateralism" would not even care to do.

The referential and localist quest of AvInd strongly contradicts at least two fundamental principles of the avant-garde: anti-realism and cosmopolitanism. AvInd, in effect, performs in societies of quasi-feudal structures, which would lead to other sorts of aesthetic (and political) answers. This reasoning only gives stronger support for the autonomy of AvInd, whose avant-garde component will be reduced to the superficial use of forms, which, at any rate, are very softened in later manifestations. Taking into account the contemporary controversies in *Amauta* and other journals, and specially the influential Mariateguian ideas, one could not help thinking that avant-garde language meant for AvInd poets simply *the* revolutionary way to express new conceptions of society as their denunciation implies a call for social change. This would fit with the novelty of image which constitutes the major imperative of their practice as well as with Castilla's softened version, as the "revolutionary" connotation has been switching from avant-garde to, so to say, neo-popularism. Now, if it is still valid to employ the term "avant-garde" for the mere use of given expressive forms, then our application of that term in the name of AvInd is still operative. If not, then we have been once more caught in the unilaterality trap. At any rate, it seems clear that AvInd is not part of any avant-garde system, nor even a subsystem of it, but is a different system in its own right.

According to what we have just said, the organizing force of this system would seem to be indigenism. In order to still justify the autonomy of AvInd, one could argue that no other form of indigenism took avant-garde, or at least this particular form of avant-garde, language as a medium. But this does not make much difference, since, as Cornejo-Polar has extensively shown (e.g., 1980), indigenism is characteristically heterogeneous, meaning that it takes its subject from some social structure (in this case, indigenous) and offers it in another mode of production (in this case, Western culture). Avant-garde would be, in that case, a particular choice within a general procedure typical of indigenism in general. It could also be advanced that indigenist poetry, as clearly opposed to indigenist narrative, does not seem to show such a systematic character as can be observed in AvInd. Again, this would not allow us to go too far, since it may well be an illusion created in literary studies because of the relative success of novels like those by Ciro Alegría, Manuel Scorza, Jorge Icaza, and especially José María Arguedas, which have been the subject of academic consideration while much poetry may still be hidden from sight simply for lack of similar attention from critical discourse. From this point of view, AvInd may well be part of some kind of a broader indigenist poetic system not properly identified until now.

There are a couple of properties of the AvInd system, however, that should be mentioned in relation to this hypothesis of its assignment to a major system, which speak rather for some degree of autonomy. Firstly, AvInd voices seem to carefully avoid presenting themselves as those of the "savers" of the victims, as it is, on the contrary, characteristic of indigenist discourse in general (see Saintoul). In this sense, AvInd seems to forestall what Escajadillo has called neo-indigenism (see also Cornejo-Polar, 1984), which is able to escape from the accusations raised against indigenism of being a new kind of paternalism ("pretending to be the voice of those with no voice"; see Barré). Therefore, AvInd did not fulfill a useful function for any particular urban sector with some kind of agrarian interests, as was typical of standard indigenism (see Rama, 1974). Some consciousness about this pioneering role can be seen in Churata's prologue to *El pez de oro*, written in a date closer to the publication than the body of the book, especially in the paragraphs about José María Arguedas and other *mestizo* writers. Related to this feature, neo-indigenism is practiced by writers with a much deeper involvement in real indigenous cultural practices, either because they themselves grew up within indigenous communities, or because they had long enough living experience among them.

Evidence supports Churata's attitude in this respect. In Bolivian literary histories, *Gesta Bárbara* is usually pictured as a major moment in national poetry, a sort of founding spot of contemporary sensitiveness. For that reason, from time to time, the group has been remembered in articles and notes in journals and newspapers. Almost all of the members of the original group have had the opportunity to recollect the years of *Gesta Bárbara*. Their respective stories show, naturally, strong similarities. Churata's version, however, shows a difference which is significant. All the other members talk with longing about the *bohemia* life and have thankful words for the gentle Potosí neighbors who allowed them to get along with it, as though considering them just naughty children. In a sense, this is the way in which the *Bárbaros* see themselves from mature age, when they have scaled important positions in Bolivian intelligentsia, and one cannot forget that, after all, they were always a part of the Potosí *elite*. Churata also takes a moment to remember this part of the *Bárbaros'* activities. But what he stresses most are the visits to the popular neighborhoods of Potosí, devoting some paragraphs to talk about the life there, colorfully and with emotion, but in enough detail to reveal his personal involvement with the values there at work.

The other feature of AvInd which distinguishes it from contemporary indigenism is equally important: Castilla's books may be considered the first, and quite lonely, relatively important manifestations of literary indigenism in northern Argentina. Whatever the reasons why this part of the south central Andean region did not show more discursive presence of the socioeconomic reality of indigenous population, the fact is that AvInd region of diffusion does not coincide with that of indigenist discourse and praxis in general, but rather, it spread independently. Therefore, even if one cannot properly disentangle AvInd from some eventual broader indigenism system, it is clear that it had a dynamics of its own. We are not able to definitely claim that it was an autonomous system, but at least in one crucial respect it behaved as such.

From these analyses, we may sketch a general picture in the following terms: the existence within the polysystem of avant-garde and indigenism as two different systems, in some aspects even opposed to each other, is the condition of possibility of the emergence of AvInd as an autonomous small system. It re-elaborates avant-garde attitude into a rhetoric semiotically charged with the idea of seeing things anew, and takes a stand more related to the proclaimed will of indigenism than with its discursive practices (in the sense that ideological discourse, by definition, does not necessarily coincide with concrete political practice). Two particular properties support the autonomy of AvInd thus characterized. On the one hand, it moved over a scope different from those of centrally controlled circuits, settling a path from the Peruvian periphery to the Argentinian periphery through some activity in the periphery of the strictly Bolivian polysystem. On the other hand, it included the practice of "going there and watching things to learn from them," to which, I think, only an orthodox and old-fashioned style of structuralism would deny status as a relevant variable for literary studies.

It is easy to accept that this "learning practice" is a presupposition of many literary systems. However, it is particularly important for AvInd, because it was the major substitute for an almost nonexistent previous discursive spatial configuration. This practice supplied the poets with the content for their work. As for the unavoidable question of where this "new" region came from, the only answer seems to be the above-mentioned South Central Andean homogeneity which is undoubtedly assumed in Castilla's neo-romantic period. Vividly experienced by the indigenous population whose cultural and economical practices constituted it, AvInd poets met this socially defined region as a consequence of their way of assuming indigenist practices. However, this region was not exactly the subject matter of AvInd, since it is not really textualized in their poems, but it constituted its social base, which explains why AvInd spread as it did and not in another way more dependent on hegemonic determination. Through AvInd, this region entered as an active variable for Latin American elite literary practices. Indeed, this entrance was by the back door, rather peripheral to the polysystem, but this does not free literary critics from the duty of being able to see it. All to the contrary, it calls us to a search for better eyes.

NOTES

1. Sections 1 and 2.2 include a re-elaboration of some material from a lecture for the Department of Spanish and Portuguese at the University of Wisconsin-Madison in January 1991. To my knowledge, the first person to "see" the system I talk about in this paper was Dr. Antonio Cornejo-Polar, who was so generous as to share his intuition with me and invite me to investigate it. Besides him, I have had invaluable help from other friends for the collection of the relevant material: Juan Zevallos-Aguilar, Edwin Guzmán-Ortiz, María Luisa Alba, and Mario Araujo-Subieta. Part of the research was made possible by a grant accorded by the Research Council of Universidad Nacional de Tucumán for the program "Tucumán en el contexto de los Andes Centromeridionales." My English version would have been even less idiomatic without the help of Janet Casaverde.

2. I use the francophone form of "avant-garde" because of the Latin American context of the poetry considered. It refers to what in English-speaking literary traditions is known as "modernism." See Bürger.

3. My translation, which is merely operative, just for the sake of introducing this poetry to English-speaking readers: "The swallow eyes of the Antuca / leave, to bound over the quinuas. // A sky of petroleum sets to flight 100 balloons of smoke. // Pecking the caramel air / a squadron evolves / of Orpheonide aircraft. // Toward the red basilicas / the sun rises to pray the *novenario*. / The lake comes out to see the sowings. / The croaking of the frogs pierces itself in the spikes. // The eyes of the Antuca / become dusty as they pass by the storehouses." *Antuca* is a proper name, a diminutive form of Antonia. The definite article which accompanies it connotes some familiarity with the character, and implies a positive affection. This is very common usage in popular Spanish. At least in this context, the construction absolutely lacks the derogatory sense which is sometimes attributed to it in some textbooks of Spanish as a second language. The *quinua* or *quinoa*, also called Puna wheat, is a variety of cereal which can endure colder temperatures than maize. The bread made with its flour can be easily stored for a long time. From the grain, an alcoholic beverage, a kind of *chicha*, is also made. The *novenario* is a catholic prayer which is repeated at the same hour for nine days. Hence the name, which could be literally translated as "ninthary."

4. See Bisio and Forni for details of exploitation of the indigenous labor force. Chaguanco is another name for a group known as the

Chiriguano-Chané complex formed by the fusion of two different groups, one of them Arawak, the other Guarani. The Chaguanco lived mainly in the eastern border of central Chaco. See Magrassi.

5. My translation: "The Mataco Indians plait chaguar knots / and yellow *fajas*. / Rivers of sun run and it seems to me / that, squatting down, they are knitting the nap time. // What a splurge of scattered light / and how burning is the forest! / The sharp silence of the Indians / comes up to us edgy as arrows. // O, how hard is the silence of the *chinas* / and how soft the hands! / If rain were to fall on them, being so brown, / they would be *chinas* of mud. // Over the *urundeles*, the moon, / they shall want to see it quite broad; / and when the rain water falls / upon the white sand, / we will have the limpid miracle / of the painted moon." *Chaguar* is a thorny plant growing in dry terrains, whose hard leaves are employed in the Chaco for making clothes such as the wide belts called *fajas* that the Matacos knit in this poem. By *chinas*, Castilla refers to the Indian women, employing a non-Indian word, but one commonly used in Argentina for peasant women. The *urundel* is a dense-topped tree of the Chaco.

6. It is an interesting coincidence that the situation in Argentine sugar mills changed toward a more liberal legislation in the second half of the 1940s, during the first government of Perón, and that Bolivian miners gained some labor rights after the mine nationalization in 1952 following a political revolution in which the miners played a significant role. In both cases, worker progress came a few years after the corresponding Castilla's book. It would be difficult, though, to argue for some kind of causal relationship between literature and politics on the basis of these cases.

7. My translation: "Like your own leafless shadow / it goes up to your mouth so that you may squeeze it. / Then over your hope / a bit of ash grows. // Your thirst is who looks for it / for its own dry and yellow sand, / but, in the end, sleep / finds no room in your red wax eyes. // I think you like it / because everything in it burns, / and if you pour ash on it / to turn it soft / that is only / for it to be put out for you / and to be transformed into moss / where your hunger may go to sleep." A mixture of ashes is usually added to the coca leaves so that more of the juice may be extracted. The way in which the poem interprets this procedure is surely a voluntary imaginary change in the perspective of things, of the type we have seen in other AvInd images.

8. This should not be taken as a complaint against works from which we have received fundamental lessons. For Latin American literary systems, see particularly the impressive work conducted by Losada.

9. I will borrow mainly from structuration conceptions of social systems (see Giddens, Pred) and models of literary institutions, pragmatically grounded in a roughly Habermasian context.

10. I must mention again the relevance of the presence of *Romancero* stanza patterns in some poems of *Copajira,* as a feature which may superficially support the claim for the "influence" of García Lorca and neo-popularism in general in that book. However, nothing like that might be adduced in relation to *Luna Muerta.* As I argue immediately below, polysystemic models may be useful for putting everything in its right place.

11. As a matter of fact, this suggestion for the internal dynamics of polysystems is heir to some concrete proposals made for Latin American history and grounded on powerful generalizations over extensive evidence by Angel Rama (1982) in his work on *narrative transculturation,* and particularly Cornejo-Polar's concept of *heterogeneity,* whose applicability to other literary systems outside Latin America is worth exploring (See Cornejo-Polar, 1982).

WORKS CITED

Barré, Marie-Chantal: *Ideologías indigenistas y movimientos indios.* México: Siglo XXI, 1983.

Bedregal, Yolanda. *Antología de la poesía boliviana.* La Paz: Los Amigos del Libro, 1991.

Bisio, Raúl, and Floreal Forni. "Economía de enclave y satelización del mercado de trabajo rural. El caso de los trabajadores con empleo precario de un ingenio azucarero del noroeste argentino." *Desarrollo Económico* 16.61 (1976): 3–56.

Bürger, Peter. *Theory of the Avant-Garde.* Minneapolis: University of Minnesota Press, 1983.

Castilla, Manuel J. *Obras Completas* Vol. I. Buenos Aires: Corregidor, 1982.

Churata, Gamaliel. *El pez de oro.* La Paz: Canata, 1957.

Cornejo-Polar, Antonio. *La novela indigenista.* Lima: Lasontay, 1980.

―――. "El indigenismo y las literaturas heterogéneas: su doble estatuto sociocultural." *Sobre literatura y crítica literarias latinoamericanas.* Caracas: Universidad Central, 1982. 67–85.

―――. "Sobre el 'neoindigenismo' y las novelas de Manuel Scorza." *Revista Iberoamericana* 127 (April-June 1984): 549–557.

Eagleton, Terry. *Ideology: an Introduction.* London: Verso, 1991.

Escajadillo, Tomás. "Scorza y el neoindigenismo: Nuevos planteamientos." *Literaturas andinas* 5–6 (1991): 5–22.

Estrella, Omar. *Brújula.* La Paz: Meridiano, 1928.

Even Zohar, Itamar. "Polysystem Theory." *Poetics Today* 1.1–2 (1979): 287–310.

Giddens, A. *The Constitution of Society. Outline of the Theory of Structuration.* Berkeley and Los Angeles: University of California Press, 1984.

Gómez-Martínez, José Luis. "La generación del Chaco y la toma de conciencia de la realidad boliviana." *Cuadernos Americanos (nueva época)* 2.2 (March-April 1988): 43–73.

Lienhard, Martin. *La voz y su huella.* Hanover: Ediciones del Norte, 1991.

Losada, Alejandro. *Creación y praxis. La producción literaria como praxis social en Hispanoamérica y el Perú.* Lima: Universidad Nacional Mayor de San Marcos, 1976.

Magrassi, Guillermo. *Los chiriguano-chané.* Buenos Aires: Búsqueda-Yuchán, 1981.

Monguió, Luis. *La poesía postmodernista peruana.* Berkeley and Los Angeles: University of California Press, 1954.

Osorio, Nelson. "Para una caracterización del vanguardismo literario hispanoamericano." *Revista Iberoamericana* 114–115 (January-June 1981): 227–254.

Palau de Nemes, Graciela. "La poesía indigenista de vanguardia de Alejandro Peralta." *Revista Iberoamericana* 110–111 (January-June 1980): 205–216.

Peralta, Alejandro. *Poesía de entretiempo.* Lima: Andimar, 1968.

Pizarro, Ana, ed. *La literatura latinoamericana como proceso.* Buenos Aires: Centro Editor de América Latina, 1985.

Pred, A. "Place as a historically contingent process: structuration and time-geography." *Annals of the Association of American Geographers* 74 (1974): 279–297.

Rama, Angel. "El área cultural andina (hispanismo, mesticismo, indigenismo)." *Cuadernos Americanos* 33 (September-December 1974):

———. *Transculturación narrativa en América Latina*. México: Siglo XXI, 1982.

———. *La ciudad letrada*. Montevideo: Comisión pro-fundación Angel Rama, 1984.

Saintoul, Catherine. *Racismo, etnocentrismo y literatura. La novela indigenista andina*. Buenos Aires: Ediciones del Sol, 1988.

Sayer, A. "The 'New' Regional Geography and Problems of Narrative." *Environment and Planning D: Society and Space* 7 (1989): 253–276.

Williams, Raymond. *Marxism and Literature*. Oxford: Oxford University Press, 1977.

Language and Crime in Yugoslavia
Milorad Pavić's Dictionary of the Khazars

Petar Ramadanović

I am going to address you not in my native Serbo-Croat, but in English, which holds that to "balkanize" means to "divide into small, often hostile, units."[1] In spite of such a prejudice of the English language toward the Balkans, the most important concern of this text lies somewhere else: what is the relation between the speaker of Serbo-Croat, on the one hand, and the states that have emerged from Yugoslavia, on the other? Croats, Serbs, and Muslims used to speak a common language before the war; now they speak "Croat," "Serbian," and "Bosnian." Serbo-Croat, the vanquished language, has no people, no folk anymore. But Serbo-Croat, the language of a ghost, the language of people who have lost their country, remains as a trace, as a witness of the un-speakable crime that is committed in the Balkans.

In this text I will attempt to trace the Serbian concept of nation through Milorad Pavić's *Dictionary of the Khazars*.[2] The book, a "lexicon novel" as it is classified by its author, although laid out in the "broken" form of a dictionary, has one focal point: the narrative about Khazars, a lost nation which disappears as its people accept one of three major religions. The protagonists are the Khazar "sect," so called "dream hunters," who inhabit a nation constituted not in space but in time. Their aim, told in three slightly different versions, Christian, Muslim, and Hebrew, is to assemble the body of "man's first father," Adam.

One of the characters in the *Dictionary of the Khazars* is an author/warrior, and Pavić explains that the final illustration in this character's book:

> showed Averkie Skila in his cage of broken-line strokes; but the zigzag saber stroke under the sign of Aries was depicted in this sketch as a passage permitting an exit from the cage or net. In the final diagram of his book, Averkie Skila is pictured exiting from the cage of his combat skills through a wound, being born from his astral prison into a new world and a new life. And inside his mute outer lips the other, inner lips laughed joyously. (101)

What is written down with saber dipped in ink, as Pavić describes Skila's weapon/pen (48), is the death that awaits on gates separating two worlds. Such a murder does indeed accompany all transitions, translations, all passing in or out of the Balkans, which are trapped in their national and regional divisions. But the translation of Pavić's novel into English and into more than twenty other languages was accompanied by an undivided international acclaim. Pavić went around the world following the fame of his novel with statements that identified Khazars in Basquia with the Basques, in Croatia with the Croats, and in Israel with the Jews. The internationalism of the *Dictionary* reached its peak in France, where one critic exclaimed: "We are all Khazars!" A second wave of interpretations of the *Dictionary* discovered that Khazars are in fact Serbs and that Pavić wrote a kind of program for national renewal. Pavić did not deny it.

In spite of the fact that Serbian nationalism and the renewal of their nation portrays Croats and Muslims as enemies, one could be safe in saying that Croats and Muslims may also be Khazars. The delimiting line between Khazars and non-Khazars is not exactly the line between two nations, but the line within the very concept of the group. And Pavić's model does not differentiate between "us" and "them," but rather between "us" and those "among us" who are denied a name and a language. Khazar, then, stands not only for the "extinct nation," but also for the concept of nation as always already threatened and thus in the need of preservation, in the need of permanent watch over the unity. And when Khazars are "baptized" into one of three major religions, they do not disappear, but are, in fact, only translating their ungrounded pagan ethnicity into a more permanent and more unified form: the nation with a book, with a name, and with a God.

Thus, what Pavić has in mind may not be very far from "the other" side of the Western concept of internationalism. But the problem of the nation/state is not that simple, and I would suggest a shift of the perspective from the relation between internationalism and nationalism to the possibility of translation. In other words, the problem that Khazars and the conflict on the Balkans possess is not the possibility for the communication and passage from one world into another, but rather the inherent impossibility for a human being not to belong to any language group. The difference that I would like to pose is, in Benjamin's terms, between likeness and kinship.[3] In nationalistic discourse, likeness is the result of the order, while kinship is the bond which facilitates the channeling of the autocratic force of the father. Yet, from the perspective of an individual, as well as from the perspective of the target language, likeness is only circumstantial, while kinship fluctuates between the moment of choice and the moment of predetermination. An individual cannot but belong to a language. However, that does not necessarily imply that the group, a nation that speaks the same language, is the only familiar ground; nor does it imply that the nation as such can satisfy all the possibilities of individual being. In other words, to be there does not mean primarily to share the death and dissolve oneself in the community, as Pavić's novel seems to suggest, but to share life. Pavić's obsession with death and its relation to ciphers may remind a sympathetic reader of certain postmodern themes, but the author's assertions really run in another direction, where the nation is an ideal group regardless of its sociopolitical organization.[4] The ideal form, the aristocratic Pavić indirectly asserts, is despotic rule in which the despot stands for the whole, signifying at the same time one and many. The despot in fact orientates, grounds, the community by giving it his name. And *Dictionary of the Khazars* is a dictionary formed on the basis of a discriminatory difference; a dictionary where property relations designates the meaning of words. The language of likeness is born, as we shall see, from the corpse.

As suggested by his depiction of Averkie Skila's death, for Pavić the figure of the ultimate, of the last, one does not signify the end, but a possibility for "an exit." And the continuation is accomplished with the help of the combat skills which inevitably create the opening. When Skila is born into a new life, behind him lies a corpse of his old life. Pavić never stops to lament the character's death, and the effect of his figure of continual passage from one world into another runs in two directions. First, the death becomes the source, the mark of life. And second, the birth is denied its status of the origin.

A similarly violent birth is repeated in the description of Daubmmanus's death. A Polish typographer, Daubmmanus dies, poisoned by the pages of the earlier edition of the *Dictionary*, with a blissful smile on his face. Pavić writes, "And then he died. Through his blissful smile the last letters he had read in the book dropped out of his mouth: *Verbo caro factum est*, 'The Word became the flesh'" (244). Daubmmanus's death gave life to letters, giving a transcendental status to the very death, which will become from the signature of the murderer, the signature of the translator:

> The hierarchy of death is, in fact, the only thing that makes possible a system of contacts between the various levels of reality in an otherwise vast space where deaths endlessly repeat themselves like echoes within echoes. (127)

To die, thus, means for the *Dictionary* not to die in vain and alone but in order to establish contact, a bond, to be read in another language. With the endless translation Pavić transcends the facts, the reality of the birth and death constituting the hierarchy with the God as its supreme monad. Yet the God is not a particular, nor even national God, but the father of us all. This notion of the total power, of the absolute authority without limits is not primarily concerned for the distribution of its might in space, but rather in time—Pavić's vast space of repetition—where endless deaths stand for the etymological rule, that is, for the proper derivation and edification of the meaning. It is the absoluteness of the power that guarantees the continuation, the future to the community informed through and within the language of likeness. Of course, time is at a standstill, frozen into the proper historical self-reflection. The image such a history suggests is the image of the hero who is always already dead, even at the moment of birth.

In turn, the real death, the demise, is infinitely deferred. The Khazar "sect" wander through time passing from one dream to another in their quest to assemble the body of "man's first father," Adam. In general, dream hunters form a pair wherein one dreams the life of the other and vice versa. They meet physically only in the time of death. And when Cohen Samuel, the Jew; Yusuf Masudi, the Turk; and Avram Brankovich, the Serb, meet on a battlefield near Kladovo, Brankovich is dead, and a pasha who led Turks asks Masudi:

> "You say you're a dream reader? . . . Well, then, can you read Cohen's dream?"
>
> "Of course I can. I already see what he is dreaming: since Brankovich is dying, he's dreaming of Brankovich's death."
>
> These words seemed to excite the pasha.
>
> "That means," he quickly concluded, "that Cohen can now experience what no mortal can: by dreaming of Brankovich dying, he can experience death yet stay alive?"
>
> "That's right," said Masudi, "but he cannot wake up to tell us what he saw in the dream." (235)

Dream hunters speak the same language of memory of the father and primordial unity. There is no unbridgeable distance, no incision to separate them. They are three in one, in death. The first dies, the second dreams his death, the third reads the second's dream, and he is able to tell it to the others. Thus, Brankovich dies only in the dream of the other, not believing in his own mortality and, furthermore, infinitely far from the (real) death. Cohen, on the other hand, cannot wake up from the dream; he cannot tell the reality of the death, but he does tell something through Masudi's lips: death is the dream, it is a collective dream that brings "us" together, and thus "we" signifies against the real which, with a completed circle, becomes death.

When Pavić introduces particular languages, Serbian—the mother tongue—is given a special characteristic:

> It has been said ever since that the Brankoviches of Erdely count in Tzintzar, lie in Walachian, are silent in Greek, sing hymns in Russian, are cleverest in Turkish, and speak their mother tongue—Serbian—only when they intend to kill. (25)

Whom do the Brankoviches of Erdely kill according to Pavić? Their mother? Their tongue? Their fatherland? Themselves? Perhaps all of them together, for the murder is oriented inward, inside the family. Death is the very familial bond. The Brankoviches love through murder, they speak through it. Crime is "allowed," possible, *conceivable* within the family where one not only kills the other but also commits suicide as if a part of the murderer always dies with the killing. The language, the bond, kills. And "we," "our" family melts together in death, transgressing all possible and all impossible—incestual—boundaries. "Every master embraces his own death," reads Avram Brankovich's coat of arms (45).

Pavić's appeal for compassion with the Serbian problem—the threat that Serbs would be annihilated by the growing Albanian population or by dissemination of the Serbian state on autonomous provinces—addressed to the international community presumed the existence of other languages and presumed also that the *Dictionary* can be translated according to international standards. The *geschlecht* formed with this concept is the one of, so to say, united nations, wherein people who do not belong to a nation—the people who do not look alike—have no representatives. Pavić writes, "woe upon those who have deserted Adam's body, the body of man's first father, for they will not be able to die with him or like him. They will become not people but something else" (*Dictionary*, 319). It is this "something else" that is most interesting in the whole nationalistic conflict in the Balkans, where these ghosts, these wanderers have no side to identify with, no death to die, and no ground to be buried in. The father, or better The Father, is the father of all of mankind except the ones that have deserted Him. Deserters are not Croats, or Albanians, but some other ilk. They have no name, certainly not Adam's, who is the normative principle of all national symbolic orders.

Besides Adam, perhaps Avram Brankovich, also called Papas, is the most intriguing father figure of the *Dictionary*. Not only because of his name, Avram, which means "the father," but also because he resembles very much the historical figure Djordje Branković (1645-1711) who, as Pavić describes him in another context, "is for a long time the last secular ruler of the Serbian people" (*Birth*, 18). Djordje Branković, a self-professed descendent of Serbian royal dynasty, is also the author of the *Slavenoserbske hronike* (Old Slavonic Chronicles), which Pavić finds to be "in general terms, the first modern and secular history of Serbs" (*Birth*, 89). This history, as all other Serbian baroque histories, tried to "awake in Europe consciousness about the need of united action of the Christian states for liberation of the enslaved peoples in the Balkans" (*History*, 334). Baroque history is not only, Pavić writes, a witness of the glorious Serbian past and Serbs' state but it is also in the service of the national future with its energetic attempts to defend Serbs from the loss of their nationhood under the Austrian Empire and Venetian Republic, and also to help them to survive under the Ottoman occupation (*History*, 334). Pavić concludes:

> The ruler [Djordje Branković] that ruled from the captivity over *the wandering nation without the state and territory* established, with the help of his historical arguments, legitimacy [of the Serbian nation] that could not be overlooked any more within the political constellation of Middle Europe. (*History*, 341; emphasis mine)

When a nation lacks territory and a ruler, Branković's *Chronicles* seem to suggest, the nation will come to exist only in the state formed after the national ground is liberated and the ruler freed from captivity. So, if Pavić's *Dictionary* is a dialogue with somebody, it is with the Serbian baroque historians who have moved the significance of the death from folk poetry's epic celebration toward the death as political argument that marks the borders of the territory. As if the baroque histories have discovered the "true" measuring system to mark the national dwelling place, they initiated the carving of Serbia on an imaginary map of the concrete terrain. And Serbia, the glorious state of the corpses, was politically, linguistically, and historically separated from other nations.

The delimitation is done also within the group, for it is up to the master to choose the principle for discrimination. Pavić poses the difference through the lips of Averkie Skila: "I am a master of sabres and I know: when you kill, it is different every time, just as it is different with every new woman you take to your bed" (*Dictionary*, 57). The one who knows *is* the master, but the argument's circularity closes up only *via* death and *via* woman "you take to your bed." It is in these two domains, on these two terrains, that mastery is being constituted. Once woman and death are compared, and perhaps equated, the difference itself becomes the property of the one who knows, that is, of the one who actually kills and thus establishes the mastery over the unknown and, perhaps, unnameable. Skila's skill seems to repeat in advance the rapes that will become one of the weapons of the war on the Balkans, the war that is, in fact, being waged against the ghosts, the ones that are denied name and property—the women, but also, the citizens.[5]

On another level of his novel, Pavić describes a fate that awaits Croats, Muslims, and all other nations that refuse to obey the Serbian Father, a level that one may call an apparent political engagement of the *Dictionary*. When Pavić leaves the seductive voice of legend and myth, such statements as the four-year-old boy's rejection of democracy appear. He says that he is sick of democracy and continues:

> Look at the results of this democracy of yours. Before, big nations used to oppress small nations. Now it's the reverse. Now, in the name of democracy, small nations terrorize the big. Just look at the world around us. White America is afraid of blacks, the blacks are afraid of the Puerto Ricans, Jews of the Palestinians, the Arabs of the Jews, the Serbs of the Albanians, the Chinese of the Vietnamese, the English of the Irish. Small fish are nibbling the ears of the big fish. Instead of minorities being terrorized, democracy has introduced a new fashion: now it's the majority of this planet's population that's being burdened. . . . Your democracy sucks. (*Dictionary*, 303)

A similar reflection of the contemporary Balkan situation appears when Pavić describes the Khazar state. It repeats in advance future Serbian arguments against their position in the Yugoslavian federation: "in their own part of the state the Khazars share bread with everybody, but in the rest of the land nobody gives them even a crumb" (*Dictionary*, 149).

Pavić needs a deeper, mythical level of narrative, a "familiar" level on which all nations are the same and together, in spite of the mutual killing and conquest, as a proof that the thing that one is born with, a language and the last name of the father, are inherent, always already there as a part of the nature that grows on the particular soil. One is born into the dream of assembling Adam's body and with the task, as it is said in Serbia, to create the Heavenly Nation. The symbolic universe of the Serbian heroic enterprise to "preserve" their nation culminates with an almost incredible proposition given by some Serbian "intellectuals." The present war atrocities, they say, should not be judged in ethical but in what they call historical terms. History is thus postulated as independent of human decision. It is neither fiction nor reality, neither lie nor truth, but rather death—i.e., history—that is beyond the grasp of an ordinary human being.

Strictly speaking, Pavić's novel does not blur the line that separates history and fiction. The historical, Djordje Branković for instance, is for him beyond any doubt and, as such, not a subject of interpretation but a normative model. Within such a system it is logical to conclude what the Serbian poet Brana Crnčević concluded: "Serbs kill in a despair, their murders are the deed between the killer and the God".[6] Thus, the present-day political principle is born: Wherever there are Serbian graves, that should be Serbia! The state, the nation, and the ground are one.

In other words, Cohen, the dream hunter, cannot experience the death (the dream) if he only stands for himself, but once he becomes the part of a trinity with Brankovich and Masudi, once he dissolves his individuality in a dream of unity, he gains the ability to "read" the death, thereby acquiring the history for the immortal nation. The same structure of a translation without end is propose by Pavić as a way to read the

Dictionary. Although he says that the *Dictionary* "can be read in an infinite number of ways" (*Dictionary*, 11), the infinity is bound by the introductory epigram/epitaph. What a reader lacks in advance, what is taken from him, is precisely the death:

> Here lies the reader
> who will never open this book.
> He is here forever dead.

With the "epitaph" Pavić distinguishes two types of reading: one within the *Dictionary* that is infinite, and one without it that is forever dead. There are an infinite number of ways to read, that is, to assemble Adam's body, while at the same time there is only one way not to read. By not reading, the reader without has chosen the death which he cannot die. The death which the reader within the *Dictionary* reads, in a manner similar to Cohen's, becomes his property. The non-reader is left without death, deathless, a ghost. And ultimately it is the body of the *Dictionary*'s non-reader that cannot die, and it is his/her corpse that is limited, doomed to have no offspring, and sentenced to disappear without a trace, killed by love and hate. The reader within the *Dictionary*, as well as its protagonists, do not die, but are transformed, translated through national death. Writing woven around death implies the "infinity" of the death reading. Yet the members of the death community, the speakers of the death language, do not see this death as disappearance, but as a triumph of the semblance over radical difference. The one left outside, the one who can perceive the nature of the death is not one of *us*. He or she does not speak the language of the book.

To refuse to read, to refuse the infinite possibility to assemble Adam's body, means to rebel against the father and to threaten the national security of that special, divine state which, according to the prediction Pavić finds in the "Fragment from Basra," may be formed in the end of the twentieth century (*Dictionary*, 138). Furthermore, the referents of Pavić's dream *Dictionary* are the battlefields of the Balkans, not the Babylonian library; some reality which is constituted through this *Dictionary* of Serbian prosecution, not a fiction that Serbian language may be dreaming of. Death is, therefore, seized by the narrative, and only by becoming the reader of the book can one retrieve his death, which returns to the body in an inverted form, as the "infinite possibility." This infinite possibility is the possibility *to* speak. The other is forever silenced.

NOTES

1. *The American Heritage Dictionary of the English Language* defines "balkanize" as follows: "to divide (a region or territory) into small, often hostile, units."

2. Milorad Pavić is a poet and a professor of literary history at the University of Belgrade, Yugoslavia. *Dictionary of the Khazars* is his first full-length novel.

3. See "The Task of the Translator."

4. The problem I am trying to address in this text is not the death of the subject but, on the contrary, the subjectivity of death in nationalistic discourse.

5. I believe that the warring factions of the Balkans are not so much determined by belonging to a particular nation/religion but on the basis of possession of ground: the ones with ground (farmers, villagers), and the others who do not have it (citizens, including women and children).

6. Quoted in Vasic's "Vreme stida" [The Time of Shame].

WORKS CITED

The American Heritage Dictionary of the English Language. Ed. William Morris. Boston: Houghton Mifflin, 1969.

Benjamin, Walter. "The Task of the Translator." Illuminations. Ed. Hannah Arendt. Trans. Harry Zohn. New York: Schocken Books, 1985. 69-82.

Pavić, Milorad. Dictionary of the Khazars. Trans. Christina Pribićević-Zorić. New York: Vintage Books, 1989.

————. Radjanje nove srpske književnosti: Istorija srpske književnosti baroka, klasicizma i preromantizma. [The Birth of the New Serbian Literature: The History of Serbian Literature, Baroque, Classicism, and Preromanticism.] Beograd [Belgrade]: Srpska književna zadruga, 1983.

————. Istorija srpske književnosti baroknog doba (XVII i XVIII vek). [The History of Serbian Baroque Literature (Seventeenth and eighteenth century).] Beograd [Belgrade]: Nolit, 1970.

Vasić, Milož. "Vreme stida" ["The Time of Shame"]. Vreme [Time]. Beograd [Belgrade], Yugoslavia, February 24, 1992.

Bibliography

Alonso, Carlos. *The Spanish American Regional Novel: Modernity and Autochthony*. Cambridge: Cambridge University Press, 1990.

Austin, Mary. "Regionalism in American Fiction." *English Journal* 21 (February 1931): 97–106.

Berry, Wendell. "The Regional Motive." *A Continuous Harmony: Essays Cultural and Agricultural*. New York: Harcourt, 1972. 63–70.

Berry, Wendell. "Writer and Region." *Hudson Review* 60 (1987): 15–30.

Biehl, Janet. *Rethinking Ecofeminist Politics*. Boston: South End, 1991.

Bredahl, Carl A. Jr. *New Ground: Western American Literature and the Literary Canon*. Chapel Hill: University of North Carolina Press, 1989.

Burke, John Gordon, ed. *Regional Perspectives: An Examination of America's Literary Heritage*. Chicago: American Library Association, 1973.

Cândido, Antônio. "Backwardness and Underdevelopment: Its Repercussions in the Writer's Consciousness." *Latin America in Its Literature*. Eds. César Fernández and Julio Ortega. Trans. Mary G. Berg. New York: Holmes and Meier, 1980. 263–82.

Cheney, Jim. "Postmodern Environmental Ethics: Ethics as Bioregional Narrative." *Environmental Ethics* 11,2 (Summer 1989): 117–34.

Cornejo-Polar, Antonio. "El indigenismo y las literaturas heterogéneas: su doble estatuto sociocultural." *Sobre literatura y crítica literarias latinoamericanas*. Caracas: Universidad Central, 1982. 67–85.

Coutinho, Eduardo F. "Regionalsm and Universalism." *Proceedings of the XIIth Congress of the International Comparative Literature Association*. Eds. Roger Bauer and Douwe Fokkema. Vol. 4. Munich: Iudicium verlag, 1990. 191–95.

Davidson, Donald. *The Attack on Leviathan: Regionalism and Nationalism in the United States*. 1938. Gloucester, MA: Peter Smith, 1962.

Entrikin, Nicholas J. *The Betweenness of Place: Towards a Geography of Modernity*. London: Macmillan, 1991.

Everson, William. "Archetype West." *Regional Perspectives: An Examination of America's Literary Heritage*. Ed. John Gordon Burke. Chicago: American Library Association, 1973. 49–75.

Fetterley, Judith, and Marjorie Pryse. *American Women Regionalists 1850–1910: A Norton Anthology*. New York: Norton, 1992.

Fisher, Philip. "Introduction: The New American Studies." *The New American Studies: Essays from Representations*. Ed. Philip Fisher. Berkeley: University of California Press, 1991. vii–xxii.

Franco, Jean. "The Nation as Imagined Community." *The New Historicism*. Ed. H. Aram Veeser. New York: Routledge, 1989. 204–12.

Garland, Hamlin. "Local Color in Art." *Crumbling Idols: Twelve Essays on Art Dealing Chiefly with Literature, Painting, and the Drama*. Ed. Jane Johnson. Cambridge: Belknap-Harvard University Press, 1960. 49–55.

Harrison, Dick, ed. *Crossing Frontiers: Papers in American and Canadian Western Literature*. Edmonton: University of Alberta Press, 1979.

Harrison, Dick. *Unnamed Country; The Struggle for a Canadian Prairie Fiction*. Edmonton: University of Alberta Press, 1977.

Jensen, Merrill, ed. *Regionalism in America*. Madison: University of Wisconsin Press, 1951.

Jones, Suzi. "Regionalization: A Rhetorical Strategy." *Journal of the Folklore Institute* 13 (1976): 105–20.

Jordan, David. "Representing Regionalism." *The Canadian Review of American Studies* 23,2 (Winter 1993): 101–14.

Keith, W.J. *Regions of the Imagination: The Development of British Rural Fiction.* Toronto: University of Toronto Press, 1988.

Kerber, Linda. "Separate Spheres, Female Worlds, Woman's Place: The Rhetoric of Women's History." *Journal of American History* 75, 1 (June 1988): 9–39.

Kolodny, Annette. *The Lay of the Land: Metaphor as Experience and History in American Life and Letters.* Chapel Hill: University of North Carolina Press, 1975.

Kroetsch, Robert. "'The Writer Has Got to Know Where He Lives': An Interview with Robert Kroetsch." *Writer's News Manitoba,* 1 (1982): 3–18.

Lewis, Martin W. *Green Delusions: An Environmentalist Critique of Radical Environmentalism.* Durham, NC: Duke University Press, 1992.

Lopez, Barry. "Landscape and Narrative." *Crossing Open Ground.* New York: Vintage Books, 1989. 61–71.

———. "The American Geographies." *Finding Home: Writing on Nature and Culture from Orion Magazine.* Ed. Peter Sauer. Boston: Beacon Press, 1992. 116–32.

Lowell, James Russell. "Nationality in Literature." *Literary Criticism of James Russell Lowell.* Ed. Herbert F. Smith. Lincoln: University of Nebraska Press, 1969. 116–31.

Mallory, William E., and Paul Simpson-Housley, eds. *Geography and Literature.* Syracuse, NY: Syracuse University Press, 1986.

Mandel, Eli. "The Regional Novel: Borderline Art." *Taking Stock.* Proceedings of the Calgary Conference on the Canadian Novel, February 1978. Ed. Charles R. Steele. Downsview, Ontario: ECW, 1982. 103–20.

Miki, Roy. "Prairie Poetics: An Interchange with Eli Mandel and Robert Kroetsch." *Dandelion* 2 (1983): 82–92.

Miller, Angela. "Everywhere and Nowhere: The Making of the National Landscape." *American Literary History* 4 (1992): 207–29.

Mitchell, W.O. "Regionalism and the Writer: A Talk with W. O. Mitchell." Patricia Brady. *Canadian Literature* 14 (1962): 51–63.

Odum, Howard W., and Harry Estill Moore. *American Regionalism: A Cultural-Historical Approach to National Integration.* New York: Henry Holt, 1938.

Plant, Judith. "Searching for Common Ground: Ecofeminism and Bioregionalism." *Learning to Listen to the Land.* Ed. Bill Willers. Washington, DC: Island, 1992. 212–19.

Podock, Douglas C.D. *Humanistic Geography and Literature.* Totowa, NJ: Barnes, 1981.

Pred, A. "Place as a historically contingent process: structuration and time-geography." *Annals of the Association of American Geographers* 74 (1974). 279–97.

Pryse, Marjorie. "'Distilling Essences': Regionalism and 'Women's Culture.'" *American Literary Realism* 25, 2 (Winter 1993): 1–15.

Ransom, John Crowe. "The Aesthetics of Regionalism." *American Review* 2 (1934): 290–310.

Rosenthal, Bernard. *City of Nature: Journeys to Nature in the Age of American Romanticism.* Newark: University of Delaware Press, 1980.

Sale, Kirkpatrick. *Dwellers in the Land: The Bioregional Vision.* San Francisco: Sierra Club Books, 1985.

Salomon, Noël. "Cosmopolitism and Internationalism in the History of Ideas in Latin America." *Cultures* 6,1 (1979): 83–108.

Sauer, Peter. "Introduction." *Finding Home: Writing on Nature and Culture from Orion Magazine.* Ed. Peter Sauer. Boston: Beacon Press, 1992. 1–17.

Sayer, A. "The 'New' Regional Geography and Problems of Narrative." *Environment and Planning D: Society and Space* 7 (1989): 253–76.

Schlereth, Thomas J. "Regional Culture Studies and American Culture." *Sense of Place: American Regional Cultures.* Eds. Barbara Allen and Thomas J. Schlereth. Lexington: University Press of Kentucky, 1990. 164–83.

Slovic, Scott. *Seeking Awareness in American Nature Writing: Henry Thoreau, Annie Dillard, Edward Abbey, Wendell Berry, Barry Lopez.* Salt Lake City: University of Utah Press, 1992.

Snyder, Gary. *The Practice of the Wild.* San Francisco: North Point, 1990.

Soja, Edward. *Postmodern Geographies: The Reassertion of Space in Critical Social Theory.* New York: Verso, 1989.

Steiner, Michael, and Clarence Mondale. *Region and Regionalism in the United States: A Source Book for the Humanities and Social Sciences.* New York and London: Garland, 1988.

Stewart, George R. "The Regional Approach to Literature." *College English* 9,7 (1948): 370–71.

Tuan, Yi-Fu. *Topophilia: A Study of Environmental Perception, Attitudes, and Values.* 2nd ed. New York: Columbia University Press, 1990.

Turner, Frederick. *Spirit of Place: The Making of an American Literary Landscape.* San Francisco: Sierra Club, 1989.

Warren, Robert Penn. "Not Local Color." *The Virginia Quarterly Review* 1 (1932): 153–60.

Warren, Robert Penn. "Some Don'ts for Literary Regionalists." *American Review* 8 (1936): 142–50.

Welty, Eudora. *The Eye of the Story.* New York: Random House, 1978.

Contributors

Peter Caccavari recently completed his doctorate at the Department of English, Xavier University, Cincinnati, Ohio.

Jill Franks is a Sessional Instructor at the University of British Columbia in Vancouver, British Columbia.

Warren Johnson is Assistant Professor of French at The University of Alabama, Tuscaloosa, Alabama.

David Jordan is an independent scholar living in Vancouver, British Columbia. He has recently published *New World Regionalism: Literature of the Americas* (Toronto: University of Toronto Press, 1994.)

Ricardo Kaliman is an Assistant Professor in the Faculty of Philosophy and Letters at the Universidad Nacional de Tucuman in Argentina.

Michael Kowalewski is Assistant Professor of English at Carleton College in Northfield, Minnesota.

Francesco Loriggio is Associate Professor at the School of Comparative Literary Studies, Carleton University, Ottwaw.

Marjorie Pryse is a professor in the Department of Women's Studies at New York State University College in Plattsburgh, New York.

Petar Ramadanović is completing his dissertation at the State University of New York, Binghamton.

Rosa Sarabia is Assistant Professor in the Department of Spanish and Portuguese at the University of Toronto.

Mark Schlenz is completing his doctorate in the Department of English at the University of California, Santa Barbara.